#1 *WASHINGTON POST* BESTSELLER
NEW YORK TIMES, WALL STREET JOURNAL, AND *USA TODAY* BESTSELLER

"Forceful. . . . It is curious how many Reaganesque themes find a contemporary echo . . . [and] it is worth recalling both Reagan's celebration of freedom and his understanding of democracy." —*Wall Street Journal*

"Bret Baier has done it again. *Three Days in Moscow* is a remarkable story about one of the most monumental moments in contemporary world history. Grand in sweep, brilliantly crafted, and riveting, this extraordinary book is also masterfully researched. It will take its place as an instant classic, if not as the finest book to date on Ronald Reagan himself!"
—JAY WINIK, author of *April 1865* and *1944*

"Bret Baier's enthralling *Three Days in Moscow* is a timely reminder at a time of resurgent US-Russian tensions of the historic role Ronald Reagan played in negotiating landmark nuclear agreements that helped end the Cold War. Baier recounts the personal diplomacy, overriding vision, and steadiness of purpose Reagan brought to his summits with Soviet leader Mikhail Gorbachev in wonderful detail. Those three days at the Moscow summit are a great foundation for his larger exploration of a defining chapter in US and world history. " —ANDREA MITCHELL, Chief Foreign Affairs Correspondent, NBC News

"Bret Baier's *Three Days in Moscow* is a riveting recounting of Ronald Reagan's gallant Cold War diplomacy during his 1988 historic visit to the Soviet Union. Every page sparkles. Baier has a great gift for writing fine narrative history anchored around impressive academic research. This is one of the best and most essential books ever written about Reagan, the man Margaret Thatcher said won the Cold War without firing a single shot."
—DOUGLAS BRINKLEY, professor of history at Rice University and editor of *The Reagan Diaries*

"Highly readable, perceptive and deeply researched. . . . [A] refreshing one volume account of Ronald Reagan's extraordinary career. . . . A well-informed account of how business is done in the White House."
—*Washington Times*

"Bret Baier gives us a clear and lively picture of Ronald Reagan, the man and the president. Read *Three Days in Moscow*, enjoy, and learn why the Gipper was such a great leader."
—GEORGE P. SHULTZ, US Secretary of State, 1982–1989

"Drawing on newly opened archives and his own revealing interviews with key figures of the time, Bret Baier deserves credit for this fascinating, thoughtful, and highly readable account of Ronald Reagan's towering contribution to his country—ending the Cold War without the firing of a shot, on terms that Harry Truman and Dwight Eisenhower could have only dreamed of. *Three Days in Moscow* should be read by everyone not old enough to have personally witnessed how this president, step by step, in public and in secret, closed down a half century of dangerous confrontation—and by those whose memories of that crucial story are imperishable."

—MICHAEL BESCHLOSS, author of *Presidential Courage*

"I associate the Brandenburg Gate, Reykjavík, and the defense buildup with the places where the Cold War was won. But in Bret Baier's uplifting *Three Days in Moscow* we learn of a critical chapter in the Reagan triumph over totalitarianism, a place and time where a new vision of freedom for all people was born. An engaging story well told by a professional with insight and empathy."

—WILLIAM BENNETT, US Secretary of Education, 1985–1988

"*Three Days in Moscow* may make you see Ronald Reagan for the first time. You may have liked his political philosophy, his personality, his beliefs on the American people, or his straightforward method of governing. But Bret Baier ties it all together in three days of conversations and speeches in Moscow that President Reagan called 'the last act.' . . . This is a remarkable book on many levels. Certainly it focuses on the man, and on Nancy, but it also lays out the role of personal diplomacy, and how it is a crucial part of winning. It demonstrates how Reagan knew to hire good people who shared his values. How to absorb the blows of the press and move on."

—MARLIN FITZWATER, White House Press Secretary, 1987–1993

"Bret Baier is not only among the most reliably honest and professional journalists in America, he is also a brilliant historian and author. *Three Days in Moscow* is a comprehensive and wonderfully written exposition of Ronald Reagan's lifelong mission to spread liberty and to end the Soviet Union. Through his original research and essential interviews, Bret walks the reader through much of Reagan's life. But it is Reagan's final summit in Moscow to which Bret rightly draws our attention, for this is where Reagan delivered his historic and electrifying speech to the students of Moscow State University and drove the final nail into the coffin of the Soviet empire, thereby ending the Cold War. Reagan's lessons must not be lost on present-day America, and thanks to Bret's marvelous book, they won't be."

—MARK R. LEVIN, #1 *New York Times* bestselling author

"[A] satisfying handling of what was arguably the highlight of Reagan's time as president. . . . Offer[s] a soothing glimpse of a time when we were led by an old-school gentleman who did not bully those who disagreed with him."

—*Express-News* (San Antonio)

THREE DAYS IN MOSCOW

RONALD REAGAN AND THE FALL OF THE SOVIET EMPIRE

BRET BAIER

with CATHERINE WHITNEY

WILLIAM MORROW

An Imprint of HarperCollins*Publishers*

A hardcover edition of this book was published in 2018 by William Morrow, an imprint of HarperCollins Publishers.

FIRST WILLIAM MORROW PAPERBACK EDITION PUBLISHED 2019.

Library of Congress Cataloging-in-Publication Data has been applied for.

ISBN 978-0-06-274843-0

19 20 21 22 23   10 9 8 7 6 5 4 3 2 1

To my sons, Paul and Daniel, and their generation,
that they might inherit the legacy of
peace that Reagan envisioned

CONTENTS

PART FOUR: DREAMS FOR THE FUTURE

INTRODUCTION

FINDING REAGAN

The long, winding road up to the Ronald Reagan Presidential Library and Museum in Simi Valley, California, is lined with banners picturing US presidents from George Washington to Donald Trump. They flap in the breeze, historical markers and patriotic flags—a reminder that the presidency is not about one man alone. As I exited my car at the top of the hill and walked toward the entrance, the hot sun beating on my back, I passed the tall bronze statue of our fortieth president at the entrance, making sure I touched Reagan's outstretched hand, which is clearly worn on the palm by the thousands of visitors every day who make the same move—a presidential high five.

That day I was on a mission. With my fantastic coauthor, Catherine Whitney, and amazing researcher, Sydney Soderberg, both of whom I truly loved working with on the Dwight D. Eisenhower book, I was in search of the next focus, the next moment in presidential history that needed reexamination, the next speech that might have changed the world but that very few people at the time or since seemed to grasp the importance of—not to mention the very real prospect that a new generation might be reading about this president in an intimate way, or in any way, for the first time.

It was an equation that seemed to work well with *Three*

Days in January, which focused on President Eisenhower's farewell address, delivered three days before John F. Kennedy's inaugural address, then bounced back to Eisenhower's life to show how he arrived at the convictions and the specific messages he expressed in that legendary eighteen-minute farewell speech from the Oval Office.

With Reagan, my interest settled on a speech near the end of his second term in office, in late May 1988, on a momentous trip to Moscow, the capital of the Soviet Union. The purpose of that visit was to hold a fourth summit between Reagan and General Secretary Mikhail Gorbachev. A lot happened on that now largely forgotten trip, but my attention was especially captured by the speech Reagan gave at Moscow State University.

I made my way back to the library, passed the entrance to the museum, and entered a room with familiar large wooden tables, similar to the setup at the Dwight D. Eisenhower Presidential Library in Abilene, Kansas. I pulled up a chair next to the gray cardboard box on the corner of the table. I flipped it open and thumbed through the contents. The folder I pulled out contained several drafts and a printout of the complete speech, along with a transcript of the question-and-answer session with Moscow State University students. I read through it but didn't truly appreciate the genius of the speech and the Q&A until I heard President Reagan deliver it. Ten steps away, I put on headphones at another table and listened to the address delivered that day. I was struck by the complete absence of rancor—no veiled threats, no chest-thumping, no insults—only a hopeful message directed at young students just starting out. Reagan was funny, optimistic, and warm in a grandfatherly way. He expressed awe at all the wonders that awaited the young students—the one catch being that freedom was a prerequisite. He seemed to relish the moment, which had been a lifetime in the making—from anti-Communist activist to president touring Red Square and speaking to Soviet students.

Most experts believe the fourth summit between Reagan and Gorbachev was essentially just the final turn and dip in a long diplomatic dance over Reagan's two terms. But looking at the text of the speech that day in Simi Valley, hearing it on audio, and eventually seeing it on video, it seemed to me to be much more than that.

President Reagan spoke to the college students in Moscow under a giant image of Vladimir Lenin, with confidence, optimism, self-assuredness, pride in his country, and knowledge that the Soviet Union's days were numbered, telling the students at one point, "I want to talk not just of the realities of today but of the possibilities of tomorrow."

And then, in the heart of Communist thought—the capital of communism—President Reagan delivered these words about freedom, not in a threatening or scolding way but in a "shining city on a hill," hopeful manner:

> Freedom is the right to question and change the established way of doing things. It is the continuing revolution of the marketplace. It is the understanding that allows us to recognize shortcomings and seek solutions. It is the right to put forth an idea, scoffed at by the experts, and watch it catch fire among the people. It is the right to dream—to follow your dream or stick to your conscience, even if you're the only one in a sea of doubters. Freedom is the recognition that no single person, no single authority or government has a monopoly on the truth, but that every individual life is infinitely precious, that every one of us put on this world has been put there for a reason and has something to offer.

The speech can still evoke a thrill. It was an audacious challenge by a US president to a Soviet citizenry rocked by economic crisis and international conflicts. The speech sounded to many listeners like a siren call, an invitation to follow a different dream.

Looking at the words of the speech and then hearing and seeing them delivered was powerful for me. I was intrigued to learn how a relentless enemy of communism had helped orchestrate such a dramatic finale to an adversary he'd once called the "Evil Empire," without firing a shot. What was in his character and temperament that allowed him to collaborate with Gorbachev in a strategy of "peace through strength"? How did he stand firm on an opposing set of principles and still negotiate? He found a way. What is the measure of a man who could so completely capture the imagination of both the nation and the world?

UNLIKE THE EISENHOWER PRESIDENCY, which was before my time, I did have some sense of President Reagan's two terms in office growing up. And it so happened I was in the Rose Garden with President Reagan just months before the Moscow summit.

I'm forty-seven, and in the fall of 1987, I was a senior in high school and the student council president at Marist School in Atlanta. With that position came the honor of representing Marist in Washington, DC, to accept a national excellence award on behalf of the school. So I traveled with Marist headmaster Father Joel Konzen to Washington for a ceremony at the White House.

I distinctly remember being struck by awe walking into the Rose Garden for the event—the sun shining, the White House gleaming, the garden manicured, the chairs lined up, the podium positioned. I can still see the White House press corps crowding into the back of the Rose Garden, a mass of television cameras, photographers, and reporters with notebooks milling around, waiting for the president to arrive.

President Reagan walked out of the Oval Office with his education secretary, William Bennett. Both men talked about the importance of education and of supporting schools that were succeeding, taking time to name and praise the schools being recognized for excellence that day, their student and faculty leaders all in attendance. When he was finished, Reagan started to walk back to the Oval Office, and ABC White House correspondent Sam Donaldson yelled out a question: "Mr. President, what is your reaction to the Bork nomination possibly dying in committee?" (Supreme Court nominee Robert Bork's nomination was on the rocks at the time, and it was the story of the day in Washington.) Reagan ignored the reporter's shouting at first but then turned and said, "Over my dead body," before going inside. The next day, Bork's nomination was rejected by the Senate Judiciary Committee by a 9–5 vote. But Bork didn't back down and the administration didn't pull the nomination, despite quickly dwindling political support. Two weeks later, the full Senate voted against Bork's confirmation 58–42. It was big news.

But in the mind of a seventeen-year-old student council president, it was irritating, obnoxious, and just plain rude of those reporters to interrupt *our* education excellence ceremony. I was so disturbed by it that I went back to Marist and penned an opinion editorial in the school newspaper, the *Marist Blue & Gold*. I was the sports editor of the paper, but the indignity in the Rose Garden had forced me to put on my news hat and to weigh in (so I thought at the time). This is part of what I wrote in an op-ed entitled "Press Needs Etiquette":

The press has to respect others around them. They had
no right to come into that ceremony and be obnoxious
by yelling questions at the President as he walked away.
I understand that they do need some way "to get the stories," but I think that respect has a lot to do with it also.

The president did not walk into the Rose Garden on October 5 to deliver a press conference; he walked in there to deliver
a speech to schools of excellence, and tell them to keep up the
good work. The press gets plenty of time as it is without using
someone else's.

Fast-forward exactly twenty years, and as chief White House
correspondent for Fox News, an older Bret Baier was back in
the Rose Garden yelling questions at then president George
W. Bush as he walked away from the podium. Older and wiser,
I understood more fully that such questions, uncomfortable as
they may be, are the bedrock of our free press. Fast-forward
ten years from there, and as Fox News chief political anchor
and host of *Special Report with Bret Baier,* I now regularly invite then education secretary and now radio talk show host Bill
Bennett on the *Special Report* panel to talk about the stories of
the day. Bennett often lists the ways in which the White House
press corps seems to have it out for President Donald Trump.
From that October 5, 1987, Rose Garden event at the White
House to now, it all comes full circle.

Which brings me back to the Reagan Library in Simi Valley.
In early 2017, I went there during my *Three Days in January*
book tour to deliver a speech about President and General Eisenhower, telling a packed house stories of a humble leader who
had never forgotten his small-town roots in Abilene, Kansas. At
a homecoming speech in 1945, General Eisenhower said, "The
proudest thing I can claim is that I am from Abilene." A few

years later, he became president. Running for a second term, shortly before Election Day 1956, President Eisenhower took questions from viewers in a made-for-TV event called "The People Ask the President." Ike again harkened back, as he often did, to Abilene, saying, "I belong to a family of boys who were raised in meager circumstances in central Kansas, and every one of us earned our way as we went along, and it never occurred to us that we were poor, but we were."

There are many similarities between the thirty-fourth and the fortieth presidents. But one of the deepest was their small-town sensibility. Marlin Fitzwater, President Reagan's press secretary, who happened to be from Abilene, Kansas, saw this connection between the two men. "Governor and then President Reagan always took the conversation back to Dixon, Illinois, where he grew up," Fitzwater told me. "I've always believed the absolute biggest and most compelling force in Ronald Reagan's life was the goodness that he saw in the American people, and that is a small-town goodness. People in Abilene and Dixon believe in each other, believe in the country, and basically they just think their friends and neighbors are good people. Reagan thought that to his last day. Presidents Reagan and Eisenhower knew themselves and knew how they felt about America. They were both just decent guys. Shared small-town values."

And with that connective tissue from the focus of my first book in the "Three Days" presidential series, I've found the second: President Ronald Reagan, his speech to students at Moscow State University during the final summit with the Soviets, and how he arrived at that point and those messages throughout his life. Its publication will come on the thirtieth anniversary of the Moscow summit, a fitting memorial at a moment in history when we once again face forces of evil on a global scale.

Like Eisenhower, Reagan is a leader we turn to still. Barely a day goes by when someone—a colleague, a viewer, a friend, a person on my social media feed—doesn't mention Reagan, wondering what he'd have to say about the world we've inherited or wishing we had him back. He continues to speak to us as we navigate these uneasy times. He would have preached vigilance. "Freedom is never more than one generation away from extinction," he said in 1961, long before becoming president. "We didn't pass it on to our children in their bloodstream. It must be fought for, protected and handed on for them to do the same."

—Bret Baier
   May 2018

THREE
DAYS IN
MOSCOW

PROLOGUE

THE WALK

May 29, 1988
Moscow

Nancy Reagan, looking poised and elegant in a dark gray Oscar de la Renta dress with a white bow-tied collar, gathered the administration staff, advance team, and Secret Service agents in an ornate living room of Spaso House. It was late in the afternoon of the Reagans' arrival day in Moscow, and they were staying at the historic yellow mansion, home of US ambassador Jack Matlock. The mood of the staff and officials who stood around Nancy was upbeat and expectant, if not a little awestruck. Here were the president of the United States and the first lady on a first-time visit to the heart of the Soviet Union, the place Reagan had once called the "Evil Empire." As Nancy wrote a decade later in her memoir, "If someone had told me when Ronnie and I were first married that we would eventually travel to Moscow as president and first lady, and would be the honored guests of the Soviet leadership, I would have suggested that he get his head examined."

The opening of relations was tentative but hopeful, a romance still in a delicate early stage, marred by tension but buttressed by a genuine chemistry between the two principals,

Reagan and Soviet general secretary Mikhail Gorbachev. The Reagan visit followed a similar trip to the United States by Gorbachev only six months earlier. During his visit, the American people had showered "Gorby" with goodwill. They found him charming and were buoyed by his growing friendship with the president, never before seen from a Soviet leader. Now it was Reagan's turn.

Beneath the pomp and glitter, Reagan understood that this wasn't a ceremonial visit. Despite their personal chemistry, Reagan and Gorbachev were combatants, playing out the endgame of a decades-long battle for the future of civilization. In the final months of his presidency, Reagan intended to show the world that the democratic principles he espoused were the only road to the future. It was a message he thought might be welcomed by the long-suffering citizenry of Moscow, whose daily lives were burdened by matters of survival—standing in long lines for poor-quality products, enduring waiting lists for the most basic housing, suffering chronic shortages of fruit, vegetables, and meat, struggling with outdated technology when it was available at all—and the heavy hand of oppressive paternalism, which told them what to say, where to go, and what to believe.

Whatever noble ideals might have existed in the minds and hearts of Karl Marx and Vladimir Lenin, the Communist system had grown corrupt and unworkable, with a legacy of famine, labor camps for perceived enemies, religious persecution, steady economic decline, and a mad expansionism that was crippling the USSR's satellite nations and threatening its very existence. Gorbachev shared many of those concerns; they were the impetus for his program of reform called perestroika, which was designed to eliminate corruption and waste and shift the command economy to a more market-based system. But progress was slow, and the sluggish and overbearing state machinery made it impossible to initiate more rapid and widespread changes. The citizens were growing restless.

"People in the Soviet Union used to say, 'We open the fridge and don't see perestroika inside,'" Daniel Aarão Reis, a professor of contemporary history at Fluminense Federal University in Rio de Janeiro, said of that time. Instead of getting better, things were getting worse. By the time of Reagan's Moscow visit, Gorbachev's popularity at home was in decline and he had many establishment enemies. "His growing loneliness reflected his conscious choice to be a reformer determined to forge ahead despite the increasing political risk," his aide Andrei Grachev wrote. He was desperate and looking for a lifeline from Reagan.

The Reagans had arrived at Vnukovo International Airport earlier in the afternoon, to be greeted by Soviet dignitaries and a crowd of US Embassy workers. In an unusual move, Soviet TV covered the arrival live—a nod to Gorbachev's program of glasnost, literally meaning "openness." As the Reagans sped toward the Kremlin in the armored Cadillac that had been flown from Washington for their use, groups of Muscovites lined the roadways to watch and wave. As they neared the center of the city, the crowds became larger, and people stood on high-rise balconies to watch. Two blimps, pulling giant Soviet and US flags, circled lazily overhead.

Reagan was relaxed and rested following a four-day stopover in Helsinki, some five hundred miles away. The American media speculated that the seventy-seven-year-old president needed a break before making what could be the most significant diplomatic trip of his presidency. But one could hardly fault Reagan for the wisdom of that strategy, which allowed him to recover from jet lag (given the eight-hour time difference) before meeting Gorbachev face-to-face on his own turf.

Arriving at the Grand Kremlin Palace, a structure of breathtaking mass and majesty, the Reagans went inside and walked up a long staircase to the second floor. They entered St. George Hall, a chandeliered marble room the size of a football field, lined with eighteen columns topped with statues featuring Russian military leaders. As they walked down the long red carpet, Mikhail and Raisa Gorbachev appeared at the opposite end, coming toward them. They met in the middle—high symbolism—smiling and shaking hands. Raisa presented Nancy with a bouquet of two dozen pink roses.

At the opening ceremony, Gorbachev gave the couple a warm welcome, and Reagan responded in kind. The two men pointedly traded proverbs. "Mr. President," Gorbachev said, "you and Mrs. Reagan are here on your first visit to the Soviet Union, a country which you have so often mentioned in your public statements. Aware of your interest in Russian proverbs, let me add another one to your collection: 'It is better to see once than to hear a hundred times.'"

When it was his turn to speak, Reagan, who had practiced the pronunciation of a Russian proverb on the plane, said, "In the past, Mr. General Secretary, you've taken note of my liking for Russian proverbs. And so as not to disappoint anyone on this visit, I thought I would mention a literary saying from your past, another example of your people's succinct wisdom. *Rodilsya, ne toropilsya*. It was born, it wasn't rushed." Gorbachev smiled, seeming to approve. It was a moment of mutual understanding.

After the ceremony, Reagan and Gorbachev met privately for a time while Raisa took Nancy on a tour. The two women had never had a warm relationship. Nancy disliked Raisa's imperiousness and penchant for lecturing her on the benefits of communism. She'd made a point of studying up on Russian culture and the Soviet Union before the visit, hoping to hold her own. The eagle-eyed press was always on the lookout for the slightest sign of a chill between the two women, and this trip was no different. Leading up to the visit, many articles were published speculating on the "wives' summit." A cartoon by *Phoenix Gazette* cartoonist Len "Boro" Borozinski depicted Nancy and Raisa arm wrestling while their husbands happily pumped hands.

As they strolled through Assumption Cathedral, the oldest church in Moscow, Raisa talked nonstop as Nancy listened with rigid posture and an expressionless face. When she was finally able to get a word in, the first lady asked if the cathedral was used for religious services.

"Nyet," Raisa replied curtly.

"Oh, yes," Nancy said with a withering tone. "The word 'nyet,' that I understand."

Coincidentally, their husbands were also talking about religion and human rights. The private meeting between Reagan and Gorbachev had not been on the schedule, and as aides hovered outside, eagerly awaiting a report from the translator, they didn't know that Reagan had decided to directly raise the issue of religious freedom. Referring to the Jews who wanted to emigrate, he asked Gorbachev, "Did it ever occur to you, on this whole question of human rights, that maybe if these Jews were permitted to worship as they want to, and teach their children the Hebrew language, that maybe they wouldn't want to leave the Soviet Union?"

Gorbachev was briefly taken aback that the president was so quick to bring up such a sensitive topic. But Reagan's comment foreshadowed a theme he would return to as a core purpose of the visit. He made a point of often bringing up religion. Turning personal, he confided to Gorbachev that there was one thing he had always wanted to do for his son Ron, who was an avowed atheist. He wished to serve him the perfect gourmet dinner, and at the end, after Ron had thoroughly enjoyed the meal, he would ask him if he believed there was a cook. He wondered how his son would answer. Gorbachev replied that the only possible answer was yes.

Now it was day's end, and they were back at Spaso House, the residence of the US ambassador, which could be considered a US oasis a mile from the Kremlin—if you didn't mind that the rooms were probably bugged. Everyone breathed a sigh of relief that the arrival had passed without incident. Until Nancy Reagan gathered everyone together.

"We thought she was just going to say, 'It's great to have you all here on this historic occasion,'" press secretary Marlin Fitzwater recalled. "But she announced, 'The president and I want to go for a walk among the people. We want to talk to Soviet citizens.'"

A hush fell over the room as everyone grasped what she was saying. No preparations had been made for a walk outside. The area she had in mind, a couple hundred yards from Spaso House, called the Arbat, was a pedestrian mall open to artists, vendors, and cafés, crowded with pushcarts selling sack dolls, vegetables, and food. The Arbat was surrounded by large limestone apartment houses, with windows facing the street. It was a security team's nightmare.

Ray Shaddick, the seasoned Secret Service detail leader (he'd been with Reagan during the assassination attempt in 1981), told Nancy that they hadn't coordinated a public stroll with the Moscow police or KGB, perhaps thinking that would settle the matter. Advance man James Hooley added his concerns. But Nancy was insistent. The president had decided that this summit would not be conducted solely in the privacy of conference rooms. He and Nancy planned to be as public as possible. "This was the last act," Fitzwater said. "He wanted to show freedom of assembly, and he wanted to talk to the Russian people. He talked about that privately all the time, and I think Gorbachev's attitude towards him was good enough to allow Reagan to think in terms of the Russian people being different from the Russian government—that they cared about the same things we cared about."

Nancy asked the Secret Service agents, the advance team, and the president's advisors to join her in her bedroom to continue the discussion. As they gathered around her bed, she said, "I don't want to hear any more talk about what you can't do and who you've talked to and what the KGB think and all of that. My question is, Can we do this or not? Yes or no?"

Everyone turned to look at Shaddick. It was his call.

Shaddick didn't say no, which Nancy took as a yes.

"Fine," she said. "We go in fifteen minutes."

They rushed out of the room to make what arrangements they could.

The Secret Service called for additional agents to come, and notified the police and KGB. Fitzwater quickly gathered the press pool and instructed them to stay close together, like a flock of ducklings, outside the embassy door so they could fall in line behind the first couple.

At 6:10 P.M., the Reagans appeared, casually walking down the spiral staircase, and were on their way. They ducked into their limo to ride the mere two hundred feet to the Arbat. It was crowded on that Sunday afternoon, and by the time they departed their vehicle, people were rushing in from every side, cheering and running toward them. The Secret Service and KGB formed a protective ring around the Reagans, but it was bedlam. In the crush of bodies, people were shouting

"We can't see you!" So Reagan climbed onto an open vegetable cart, pulling Nancy up beside him, as the crowd swelled forward. Reagan didn't have a microphone, but he shouted to be heard, calling out, "I'm so happy to be here . . . to meet the Russian people . . . to say hello." His voice was swallowed up by the cheers.

Above the street, faces appeared at the windows of the buildings, and then bodies began to stream out the doors as people came from their apartments, calling, "Mr. President! Mr. President!"

There were suddenly thousands of people on the Arbat, and there was a sense of quickly growing danger, of things spiraling out of control. "This is either going to be the greatest performance in history, or it's going to be a disaster," Fitzwater thought. "Somebody's going to get hurt."

At that point, the KGB agents started to panic. They were not used to crowd control issues in Moscow, where the population mostly kept in line or out of sight when the KGB was around. While Reagan was shouting from the cart, "This is an example of free assembly!," the KGB was seeing it as a grave threat to the established order. As the crowds pushed forward, Secret Service agents pulled the Reagans down from the cart, shouting "Get down! We're going back to the house!" They set off, with the crowd rushing after them, including the press pool, with the indomitable sixty-seven-year-old Helen Thomas in the lead.

Then the KGB agents, whose stony brutality was well known to the citizens, began randomly attacking people in the crowd. Fitzwater and Deputy Chief of Staff Kenneth Duberstein were pushed outside the president's cordon. Duberstein got hit on the head with a billy club. Several reporters were knocked down by security agents, one was punched in the face, another was slammed into a concrete trash receptacle, still another was bear-hugged and almost choked by his camera strap. But still the crowd came forward toward the Reagans, only to be roughly beaten back by the agents.

One of the KGB men grabbed Helen Thomas, who stumbled and cried out. Nancy saw it and stepped back, shouting "She's with us!" and pulled Helen from his grip. "Come on, Helen," the first lady cried, hanging on to the dazed reporter. She held on to her all the way to the door. "You owe me one," she said, before releasing the tempest-tossed Helen back to the press pool.

The group entered Spaso House, everyone feeling the aftershock, thinking of how close they'd come to a crisis. "Just a couple more shoves and pushes, and it would have been a disaster," Fitzwater said.

Nancy turned to him. "Well, Marlin, what do you think?" she asked.

They all stared at him, waiting for the press secretary's verdict on the incident. "Well," he replied, "we just lost the last best chance of getting rid of Helen Thomas." That broke the ice.

The Reagans didn't seem at all ruffled. In fact, they looked quite pleased and even exhilarated by the experience. Forget the KGB's reaction; the main event for them had been the wonderful outpouring of love from the Russian people and the photo op that was created by the incident. It was a form of payback for Gorbachev's clever move while in the States six months earlier. Driving through Washington on his way to the White House, Gorbachev had spontaneously hopped out of his vehicle on Connecticut Avenue to greet lunchtime crowds and was mobbed by wildly cheering Americans crying, "We love you!" It was a major PR coup, and now the Reagans had done the same in Moscow.

"It was clearly an effort by the president to duplicate what Gorbachev had done when he stopped on Connecticut Avenue," said Chris Wallace, who was a young reporter covering the Moscow trip for NBC. "It was his way of saying 'If you're going to charm my citizens, I can do the same to you.'"

But one-upmanship wasn't Reagan's only motivation. In the early hours of his Moscow trip, he was laying the groundwork for a more profound endeavor. Although the continuation of arms control negotiations was the stated agenda, his aim was more cinematic—an effort to touch Russians at their core, their very humanity. What did all people have in common? Greater than the fear of war or the pride of supremacy were the basic human values of life, liberty, and the pursuit of happiness. And although those values were central to the American creed, that did not mean they were owned exclusively by Americans. Like struggling plants straining toward the light, the Soviet people, too, desired those life-affirming benefits.

In the midst of those desires, it was a sobering reality that the arms race was a constant threat. Early in their relationship, Reagan had told Gorbachev, "We represent two countries that could initiate another world war. Or, we could make sure that there would not be another world war." It had been that way since the beginning of the nuclear age, but Reagan hoped that Gorbachev would be a more honest broker than his predecessors. Now they would meet in their fourth summit, having wrestled mightily with the questions of war and peace, but also with identity. What were these two great nations going to be in the future? Reagan wanted to take a step out into the unknown and make a personal appeal, to open a window for the people of Russia—to tell them right to their faces, "Look! The world is changing; there's a choice before you. Choose freedom."

"Sometimes the best act is the final act," Reagan had told reporters as he boarded Air Force One for Moscow. That's the way he saw this trip. He had just three days to make his appeal and forge an opening; three days to let the Russian people take a personal measure of the possibilities of democracy, which was mostly an ideological abstraction, if not an abhorrent philosophy, to them. He had been preparing for this moment for most of his life, and he had to make it count.

PART ONE

REAGAN'S DESTINY

CHAPTER 1

DREAM MAKER

Ronald Reagan often told a story about his childhood that captures a key aspect of his unique appeal. As the drum major for the YMCA boys' band in Dixon, Illinois, a position he had secured because he didn't play a musical instrument, he was out front during a small-town parade for Decoration Day, marching behind the marshal, who was on his horse. At one point the marshal turned his mount around and rode back to check on the line of marchers. "I kept marching down the street," Reagan wrote, "pumping my baton up and down, in the direction I thought we were supposed to go. But after a few minutes, I noticed the music behind me was growing fainter and fainter." Turning, he found that he was marching alone. Unbeknown to Reagan, the marshal had returned to the front of the band and directed them to turn a corner. "It wasn't the last time, incidentally, that people have said I sometimes march to a different drummer," Reagan observed.

Reagan was an enigma in the political world, a complex person who defied labels. He could be called a sociable loner, a man of amiable warmth who was most content in his own company. "I've always said that Ronald Reagan would make a superb hermit," Lyn Nofziger, an early aide and confidant, said. "He really didn't need anybody . . . he was not a typical gregarious politician."

This paradox of his personality has fascinated pundits and historians for decades. The search to know the real Reagan has thwarted his closest friends and allies, presidential historians, and even sometimes his beloved wife, Nancy, who wrote that he built a wall around himself that even she sometimes felt: "He lets me come closer than anyone else, but there are times when even I feel that barrier."

The journalist Robert Draper referred to his "sunny aloofness," capturing a certain remoteness that Reagan himself acknowledged. "I've never had trouble making friends," he explained, "but I've been inclined to hold back a little of myself, reserving it for myself."

He was a handsome actor—in the style of Robert Taylor, his agent suggested—who never quite clicked as a romantic leading man on the big screen, yet as a politician he was idolized. He was sentimental and loving, penning long letters to strangers, yet his own children often felt rebuffed by him. He was mocked by his critics for being an empty suit, yet he was a careful, studious chief executive—a voracious reader and talented writer who often left his speechwriters in awe. He was surrounded by loyal advisors, some of whom stayed with him throughout his political life, yet he had few if any real friends apart from Nancy. He projected a welcoming demeanor, yet on the inside he was tough as nails. Martin Anderson, a policy advisor, once depicted him as "warmly ruthless." He revitalized the conservative movement, achieved bold economic goals, and set the stage for the end of the Cold War, yet he was habitually underestimated. He *did* march to a different drummer, yet he captured the imagination of the nation and the world and counted as allies the most substantive political figures of his era. In her eulogy to him, British prime minister Margaret Thatcher spoke of his special nature: "In his lifetime, Ronald Reagan was such a cheerful and invigorating presence that it was easy to forget what daunting historic tasks he set himself."

He has been likened to Franklin D. Roosevelt in his gift for communication, especially the way he could reach out across the airwaves and impart a vision and sense of purpose to the American people. He shared with Eisenhower a hardscrabble childhood, a human touch, and a restrained ego. Like Ike, he despised pretention and was skeptical of praise. He might grimace were he alive today to observe the almost religious reverence with which he is regarded in Republican circles. Adulation embarrassed him, and he couldn't tolerate people being obsequious in his presence. A small plaque on his Oval Office desk read, "There is no limit to what a man can do or where he can do it if he doesn't care who gets the credit."

In his early life, Reagan wasn't a person of grand ambitions. He wrote that he would have been happy to spend his life as a sports announcer. He was drawn to politics through passion and ideas, and he was as surprised as anyone when they connected with the public. "I thought I married an actor," Nancy wrote in her memoir. "I honestly never expected that Ronald Reagan would go into politics."

It's interesting to speculate how this reserved, complex man, who did not wear his high ambitions on his sleeve, grew up to be a president of such iconic stature and achievement. But clues can be found in his upbringing, with its blend of moral conviction, homespun values, and struggle.

RONALD WILSON REAGAN WAS born on February 6, 1911, in a modest apartment above the Pitney General Store in the small farming town of Tampico, Illinois. The family legend has it that his father, Jack, took one look at him, bawling his head off, and said, "For such a little bit of a fat Dutchman, he makes a hell of a lot of noise, doesn't he?" Thus his nickname, Dutch, an odd moniker for the son of an Irishman whose ancestors, the O'Regans, hailed from County Tipperary, and a Scots-English mother. The nickname stuck, though it was seldom used after he entered politics. It didn't fit the rosy-cheeked Irishman all that well. Reagan's brother, Neil, two and a half years older, also had a nickname, Moon, given him in high school, after the comic strip character Moon Mullins, which stayed with him for life.

Jack and Nelle Reagan, whom their children called by their first names, were attractive people—Jack was tall, dark-haired, and muscular, and Nelle was small and auburn-haired with bright blue eyes. He was a Catholic, and she was a Protestant (Disciples of Christ), both devout in their religious beliefs and practices. In reminiscences Reagan spoke of an all-American childhood and liked to recall happy times and boyish adventures. He loved and admired his parents, even though Jack, a shoe salesman whose big dreams were frequently dashed, struggled to provide for the family. "He loved shoes," Reagan wrote, saying his father had even studied about them in correspondence courses. "He might have made a brilliant career out of selling, but he lived in a time—and with a weakness—that made him a frustrated man."

That weakness was alcoholism. Jack's battle with drink was a constant theme of Reagan's childhood, but mostly it was kept in the background, until the day at age eleven when Reagan came home alone one cold, windy night to find his dad sprawled on the front porch, passed out drunk. "I wanted to let myself in the house and go to bed and pretend he wasn't there," Reagan recalled, with some sympathy for that young boy. Instead, he dragged his slumbering father inside and somehow got him into

bed. The confrontation with the hard truth of his father's struggle stayed with him, but he never condemned him. Nelle had
taught her boys not to disparage their father for his drinking; it
was a sickness, not a moral failing, she said, and they learned
to see it that way, too.

The frequent moves of his early childhood and his father's
alcoholism did not engender the typical expressions of resent-
ment or fear. For that reason, Reagan's memories of his father
were warm and loving. In two memoirs, he went out of his way
to highlight the aspects of Jack's character that showed him
in a positive light. But his biographer Lou Cannon observed
that those facets of his upbringing might have contributed to
his habit of keeping people at an emotional arm's length. "If
you're the child of an alcoholic, you see things you don't want
to remember, and you certainly don't want to tell anybody,"
Cannon said. "Its main impact on Reagan was to create a kind
of inward part of him that was a very, very important part of
his character."

Although Jack's dreams went unfulfilled, he was a hard
worker who believed that stability was always around the corner. They moved from place to place during Reagan's early
life—six moves in his first nine years. That itinerant life might
have contributed to Reagan's sense of himself as an outsider.
Perhaps it was also responsible for his gift for reinvention.

There was never enough money, even with Nelle supple-
menting their income with sewing. But Reagan said, "I learned
from my father the value of hard work and ambition, and
maybe a little something about telling a story. From my mother,
I learned the value of prayer, how to have dreams and believe I
could make them come true."

The family finally settled in Dixon, Illinois, on the south side
of the Rock River, when Reagan was nine. Dixon was a classic

exemplar of the American heartland. The family home at 816 South Hennepin Avenue, a modest two-story white frame house with a wide front porch, where they lived for three years, was later restored and designated by Congress as his official boyhood home, a national historic site. In 1984, President Reagan returned to Dixon on his seventy-third birthday and spoke of his boyhood. "Times were tough," he told the audience. "But what I remember most clearly is that Dixon held together. Our faith was our strength. Our teachers pointed to the future. People held on to their hopes and dreams. Neighbors helped neighbors. We knew—my brother, Moon, and I, our mother and father, Nelle and Jack, saw to that—we would overcome adversity and that after the storm, the stars would come."

Looking back on his childhood, Reagan could never resist casting a rosy glow over the experience. He loved to describe his heartland upbringing as being an essential American story, full of character-building experiences. He even wrote of his early childhood, "My existence turned into one of those rare Huck Finn–Tom Sawyer idylls. There were woods and mysteries, life and death among the small creatures, hunting and fishing; those were the days when I learned the real riches of rags." Most of all, he loved football, which he considered "a matter of life and death."

He was also a voracious reader. In a letter to a librarian shortly after he became president, he recalled his love of books. At least once a week after dinner he would take a long walk to the library, where he would spend a lot of time browsing before choosing two books to check out. He enjoyed a wide range of books, from Mark Twain to Horatio Alger to the Tarzan books and the Rover Boys, a popular adventure series. The Dixon Public Library, he declared, was his "house of magic."

Those who idolize Reagan as the standard-bearer of conservatism might be surprised to learn that his most important early influences were not Republican—showing that patriotism can transcend party. Not only were his parents Democrats, they became fervent supporters of FDR, who earned their respect with his programs to rescue the country from the Great Depression. Jack Reagan was employed by the Works Progress Administration (WPA) coordinating food distribution to the poor. His father's son, Ronald Reagan cast his first vote ever for FDR and remained loyal to him and then to the Democratic Party for twenty years. Certain liberal principles were appealing to him. His parents, he said, believed literally in the equality of all people, a progressive ideal in an era when Jim Crow was at its height. Reagan recalled the time when the film *The Birth of a Nation* came to town. The film portrayed blacks, who were played by white actors in blackface, as aggressive and threatening to white women, while elevating the Ku Klux Klan as a patriotic group. Jack Reagan said, "I'm damned if anyone in this family will go see it." Regularly, during Reagan's childhood, his father and mother reached out to blacks, welcoming them into their home and lending them their support. Reagan recounted another incident during his college years when his football team was away from campus, requiring an overnight stay in Dixon. When the hotel manager refused to take a black teammate, Reagan promptly invited him to his house, where he knew he'd be welcome. The moral principle of equality for all and respect for each person's human dignity was burned into Reagan's very being, and he carried it throughout his life. He was deeply pained when critics later accused him of racial insensitivity.

Although many aspects of Reagan's early emotional life are mysterious, one thing is clear: the powerful influence of his mother. Nelle Reagan, outgoing, generous, and creative, nurtured Reagan's dreams and helped shape his character. As Bonnie Angelo, the author of *First Mothers: The Women Who Shaped the Presidents*, put it, "When the credits roll on the Reagan life story, Nelle Wilson Reagan should be listed as director, producer, and head of casting." Not only did she instill in him the optimistic spirit that made him such an attractive politician, she also trained him for public performances, involving him in the small plays she loved to put on for her church and demonstrating her own theatrical skills in amateur performances. A constantly positive presence despite the trials of poverty and a flawed husband, she became Reagan's central model for living a life above the fray. In her eyes, anything could be accomplished, no matter how difficult.

The source of Nelle's boundless spirit was her deep faith; its payoff was an opportunity for her children to rise. As Reagan wrote, "She had a natural and intuitive intelligence that went a long way toward overcoming a shortage of formal schooling. She had a drive to help my brother and me make something of ourselves."

Nelle was also a writer, penning many poems and sonnets, such as this one:

To higher, nobler things my mind is bent
Thus giving of my strength, which God has lent,
I strive some needy souls unrest, to soothe
Lest they the paths of righteousness shall lose

In another era and under more fortunate circumstances, Nelle might have been famous in her own right. Instead, she had a son whose star shined on her behalf.

Like his mother, Reagan had poetic tendencies, and one poem, published in his high school yearbook, *The Dixonian*, reveals the inner conflict between suffering and joy that he would return to many times in his life.

Life

I wonder what it's all about, and why
We suffer so, when little things go wrong?
We make our life a struggle,
When life should be a song.

Reagan was drawn to a heroic ideal and throughout his life often pointed to his summers as a lifeguard, which began in 1926, when he was fifteen, and continued for the next seven years, at Dixon's Lowell Park, a beach on the Rock River, where, he said, he had saved seventy-seven lives. It seemed that he was as proud of that achievement as anything else in his life. As president, he wrote a letter to a woman whose son had reached out to say that Reagan had taught his mother to dive, saying "Just between us I think maybe lifeguarding at Lowell Park was the best job I ever had." But he also learned a lesson: people didn't always appreciate being saved. He wryly noted that "almost every one of them later sought me out and angrily denounced me for dragging them to shore." Perhaps it was a perfect training ground for politics, planting a seed in Reagan's mind that government "help" wasn't always welcome or effective.

As he reached the end of his high school years, Reagan was determined to go to college, a lofty goal in his circumstances. In 1928, on the eve of the Great Depression, midwestern farming communities were struggling, and certainly Reagan's family didn't have extra funds for his education. But he set his sights on Eureka College, seventy-five miles from home, and secured a football scholarship for half his tuition, which was $400. The remainder he paid for with his lifeguarding savings, and he was

given a job to cover his board, first washing dishes in a frater-
nity house. By his junior year, he was working as a lifeguard
and official swim coach.

Eureka was a small college, run by the Disciples of Christ,
with only two hundred and fifty students, but it was Reagan's
introduction to a wider world. It was at Eureka during his
freshman year that he first found his public voice and had his
initial experience with political persuasion. Facing a financial
crisis, the college president had announced a plan to make deep
academic cuts that would decimate the faculty and leave gradu-
ating seniors without enough courses to fulfill requirements for
their majors. The college was in an uproar over the announcement. The students threatened to strike, and Reagan joined the
strike committee as the freshman class representative.

When it was time for the students and faculty to vote on
the strike motion, it was decided that a freshman should sell
the idea, and Reagan found himself standing before a raucous
crowd, summoning the courage to speak. "I discovered that
night that an audience has a feel to it, and in the parlance of
the theater, that audience and I were together," he wrote later.
By the time he was finished, the crowd was on its feet, voting
by acclimation to strike. "For the first time in my life, I felt my
words reach out and grab an audience, and it was exhilarating,"
he recalled, noting with satisfaction that the threat of a strike
worked. The college backed down from its original plan, and
the faculty jobs were saved.

From then on Eureka refused to let the financial weight of
the Depression sink it. In a 1957 commencement address at the
college, Reagan spoke of the Depression-era hardships it had
endured and overcome. "We attended a college that made it
possible for us to attend regardless of our lack of means, that
created jobs for us, so that we could eat and sleep, and that

allowed us to defer our tuition and trusted that they could get paid some day long after we had gone," he told the students who were living in more comfortable times. "And the professors, God bless them, on this campus, the most dedicated group of men and women whom I have ever known, went long months without drawing any pay. Sometimes the college, with a donation of a little money or produce from a farm, would buy groceries and dole them out to the teachers to at least try and provide them with food." He was unabashedly proud of his college, and in later years he would often speak of the courage of institutions such as Eureka that had made the pursuit of one's aspirations possible even during the nation's darkest times.

Reagan wasn't a particularly good student—he graduated with a C average—but he was fully engaged, playing football, swimming, performing with the drama and debate clubs, and being elected president of the student council. He was learning to put aside self-doubt, to form an identity. By the time of his graduation in 1932, he knew he wanted to be a performer. But how exactly that would happen eluded him. First he needed to get a job. Borrowing his father's car, he set off on a circuit of radio stations within a hundred-mile radius of Dixon and at one point found himself at WOC in Davenport, Iowa, seventy-five miles away. It was a popular station with the motto "WOC Davenport, where the West begins, in the state where the tall corn grows." It happened that the station was looking for a sports announcer, and when it tested Reagan it saw he had a knack for bringing the thrill of a game home, creating the visual pictures that kept listeners tethered to their radios. That was no easy task. It required reading the ticker descriptions of a game and then painting a live picture for listeners without seeing the game itself, elaborating where necessary to dramatize every pitch. Reagan was hired for a sum of $10 a game, and over the next four years he gained a following and advanced to WHO in Des Moines, where he secured a good salary for the time and happily immersed himself in the world of broadcasting national baseball and football games.

That might have been the fulfillment of his dreams. But on a trip to Los Angeles in 1937 to cover spring training for the Chicago Cubs, Reagan was introduced to William Meiklejohn, a movie agent. Meiklejohn took one look at the handsome six-foot, one-inch tall young man with the wavy dark hair and golden voice and was interested in him, although for Reagan the meeting was a blur—literally. He'd been advised to ditch his glasses for the occasion, and he could barely see without them. (When he'd received his first pair of glasses as a child, he'd been amazed to see that trees had leaves!)

With Reagan sitting there, Meiklejohn picked up the phone and called Maxwell Arnow, a casting director for Warner Bros. He told him, "I have another Robert Taylor sitting in my office." Arnow was doubtful, but he agreed to a screen test. Reagan remembered his discomfort during the test, which he compared to being examined like a slab of beef. He wasn't encouraged. But when Jack Warner, the powerful head of Hollywood's most prominent studio, viewed the test, he liked what he saw. Before Reagan returned home, he'd been offered the chance of a lifetime: a seven-year contract with Warner Bros. for $200 a week.

Reagan once joked that his first role might have been called "The Remaking of Dutch Reagan." The hair, makeup, and wardrobe pros were brutal about detailing his flaws. They said his body was out of proportion: he had a small head, short neck, and large shoulders. The problem was solved by calling in Jimmy Cagney's tailor, who had devised a solution for the similarly challenged star, a collar design that spread wider than normal. From then on, Reagan wore shirts with broad collars that put his head and shoulders into balance. Not many people would ever remark that Reagan had a small head. With the right tailoring, he appeared larger than life in all respects.

Reagan brought his parents to California and set them up in a house, where they helped handle his fan mail. They were happy there until Jack's premature death in 1941, which was attributed to his drinking and two-to-three-pack-a-day cigarette habit. Nelle lived on until 1962, when she died at age seventy-nine of complications from Alzheimer's disease. Reagan was glad to have his parents close at hand, and he was as proud as any son could be that he could give them some comfort in their later years after a lifetime of struggle.

As a contract player, Reagan amassed a respectable body of B movies, most of them forgettable. But there were exceptions, films that gained a revival of sorts once he became politically famous. The first of these was a 1940 movie called *Knute Rockne, All American*, the story of a great Notre Dame football coach of the 1920s, played by Pat O'Brien. The key scene in the film involved his star player, George Gipp, played by Reagan. Gipp was grievously ill, and as he lay on his deathbed he told his coach, "Rock, sometimes when the team is up against it and the breaks are beating the boys, tell them to go out there with all they've got and win just one for the Gipper." The line "Win one for the Gipper" became a campaign slogan for Reagan, and he was often referred to as the Gipper during his political life.

A decade later, Reagan made another movie that captured the public imagination during his presidency, mostly because of the contrast between dignified governance and comedic hijinks. *Bedtime for Bonzo* was a lighthearted comedy about the efforts of a psychology professor, played by Reagan, to teach human values to a chimpanzee. As president, Reagan would occasionally watch the movie and get a little emotional. Those invited to join him during movie nights at Camp David sometimes balked at his choice of film. Worried that the press would mock him if they found out he'd been watching *Bedtime for Bonzo* again, Fitzwater once suggested another movie. Reagan called him a coward and insisted on his movie choice. "Marlin, I loved that chimp," he said, with tears in his eyes.

But the movie that made the greatest emotional impact on Reagan was *King's Row*, a 1942 drama about the hardships suffered in a small American town at the turn of the twentieth century. More than any other project, *King's Row* taught Reagan how to reach inside for human truth even when playing a fictional character. In the film, Reagan played the role of Drake McHugh, whose legs are amputated by a sadistic surgeon. Reagan agonized about that scene, trying to feel the reality of the terrible moment when McHugh awakes to find his legs gone. The prop department cut a hole in his mattress, and lying there with his legs visibly gone, Reagan felt a very strange sensation—an empathy he'd thought was beyond him. When the scene played and he delivered his famous line—"Where's the rest of me?"—he recalled having felt real alarm. It was the first film he'd done where there was anything approaching Oscar buzz, and he titled his 1965 Hollywood memoir *Where's the Rest of Me?*

In 1940, Reagan married a fellow contract performer, Jane Wyman, whom he had met while filming *Brother Rat* in 1938. The marriage lasted nine years, and Wyman became much more successful than her husband, winning an Oscar for *Johnny Belinda* and receiving four Oscar nominations during her career. Television viewers would later know her as the iron-willed head of a California winery in the popular television series *Falcon Crest*. They had two children, Maureen, born in 1941, and an adopted son, Michael, born in 1945. Both children suffered some alienation from their father before coming to a more positive resolution with him later in their lives.

Much has been made of Reagan's difficult relationship with his children. One can feel some compassion for a man who surely loved his kids and meant well but never quite knew how to reach them. There's no way of knowing what really was in his heart, much less what happened in his marriage, as he didn't write or speak of it. (In his memoir, *An American Life*, Reagan devoted only a slim paragraph in passing to the topic of his marriage and first two children.) Jane Wyman remained silent until Reagan's death, when she gave a brief public statement, deeming him "a great president and a great, kind and gentle man."

Until he met Nancy, his primary focus was on career, not family, and even his devotion to his wife did not always extend to his children. To be fair, fatherhood in 1940s and 1950s America was not always hands-on. Add to that the environment of a household with two Hollywood stars, whose children were often relegated to the care of housekeepers and nannies, and later to boarding schools, and a lot of the distance is explained.

As Michael wrote in a memoir when he was forty-two, pointedly titled *On the Outside Looking In*, his adopted status made him feel insecure, and he always struggled to measure up. "In every story the family tells about Dad, he always emerges heroic," he wrote. "I have never heard of him doing anything wrong. There was no way a child of his, especially one who was adopted, could live up to the image of the man who never made a mistake." The distance between the two was public, increasingly so during Reagan's presidency, when it caught the attention of the press. "Are you and your son Michael closer to resolving your differences?" Sam Donaldson called out at the end of one press conference, receiving no response as Reagan left the room. He refused to talk about his children, much less allow the press to psychoanalyze his parenting flaws. His children were less circumspect. However, by the time their father was suffering from Alzheimer's disease, Michael and Maureen had come to terms with him and were able to express their love for him—and he, in his own way, for them. "At the early onset of Alzheimer's disease my father and I would tell each other we loved each other, and we would give each other a hug," Michael wrote in his later book, *Lessons My Father Taught Me: The Strength, Integrity, and Faith of Ronald Reagan.* "As the years went by and he could no longer verbalize my name, he recognized me as the man who hugged him. So when I would walk into the house, he would be there in his chair opening up his arms for that hug hello and the hug good-bye. It was truly a blessing from God."

Maureen, who preceded Reagan in death—of cancer in 2001—also had warmer sentiments to express in later life, when she wrote of her admiration for her father, feeling he had achieved so much. As we'll see later, his children with Nancy had a different, but no less difficult, dynamic.

THE JAPANESE ATTACK ON Pearl Harbor changed the trajectory of Reagan's career. Before *King's Row* was released, the United States was at war. Reagan had been in the Army Reserves since 1937, although his poor eyesight had precluded his joining the war effort directly. However, within months of December 7, 1941, he was ordered to report for duty. He was assigned to a new unit creating training films for combat camera crews and producing patriotic films. For part of the war he was located at "Fort Roach," so named because the unit, commanded by Jack Warner, worked out of the Hal Roach Studios in Culver City, California. He was promoted to first lieutenant and then captain, and the unit produced some three hundred training and propaganda films during the war.

Reagan came out of World War II passionate about the fight against fascism, preaching the dangers of neo-fascism. He'd given little thought to communism at that point—after all, the Soviet Union had been an important ally during the war. That soon changed as he began participating in Hollywood organizations and found himself encountering a Communist undercurrent. Communist sentiments had been around Hollywood's labor unions for decades, to little effect, but rising Cold War tensions after the war heightened the danger of increased Communist influence in the entertainment industry. Nazism was defeated, but now there was a new fear, that the emboldened Soviet Union, under Josef Stalin, would make a direct attempt to control the American movie industry. Many people felt that unionism was a socialist construct. Reagan, a liberal Democrat and union man, experienced a growing shift in sentiment, a feeling that the world, rendered less dangerous by the defeat of Adolf Hitler, might be subjected to a Soviet threat.

As a self-proclaimed "near hopeless hemophiliac [bleeding heart] liberal," Reagan might have been fair game for recruitment by Communist sympathizers. But he was generally unaware of any efforts in that regard and even unknowingly joined organizations that were increasingly believed to be Communist fronts.

Reagan had been an alternate on the Screen Actors Guild board before the war; he resumed his position afterward and was soon elected as a full board member. Union conflicts at that time were severe. The strike of 1946 was a wake-up call. The strike was called by the Conference of Studio Unions (CSU), led by a far-left organizer, Herb Sorrell, who was suspected of being a Communist sympathizer. CSU's aim was to create a power base that would undermine the Screen Actors Guild and the other craft unions. But it soon became clear that CSU's strike was a fraud; it had been designed purely as a power move, with no interest in improving wages and conditions. Reagan was among those criticizing the strike, and he even urged members to cross the picket lines. For that he was threatened—"Your face will never be in pictures again," one anonymous caller vowed. But actually crossing the picket lines was a treacherous matter. There was some violence, but Reagan and others in the Guild kept the lines of negotiation open. The strike was finally ended, but in its aftermath a new possibility was advanced: that Moscow was behind the effort to disrupt and take over the reins of power in Hollywood.

Reagan's resolve during the strike impressed the SAG board, and in 1947 he was chosen to replace Robert Montgomery as president. Increasingly, he began to pay attention to the political environment and his role in it. "I didn't realize it," he wrote in his memoir, "but I'd started on a path that was going to lead me a long way from Hollywood."

CHAPTER 2

A POLITICAL EVOLUTION

The hearing room in the Cannon House Office Building was mobbed with press and onlookers, there for the riveting spectacle of real "American royalty," flown in from Hollywood to testify before Congress. It was October 23, 1947, the fourth day of hearings of the investigation by the House Un-American Activities Committee (HUAC) into communism in the motion picture industry. Spectators shoved their way in, jostling for position to witness the testimony of Gary Cooper, Robert Montgomery, and Ronald Reagan.

When it was Reagan's turn to testify, he sat upright and serious, peering at the committee members through horn-rimmed glasses. He might have been contemplating the journey that had brought him to this point, front and center in the investigation into the influence of Communists in Hollywood. It was, without a doubt, a central issue of his life.

The formative effect on Reagan of this early experience with communism cannot be overestimated, and he would make references to it throughout his life and presidency. In time, he came to see that too often, the use of terms like "Red Scare" and, later, "McCarthyism," were attempts to hide the historical record about Soviet attempts to undermine American democracy and commit espionage against the US government. Yet early on,

Reagan saw it in a far more nuanced way. He disagreed with the Communist ideology, but he believed that people had a right to believe in any ideology they chose. On the other hand, when that belief system turned into subversive activity that worked against the interests of the United States, that was a different matter.

Reagan could see that the congressional focus on Hollywood and communism had some resonance with ordinary Americans. "Perhaps part of it was the thought of shelling out money at the box office to support some bum and his swimming pool while he plotted the country's destruction," he wrote.

As the head of the Screen Actors Guild, Reagan's dilemma was how to straddle the line. He honestly believed that the Communist Party USA, and by extension the Soviet government, was trying to take over Hollywood using cutouts—willing surrogates. At the same time, he wanted to protect those people who were being falsely accused, and he was worried that HUAC's broad sweep would envelop the innocent as well as the guilty.

"Suddenly," he wrote, "subpoenas descended on Hollywood like a first snow of winter." Forty-one witnesses, among them the most famous names in Hollywood, were called to testify. Some, like Reagan, were viewed as "friendly" witnesses. But others refused to cooperate. Among the latter were the so-called Hollywood Ten—writers John Howard Lawson, Alvah Bessie, Lester Cole, Ring Lardner, Jr., Albert Maltz, Samuel Ornitz, and Dalton Trumbo; writer/producer Adrian Scott; writer/director Herbert Biberman; and director Edward Dmytryk. They announced that they would not testify and were held in contempt of Congress. They were briefly imprisoned, and their careers came to a halt. The atmosphere in the industry was by turns defiant and terrified. The thing was— and this worried Reagan—it wasn't just members of the Communist Party whose reputations and livelihoods were at stake;

anyone whose name came up in any context, via any hint or suggestion, was subject to intense scrutiny. There was too much room for error, especially when the grip of hysteria took hold. Not only that, it wasn't illegal to be a Communist, and the most sacred freedoms of American life allowed free speech, even the right to speak out against the government when you disagreed with it. Any fight against the Communist threat had to be conducted with a reverence for constitutional principles.

Now. as he sat before the congressional committee, Reagan attempted to articulate his strong aversion to communism, while making a robust defense of democratic freedoms. When Robert Stripling, the chief investigator for HUAC, asked him, "Mr. Reagan, what is your feeling about what steps should be taken to rid the motion-picture industry of any Communist influences, if they are there?" he gave what many judged to be the most thoughtful, balanced analysis of the hearings:

Well, sir . . . 99 percent of us are pretty well aware of what is going on, and I think within the bounds of our democratic rights, and never once stepping over the rights given us by democracy, we have done a pretty good job in our business of keeping those people's activities curtailed. After all, we must recognize them at present as a political party. On that basis we have exposed their lies when we came across them, we have opposed their propaganda, and I can certainly testify that in the case of the Screen Actors Guild we have been eminently successful in preventing them from, with their usual tactics, trying to run a majority of an organization with a well organized minority.

So that fundamentally I would say in opposing those people that the best thing to do is to make democracy work. In the Screen Actors Guild we make it work by insuring everyone a vote and by keeping everyone informed. I believe that, as Thomas Jefferson put it, if all the American people know all of the facts they will never make a mistake.

Whether the party should be outlawed, I agree with the gentlemen that preceded me that that is a matter for the Government to decide. As a citizen I would hesitate, or not like, to see any political party outlawed on the basis of its political ideology. We have spent 170 years in this country on the basis that democracy is strong enough to stand up and fight against the inroads of any ideology. However, if it is proven that an organization is an agent of a power, a foreign power, or in any way not a legitimate political party, and I think the Government is capable of proving that, if the proof is there, then that is another matter . . .

I happen to be very proud of the industry in which I work; I happen to be very proud of the way in which we conducted the fight. I do not believe the Communists have ever at any time been able to use the motion-picture screen as a sounding board for their philosophy or ideology.

Unlike other friendly witnesses, such as studio head Jack Warner and director Elia Kazan, he did not name names during his testimony. He had made his position clear: In opposing communism, the best thing to do was to make democracy work. In this, he laid down a marker that would stand during his political life: that the fight against communism would succeed only if Americans remained true to their ideals.

Sitting on the committee that day was a freshman congressman from California named Richard Nixon, who had been appointed to HUAC as one of his first assignments. The following year, Nixon's aggressive pursuit of Alger Hiss, a former State Department official accused of being a Communist operative, made him a household name and paved the way for a successful Senate run. Interestingly, Nixon did not ask a single question of Reagan that day. In 1947, few could have guessed that either Reagan or Nixon, much less both of them, would one day reach the heights of the presidency.

The fallout from the hearings was dramatic. Meeting in New York City the next month, studio heads devised the "Waldorf Statement," named after the hotel where the meeting took place. It contained a vow to deny employment to anyone who refused to cooperate with HUAC or who was suspected of being a Communist—including the Hollywood Ten. The action formalized the Communist blacklist, an idea Reagan supported in spite of his doubts about its fairness.

His activism also had a more personal impact: when he returned to Los Angeles after testifying before HUAC, he found his wife packing his bags. Their marriage was over, she told him. The reasons were open to speculation but never fully aired in public: the loss of their third child, Christine, who had died the day she was born; an affair on Wyman's part; Reagan's increasing political passion, which bored his wife; or just the fact that they had grown apart. Their early infatuation, burnished by the silver screen, could not survive the complexities of real life. Reagan was devastated by Wyman's decision—he hadn't seen it coming—but he responded to his heartbreak by throwing himself even more determinedly into his work.

As the president of SAG, Reagan continued to struggle with his conscience. It was an issue never resolved in that troubling era: how to reject the evils of communism while holding high the American values of free speech and creative autonomy. But in the following years he became more convinced than ever that the Communist threat was real.

In hindsight, the scourge of the Hollywood purge might seem overwrought and misdirected, even as Joe McCarthy's actions did—not to mention that it destroyed thousands of careers. Reagan abhorred many aspects of the Communist witch-hunt in Hollywood. Any validity the investigations might have had was undermined by the investigators' reliance on innuendo, anecdotal evidence, and political partisanship. While a later release of the HUAC investigation results showed Communist leanings and Party memberships in Hollywood, it was never determined whether the attempted takeover had made any headway. However, having lived through those years, Reagan never abandoned his conviction that communism was a great threat to the American way of life.

Ironically, it was blacklist mania that introduced Reagan to Nancy Davis, who would become the love of his life. As they both told the story, in 1949, Nancy was an up-and-coming young actress with a worrisome problem: reading the trade papers one day, she saw her name on a list of Communist sympathizers in Hollywood. That was no small matter; even the barest hint of an association with the Communist Party was enough to get a person blacklisted, thus ending their career. She was horrified. The Nancy Davis listed was not her but another person in the industry with the same name. She appealed to Mervyn LeRoy, the director of *East Side, West Side*, the movie she was filming, and he took her case to Reagan, who promised to take care of it. Nancy was relieved to have the Guild on her side, but she was also interested in meeting the handsome bachelor. She told LeRoy she'd feel much better if Reagan explained things to her himself. Obligingly, he called and asked her to dinner.

When she opened her door, she found herself looking up into Reagan's handsome face and teasing blue eyes. He was leaning on a crutch, the result of having broken his leg at a charity baseball game, but that just made him seem more dashing. Their date lasted until three in the morning. "If ever God gave me evidence that He had a plan for me, it was the night he brought Nancy into my life," Reagan wrote. But it was hardly a whirlwind romance. Reagan still felt burned by the end of his marriage, and Nancy gave him the time and space he needed. Their courtship stretched out over two years, until Reagan's doubts dissolved. "Let's get married," he said one night over dinner. Nancy took his hand and looked into his eyes. "Let's," she replied. They married on March 4, 1952, in a small church ceremony with only five people in attendance. Their first child, Patti, was born in October, followed by Ron in 1958.

By the early 1950s, Reagan was facing an identity crisis. His acting career was winding down. Even when scripts came his way, he found them uninteresting and rejected them, along with some big paydays. Television beckoned, but he dismissed the idea of a series. He needed to find a way to make money, but how? Then, in 1954, he received an intriguing proposal from MCA Television. The General Electric Company was backing a new series called the *General Electric Theater*, an original weekly production adapting novels and plays to the TV format. It needed a host to pull the whole thing together, and Reagan was offered the role. He thought it sounded like a classy idea and decided to take it.

In a move that would provide him with financial security, he was also offered part ownership of the show. For eight years he was the face of the *General Electric Theater*, welcomed into the homes of millions of Americans every Sunday night. But it was his travels to GE plants across the country that broadened his education in working-class concerns and simultaneously provided him with his first political platform. The tours, originally devised as a goodwill gesture by GE, allowed him to speak to hardworking Americans across the country about their values, trials, and aspirations. In time, he visited all 139 GE plants and spoke to more than 250,000 workers. Often, at the end of his speeches, he would stay to talk to the audience. He wanted to listen to their stories. "Those GE tours became a postgraduate course in political science for me," he wrote. "I was seeing how government really operated and affected people in America, not how it was taught in school."

Reagan was creating a political ideology during that time, a conviction that big government was the problem not the solution to America's troubles. He also continued to develop a theme that had been with him since the 1940s: the threat of communism to the American way of life. By then, the arms race between the United States and the Soviet Union had spiraled into a cold war, both nations living under the threat of nuclear destruction. "Whether we admit it or not, we are in a war," he told an audience in 1962. "This war was declared a century ago by Karl Marx and reaffirmed by Lenin when he said that communism and capitalism cannot exist side by side." Aiding and abetting it, he believed, were liberals who envisioned a society growing closer and closer to socialism. He found the response of his audiences gratifying.

Frequently, on the road, he wrote Nancy colorful, romantic letters, addressing her variously as "Nancy Pants," "Mommie Poo Pants," "Mommy," and "My Darling."

"I love you & miss you and I mean it differently than ever before," he gushed in a typical letter. "I've always loved you & missed you, but never has it been such an actual ache. The clock is standing still and April 16th seems a year away. . . . I'm all hollow without you and the 'hollow' hurts."

On one train ride home, he jumped off in Albuquerque, New Mexico, to send a telegram:

POWDER DOWN YOUR LIPSTICK. I AM ON THE
DOWNHILL SIDE OF ALBUQUERQUE. I LOVE YOU.

Their devotion was complete, a tight circle of romance that could sometimes seem to exclude their children, which caused tension. "Every family has problems, and we were no exception," Nancy wrote in a candid reflection many decades later. "What I wanted most in the world was to be a good wife and mother. As things turned out, I guess I've been more successful at the first than the second."

Patti and Ron might have agreed. A letter to Patti when Reagan was away filming a movie and she was not even two years old is telling: "I'm counting on you to take care of Mommie and keep her safe for me because there wouldn't be any moon or stars in the sky without her."

"He was easy to love, but hard to know," his son Ron wrote of him. "He was seldom far from our minds, but you couldn't help wondering sometimes whether he remembered you once you were out of his sight."

The net result was two defiant children and two disaffected stepchildren, none of whom was particularly interested in defending Nancy. Maureen and Michael blamed her, not entirely fairly, for their distance from their father. Patti and Ron blamed her for being the recipient of their father's worship while they often felt like afterthoughts or intruders in a great love affair.

But it wasn't just that. As they grew older, Patti and Ron also had to share their father with the nation, and that furthered the rift, especially since they were both liberals who disagreed with his politics and most of his policies.

In a thoughtful interview with Katie Couric after Reagan's

death, Patti acknowledged having had "an odd sibling rivalry with America. America had taken my father from me." But her mother bore the brunt of her anger, and their relationship began a tentative healing only in the last years of Nancy's life. Both children came to see their mother as an extension of their father, never separate in her own right. "I think you could make the case," Ron told the *Today* show's Matt Lauer, "that the Reagan we came to know would not have existed without Nancy Reagan."

Sharing Dad with the nation was their lot in life, because by the early 1960s, Reagan was making a transition. A cynical view of his emerging political popularity was that he was an attractive, engaging actor who knew how to tug at the heartstrings by persuasively delivering good lines. But his years as the head of the Screen Actors Guild and his on-the-road tours for GE had given him a clarity about his own beliefs and where they fit into the political spectrum. In a sense, he came to politics with a purity of vision—not through party alignment but through the power of conviction. He believed what he said.

His official entrance into politics came in 1964 with Barry Goldwater's campaign for president. Goldwater had positioned himself as the standard-bearer of a Republican revival, but he was a polarizing figure, an extremist in a party of cautious moderates. As the cochairman of the Goldwater campaign in California, Reagan, who was then the popular host of *Death Valley Days*, was doing his part on the stump, and he was gaining attention from party leaders. More than one of them privately wondered, "Why can't he be our candidate?" Reagan's optimism and personal charm were a breath of fresh air.

A week before the election, the faltering Goldwater campaign, somewhat reluctantly, agreed to let Reagan give a televised speech to the nation, financed by well-heeled California supporters. He called it "A Time for Choosing," and it would become one of the most famous speeches he ever made:

> This is the issue of this election: whether we believe in the capacity for self-government or whether we abandon the American revolution and confess that a little intellectual elite in a far-distant capital can plan for our lives better than we can plan them ourselves. . . .
>
> You and I have a rendezvous with destiny.
>
> We'll preserve for our children this, the last best hope of man on earth, or we'll sentence them to take the last step into a thousand years of darkness.

There was a tremendous outpouring of response to the speech—*Time* magazine called it "one bright spot in a dismal campaign," which must have annoyed Goldwater, who was fighting for his political life. "I didn't know it then, but that speech was one of the most important milestones of my life," Reagan wrote.

The speech also caught the attention of Dwight Eisenhower, who had spent the years since he had left office in 1961 laboring behind the scenes to restore his party. Eisenhower was no great fan of Goldwater, whose views, he felt, were unrestrained and whose rhetoric was careless. "I have a feeling that that man is dangerous," he once told a journalist. His eventual endorsement was reluctant—a concession made out of party loyalty. He was already calculating how to remake the party after a certain defeat. Watching Reagan, he began to think that he might be seeing a new standard-bearer for Republicans.

Like Eisenhower, Reagan appealed to America's patriotic

spirit and optimistic sense of itself. Americans liked him, just as they'd liked Ike. Eisenhower was drawn to him, too. Perhaps he saw something of himself in Reagan, a nonpolitician and a political independent who as a Democrat had voted for Ike in 1952. (In this sense, you could say that Reagan was the original "Reagan Democrat"!) By the 1960s, Reagan had become a Republican, saying "I didn't leave the Democratic Party; the Democratic Party left me."

Reagan's dramatic appeal wasn't enough to make a difference in the election. Goldwater was slaughtered by the incumbent, Lyndon Johnson, who earned 61 percent of the popular vote and 486 electoral votes. After the election, many Republicans, conducting a 1964 version of a party autopsy, believed that the conservative strain had been decisively defeated. But others recognized alternative reasons for the loss, not the least of which was Goldwater himself, a poor candidate incapable of rousing excitement beyond his base. His most famous statement—"Extremism in the defense of liberty is no vice . . . moderation in the pursuit of justice is no virtue"—had alienated the moderate wing of the party and scared off many Americans who might otherwise have been looking for an alternative to Johnson.

There was also the matter of timing. Only a year after Kennedy's assassination, with President Johnson receiving favorable reviews, it's likely that the nation lacked the stomach for another transition so soon.

But in spite of the loss, the Goldwater campaign marked the start of a movement. Fifty years after the fact, the political analyst Larry Sabato cited the lasting effects of "a race that produced a significant switch in both Northern and Southern party loyalties; pushed Democrats to the left; created the modern conservative GOP that took a giant step to the right with

Goldwater; made polished, vicious negative advertising the campaign tool of first resort; and showed the collective power of ideologically driven, broad-based grassroots organizers and small donors."

Undoubtedly, Reagan's speech launched him as a voice of the conservative movement. Goldwater's failed candidacy taught Republicans a lesson that Reagan would fervently embrace for the rest of his career: you don't win hearts and minds by being angry, gloomy, and dour; you win them with a blend of solid principles and relentless optimism. "He believed basically what Barry believed," the political consultant Stuart Spencer said. "He said a lot of the things that Barry said, but he said them differently. He said them in a soft way, in a more forgiving way. Style was the difference. Barry was a hard-nosed, up-front Arizonan cowboy, and that's what scared people."

After the election, Reagan returned to his ordinary life of giving speeches and hosting *Death Valley Days*. But his speech for Goldwater and his campaign presence had caught the attention of party leaders and supporters. One of them, Holmes Tuttle, a California auto dealer and Republican contributor, came to see Reagan one day, along with a group of like-minded men. They proposed that he run for governor in 1966 against the entrenched administration of Edmund "Pat" Brown, who would be making a try for a third term. Brown was considered a daunting foe. In 1962, he'd defeated Richard Nixon by three hundred thousand votes—a stunning loss for Nixon, who had thought he had a sure shot at victory.

Reagan laughed. "You're out of your mind."

Reagan enjoyed giving speeches and talking to people, but he still did not view himself as candidate material. "I'm an actor, not a politician," he said, promising that if the party found a candidate, he'd go on the road for its choice. He loved his life; he didn't want to run for office, and Nancy wasn't sold on the idea either. But they kept coming back to him, and finally he agreed to deliver some speeches around the state. To his surprise, audiences began asking him, "Why don't you run for governor?" He'd give his practiced response: "I'm an actor, not a politician." But the public interest was beginning to have an effect. "How do you say no to all of these people?" he asked Nancy. Six months after he began giving speeches, he called Tuttle. "Okay, I'll do it." He hired Spencer to run his campaign.

In truth, his timing could not have been better. There wasn't much happening in his television career; hosting *Death Valley Days* wasn't fulfilling. In addition, he had a lot to say about the state of California, which was embroiled in student upheavals and racial unrest.

From the start, Reagan was barraged with criticism that not only was he too right wing, but, God forbid, he was an *actor*. He was most annoyed by the charge that he had no ideas of his own and was merely propped up by canned talking points that someone else had written for him. After all, he'd been on the circuit, speaking his own mind, for years. To still the criticism, he increasingly began giving shorter speeches and devoting more time to question-and-answer sessions with his audiences. You couldn't fake that give-and-take. You had to know your stuff. And if his advisors were initially nervous about the dangers of spontaneity, they need not have worried. He was a natural. His sense of humor helped. A big part of his appeal was his ability to be self-effacing. For example, he quipped (in reference to his second-lead status in Hollywood), "When Jack Warner, head of Warner Brothers, first heard that I was running for Governor of California, he said, 'No, no. Jimmy Stewart for Governor; Reagan for best friend.'"

His campaign press aide Lyn Nofziger, a former newspaperman, recalled that as they started traveling the state, Reagan's connection to ordinary citizens became clear. "There was something about him that appealed to the people he talked to. I've never been able to put a finger on it. It's probably that word *charisma*, which is a word that I absolutely hate." Once he'd been out with Reagan two or three times, he became convinced that he could be elected.

Reagan's most loyal aides acknowledged that he wasn't a mastermind or genius political strategist. He knew how to delegate those roles. What he was, according to Spencer, was "the best communicator I've seen in my political life and that starts with Roosevelt, who was good. That's how good I think he was."

Reagan had authenticity; it wasn't an act. The people could feel it. Even those who disagreed with his positions could find it hard to resist his plainspoken sentiments and his ability to use humor to make a point. He could draw in a crowd. He looked camera ready, and most people assumed he wore makeup and dyed his hair. When a supporter wrote urging him to wear less makeup and not dye his hair, he replied graciously, "But there is a problem—I don't have a makeup man or wear makeup and would have to dye my hair to have grey at the temples." He added that he hadn't even used makeup when he was in pictures and on TV.

Spencer viewed Reagan's comfort with television as a clear plus. "There are lots of people that are good on the stump speaking, but they can't translate it to television. Reagan was different. He knew all the tricks, knew how to present himself."

Eisenhower watched Reagan's campaign for governor with interest and even wrote him some talking points for speeches. He had one piece of advice that stands out: he told Reagan to be expansive rather than narrow in his appeal—to impress upon the people of California that he would be governor of *all* of them, that there was no place for the divisiveness of special interests, and that they were all Americans.

The strategy worked. Reagan easily defeated his primary opponent, former San Francisco mayor George Christopher, to win the Republican nomination. He penned a grateful handwritten note to Eisenhower:

Dear Mr. President,

Now that the shouting has died (at least for a while) I want to thank you for your invaluable advice and suggestions. I realize of course this was offered within the framework of neutrality, and was born of your great interest in and devotion to the cause of Republicans.

Nevertheless, my TV appearances profited by a reduction in verbiage and the resulting slow pace drew some appreciative comments. Thanks to you, the creative society was described more understandably as a "do things" society.

Most of all however I am deeply grateful for your willingness to share your time, thoughts and philosophy with me.

To his peril, Governor Brown thought Reagan would be an easy candidate to beat and was pleased when he won the Republican nomination. "Ronald Reagan for Governor of California?" he wrote years later. "We thought the notion was absurd and rubbed our hands in gleeful anticipation of beating this politically inexperienced, right-wing extremist and aging actor in 1966."

During the campaign, Brown often mocked Reagan the

actor, taking cheap shots, which might have pleased his high-minded base but became disastrous with the airing of one TV commercial entitled "Man vs. Actor." In it Brown was shown telling a group of schoolchildren that he was running against an actor, and the man who had shot Abraham Lincoln was an actor!

The effort to paint Reagan as an extremist backfired terribly, said Reagan advisor (and future attorney general) William French Smith, "because when Reagan goes on television and makes a speech or what have you, one impression he does not create is of being an extremist of any kind. So that campaign just fell absolutely flat. And by the time they realized that it was just almost too late, and they couldn't do anything right."

Reagan was genuine and charming. He really liked people, and they could feel it. Once Nixon had advised him that when he was out doing events, he should keep his distance from the people. "Never eat with them. Go up to your room and have a steak and a good wine and then come down when you're announced." Reagan replied, "Well, Dick, you know, I kind of like to be with them."

Reagan portrayed Brown as ineffective at addressing California's multiple crises, including economic decline, urban blight, and campus unrest. Eight years of promises had yielded few results, he claimed. "Keeping up with Governor Brown's promises is like trying to read *Playboy* magazine while your wife turns the pages."

The election was a clash of ideologies, as Reagan biographer Matthew Dallek wrote:

Reagan was a card-carrying conservative, Brown a proud liberal. For Reagan, opposing communism was paramount. For Brown, anticommunism was but one issue in foreign affairs and a nonissue at home. Reagan saw the welfare-state policies of recent decades as a slippery slope toward socialism. Brown viewed governmental programs as the best way to achieve a "great society."

Each was battling for the soul of the state and, at least in Reagan's mind, the nation.

A month before the election, *Time* magazine published a cover story, "Ronald for Real," which captured some of Reagan's special campaign magic:

> Crisscrossing California from Roubidoux to Rialto, from Taft to Twentynine Palms, Republican Ronald Reagan, 55, has been running 18 hours a day as if the Dead End Kids were after him (they were in at least two of his movies). And to the surprise of Republican pros and the chagrin of the Democratic hierarchy, the candidate from Warner Bros. has turned out to be the most magnetic crowd puller California has seen since John F. Kennedy first stumped the state in 1960. . . .
>
> A polished orator with an unerring sense of timing and his listeners' mood, Reagan can hold an audience entranced for 30 or 40 minutes while he plows through statistics, gags and homilies. At times—although there is only six years' difference in their ages—he does a stagy caricature of an ancient-sounding Pat Brown that is true to the last creaky quaver.

On Election Day, November 6, Brown predicted he would win by more than the three hundred thousand votes he had defeated Richard Nixon by in 1962. The polls showed a tighter race. When the votes were counted, Reagan won by almost a million votes. On January 3, 1967, at one minute after midnight, he was sworn in as governor of California.

ONCE IN OFFICE, REAGAN surrounded himself with a tight group that stayed with him in one way or another for the rest of his political life. The team was headed in the first two years by Chief of Staff William Clark, a former Catholic seminarian and lawyer who had been drawn to Reagan after hearing his speech on behalf of Goldwater. Clark recruited a young Republican Party operative named Michael Deaver, who became so close to Reagan and Nancy that he was practically their alter ego. Press aide Lyn Nofziger became director of communications, and Caspar Weinberger, who would rise to prominence during Reagan's presidency, was director of finance in the early years.

In the third year, Edwin Meese replaced Clark as chief of staff. Meese, the deputy district attorney of Alameda County in Northern California, had caught Reagan's eye with his strong handling of campus unrest at Berkeley.

Reagan's governing style, Meese said, was "government by cabinet." He was not a lone wolf. Cabinet meetings were held several times a week, sometimes throughout the day. Also influential was his "kitchen cabinet," a group of well-heeled advisors who had his ear and bolstered his political fortunes. These included, most prominently, Holmes Tuttle, who'd first convinced him to run; Henry Salvatori, a geophysicist and oil company founder; Justin Dart, a consumer products giant and chairman of the board of the University of California; and Alfred Bloomingdale, a department store magnate whose wife, Betsy, became Nancy's best friend for life.

As governor, Reagan's daily fare was made up of domestic issues. But he never lost sight of his global perspective and ideals. "He had to face up to a lot of dirty housekeeping problems as governor," said Spencer. "But he had this vision of America that all these things we have—Democratic party, Republican party, this and that and everything, our warts and our good things—we're not going to have any of those if this Communist threat proceeds through the world. . . . He never talked about his goals, but when you look back on it, his goals never changed. He only had one item that really bothered him, and that was the Communist threat. Everything else was second tier. He conducted himself with that in mind as governor as well as president."

CHAPTER 3

THE GREATEST STAGE

In 1962, after losing the California gubernatorial election to Pat Brown—his second electoral humiliation in three years—Richard Nixon had promised the press, "You won't have Nixon to kick around anymore, because, gentlemen, this is my last press conference." The press and everyone else took him seriously. ABC aired a thirty-minute program entitled "Political Obituary of Richard Nixon." But on February 1, 1968, Nixon announced that he was running for president for a second time. In an open letter to the people of New Hampshire, he wrote that his eight years out of government had allowed him a chance to reflect upon and study the nation's issues, and he believed he was prepared with some answers.

"For these critical years, America needs new leadership," he said, ignoring the fact that he was anything but a fresh face. His critics immediately began to joke about the "new" Nixon, the magically resurrected political figure from the Eisenhower era, and many Republicans were outspoken in their desire for an alternative. With Nixon's record of losing elections, they were fearful of blowing their chance.

The Republicans had been strategizing for a long time about 1968 and thought that incumbent president Lyndon Johnson's sagging popularity and the deep divisions in the Democratic

Party presented a golden opportunity. But it was a complicated scenario. At the beginning of 1968, the political landscape was treacherous, filled with land mines: the increasingly disastrous war in Vietnam, the inflationary repercussions of that expensive war and an ambitious domestic agenda that could not be paid for, and a roiling cultural revolution growing louder, with protests by antiwar and civil rights demonstrators flooding streets and campuses. Partisans on both sides of the political divide were restless. And no one could foresee the events that would rattle the nation in the coming months: President Johnson's surprise announcement that he would not seek reelection, the assassination of Martin Luther King, Jr., the tantalizing rise and shocking death of Robert F. Kennedy. RFK had been a Johnson nemesis and pied piper of young voters, and soon after his death a riotous Democratic National Convention in Chicago tore the party apart.

Nixon's carefully considered run had been in the works for years, at least since the 1966 midterms, but now there wasn't much time. With only six months to the Republican National Convention and nine months to the general election, it was a compressed campaign season. But the Republican Party, too, was divided between the hard-line conservative heirs of Goldwater and the more liberal, often antiwar wing.

Early on, a liberal opponent to Nixon emerged in Michigan governor George Romney. Like his son Mitt forty-four years later, Romney was the picture of American rectitude, a devout Mormon with executive governing experience who looked and acted the part. But his candidacy did nothing to appeal to the growing conservative wing of the party. Romney was quickly eliminated after a fatal gaffe. Previously a strong supporter of the war in Vietnam, he now held the opposite position, explaining his flip-flop as being the result of a visit to Vietnam in 1965.

"When I came back from Viet Nam, I'd just had the greatest brainwashing that anybody can get," he told a Detroit television interviewer. The image stuck and took root, and the public never looked at him the same way again. He became the man who had been brainwashed in Vietnam. New York governor Nelson Rockefeller stepped into the liberal void with an antiwar platform that never gained traction.

Quietly, without much fanfare, a conservative dark horse was emerging. Ronald Reagan was in his second year as governor, and his closest allies had been strategizing about his presidential prospects since 1966. Indeed, "Reagan for President" signs had been seen on election night. There was no other candidate who appealed to Republican conservatives the way Reagan did. But was the party ready? Was *Reagan* ready?

The temptation to enter the fray was clearly there, debated frequently by Reagan's advisors. Nofziger described two camps, one in favor of a run, one opposed:

> There was a split in the Reagan team. I don't mean that badly, but there are people who felt, *You've been elected to be governor, stay here and be governor.* And there were people like me who thought, *Well, this guy has got something, but if he's governor for six years or whatever, who knows what will happen? It seems to me that he's on a roll here right now. He's won this governorship handily. He's the governor of the biggest state. He's well known across the country. Let's go ahead and push him because we have a shot.*

Reagan was convinced that he should at least dip a toe in as a "favorite son." In the era before binding primaries, the favorite-son system was a way for states to gain influence in the national political process. Basically, a state anointed a favorite-son candidate, and only he was on the primary ballot. He would then arrive at the convention with the state's votes in his pocket, which presumably he'd hand to the candidate of his choice. The favorite son was not considered to be a real candidate. When Reagan announced his candidacy, he made it clear that he wasn't serious about challenging Nixon, only trying to avoid a bitter primary fight in California between Nixon and the other contenders. However, his insistence that his favorite-son candidacy was not real was not very convincing to the presumed head of the ticket, in this case Nixon. There was always the chance that the voters might fall in love with the insurgent and show up at the convention ready to do battle. A challenge is a challenge, no matter how you dress it up.

Reagan did have one thing going for him: unlike Nixon, he had no ugly political baggage. He was a fresh face, but he also had evolved as a public persona who could articulate the issues of the day. Paul Laxalt, the governor of the neighboring state of Nevada, had come to respect Reagan, and the two men had developed a close partnership. Laxalt called him an instinctive politician whose "motive was just as pure as it could be. No outside agenda. He had a fundamental philosophy, which evolved during the General Electric days when he went all around the country as a spokesman for them. He was a vehicle, their vehicle, for private enterprise, extolling the benefits of private enterprise and all the evils of excessive government. He had had a very simple philosophy that he had developed, and that made it very easy for him wherever he went. He never really had to remember what he said last."

In fact, Laxalt noted, some of his stories were so well worn that those closest to Reagan would beg for mercy when he launched into one of them—*Oh no, do we have to listen to this again?* "He'd always remind us, as any good actor would, you've heard this before, many times—probably too many times, in your estimation—but that person in that group I'm talking to is hearing it for the first time."

As a craftsman of politics, "he wasn't even in the same league as Richard Nixon," Laxalt said. "But in terms of having a message and communicating with the people? In my estimation, I've never seen anybody quite as effective as him."

That said, Reagan had two challenges on the national stage. The first was the wide perception, largely based on his fiery support for Goldwater, that he was an extremist. The second was his history of vacillation. As Eisenhower put it in a letter to Walter Thayer, a close confidant, in late 1966, "His biggest trouble is that he has a past record that is rather checkered with flea hopping from one end of the political spectrum to the other."

But Reagan continued to intrigue Eisenhower, and from Nixon's perspective, the former president was sending mixed messages of his own. A story Eisenhower related in his diary is telling: In March 1967, soon after Reagan had become governor, he and Ike were together at the Eldorado Country Club when they decided to hold an impromptu press conference. One of the reporters asked Eisenhower his opinion of Nixon, and Ike replied that he was one of the ablest men he knew. The reporters gathered had not heard the question correctly, and they thought Ike's words were describing *Reagan*. The story of Ike's praise for Reagan even made it onto the evening news with Walter Cronkite. Eisenhower issued a correction, but Cronkite never did, so for most of the nation the original version stuck: Ike liked Reagan. He wasn't so sure about Nixon.

It's especially notable that Eisenhower did not publicly endorse Nixon until right before the Republican National Convention, perhaps leaving himself room to change his mind. Intimidated by this silence and possibly fearing a negative answer if he made a direct request, Nixon never asked for his backing. By then Eisenhower was gravely ill, living in a hospital suite at Walter Reed Army Medical Center. Eisenhower, the only living Republican ex-president (Herbert Hoover having died in 1964), perhaps gave a thought to his own legacy and was no longer certain that Nixon was the man to carry the party forward. A lot of time had passed since Nixon's failed campaign of 1960.

In the end, Nixon never had an opponent who could mount a real challenge. The party establishment was behind him, and the decisive action that earned important support on the right was his selection of the conservative Spiro Agnew as his running mate. Southern delegates had made it clear that if he chose a moderate or liberal, they would abandon him for Reagan.

At the Republican National Convention in Miami Beach in August, Nixon easily captured the nomination. As balloons cascaded down on the delegates and horns blared, Reagan might have felt disappointed that he hadn't made a stronger showing. But he told his aides he didn't feel bad about it. He just hadn't been ready. In the meantime, he said, party unity was the most important thing.

Writing about the political convention later that year, Norman Mailer had a prophecy: "For years in the movies Reagan had played the good guy and been proud of it. If he didn't get the girl, it was because he was too good a guy to be overwhelmingly attractive. That was all right. He would grit his teeth and get the girl the next time out."

BACK TO WORK IN California, Reagan honed a governing style that was part staunch conservatism and part idealism—thus his fondness for John Winthrop's image of a "city upon a hill," a posture Steven Hayward of the Heritage Foundation refers to as his "idiosyncratic conservatism." Reagan had showed his unconventional conservatism almost right out of the gate. In their first year in office, he and Laxalt bonded over, of all things, a tax increase. "I'll never forget it," Laxalt later said, recalling the irony of two conservative governors making such a pact. "First I told him, 'Ron, I've come to a real bad conclusion here, but I don't think I can avoid it. I think we're going to have to go for a tax increase.' He said, 'You know, Paul, we've come to the same conclusion.' So we both went for a tax increase, and we used to joke about it because the tax increase rejuvenated our respective economies, and the people who succeeded us as governor had all the money in the world for years. But we bit that bullet."

One of Reagan's main goals as governor was welfare reform, and California was one of the first states to tackle it on a massive level. Even here, he operated more pragmatically than ideologically. Peter Hannaford, a public relations specialist and close aide of Reagan toward the end of his second term, recalled that Reagan once told him his strategy on welfare reform: "You know, if I can get 70 percent of what I want on a particular program, I'll take it, because I figure it will work well enough that I can go back next year and get the other thirty." That strategy, Hannaford said, was quite effective in that Reagan got a lot more than he gave. In the process, the welfare system became more efficient. "It became a model for many other states and was really the bellwether for his constant call as president for welfare reform on a federal level."

Hannaford had an interesting insight into Reagan's governing style, which he believed was honed in his years as president of the Screen Actors Guild. During his tenure, there had been some very intense negotiations with the studios and their high-powered lawyers, while the Guild had had just Reagan, a couple of officers, and a lawyer. Reagan told Hannaford:

> An interesting thing about negotiating I discovered was you'd go at it hammer and tongs. And one side would say, "We can't possibly accept that proposal under any circumstances." You'd reach some point—you could just sense it in the room—when the moment was ripe for a compromise. But the tempers had been so strong, and the declarations so strong, that you couldn't do it right then and there. So, somebody would say, "Excuse me, I have to go to the bathroom." And someone would go to the bathroom. Then somebody on the other side would go to the bathroom. And in the bathroom, they'd say, "What do you think about so-and-so?" And first thing you know, we've got the beginnings of a settlement. You'd have to sense when the moment is to make the break in the tough position that you've taken and when the other side is willing to do the same thing. A lot of it is a matter of face—in other words, how it's going to look.

In 1974, as he was nearing the end of his second term as governor, Reagan was considering his next act. He had decided not to seek a third term. (He was succeeded by his secretary of state, Jerry Brown, the only son of Pat Brown. As of this writing Brown is governor for a second time; he succeeded Arnold Schwarzenegger in 2010. Term limits will prevent him from running again in 2018.) Out of the governor's office, Reagan was looking for a strategic way to stay in the public eye. An old radio guy from Hollywood named Harry O'Connor had been whispering in his ear. He told Reagan he could get him onto the radio for a five-minute daily commentary, and Reagan liked the idea. But while he was considering it, Michael Deaver got a phone call from Walter Cronkite. He proposed a slot for Reagan on CBS, doing a five-minute commentary on the evening news twice a week, alternating with Eric Sevareid. Deaver thought it was an incredible offer and he enthusiastically presented it to Reagan.

When the time came to make a decision, Deaver thought it was going to be "a slam dunk" in favor of the TV show. Who would turn down a chance to appear on the *CBS Evening News* twice a week? But Reagan said, "I'm not going to do it. I'm going to do the radio show."

"What?" Deaver was stunned.

Reagan explained, "Mike, people will tire of me on television. They won't tire of me on the radio." How he knew that, Deaver couldn't imagine, but he later acknowledged that he had been absolutely right. From 1975 to 1979, Reagan delivered 1,027 addresses, and between 20 million and 30 million listeners heard him every week.

On the radio, people were drawn to his storytelling, as he regaled them with the failures of government bureaucracy. "To err is human," he told them. "It takes a government to really louse things up." He was a master of the pinpointed anecdote, the tale of some ordinary person just trying to get by who was stymied by some regulation or red tape. *Newsweek* called him "the most kinetic single person in American political life."

Repeatedly, Reagan articulated a central premise: "It's time for us all to realize that government is not the answer to our economic problems. Government *is* the problem." Another favorite theme was the evil of communism, a precursor of the battles he'd one day wage as president. His platform was the American way as an ideal still to be fully realized.

RUNNING AGAINST A SITTING Republican president was nearly unheard of, and even Democrats usually pulled their unruly factions together behind the White House—1968 having been a notable exception. So why was Ronald Reagan willing to walk out on that ledge in 1976?

His friends and advisors would later agree that he had one overarching reason for challenging President Gerald Ford in 1976: détente with the Soviets. It had been Nixon's policy, and now it was Ford's, formalized in the Helsinki Accords in 1975. Reagan believed that the president's concessions to Soviet general secretary Leonid Brezhnev had been damaging to human rights and extended Soviet power in the region. He saw détente as a one-way street that had enabled the Soviets to grow stronger at our expense. The accords had placed them on an equal playing field, no longer allowing the United States to negotiate from a position of strength. It was a kumbaya moment, an embrace made without good faith by the Soviets.

Reagan wasn't the only one who felt that way. Ford's own secretary of defense, James Schlesinger, opposed the negotiations and, when Ford fired him, publicly stated that Ford was "soft" on communism. Reagan thought Schlesinger had been fired because Ford did not want to deal with the growing imbalance of nuclear arsenals. The goal, Reagan argued, should be to fight the Communists, not to appease them.

Over dinner one night in 1975, Reagan told Laxalt, now a US senator, that he was thinking about running against Ford. He asked for his advice.

"You shouldn't be making any moves here unless you're serious about it," Laxalt said. "Running for President is serious
business. Running in California as governor was serious, too,
but this is a little bit more significant." He suggested doing a lit-
mus test to gauge Ford's political vulnerability and whether the
public would be receptive to Reagan. The results were positive,
and Reagan told Laxalt he was going to go for it. He asked Laxalt to chair his campaign, and Laxalt agreed—a daring move
on his part as the party establishment was behind Ford.

A youthful, vibrant sixty-four, Reagan *was* serious. Like the
lifeguard of his youth, he was determined to save the party, even
if it didn't always realize it needed saving. The party had been
sandblasted, and the old alliances no longer existed. Watergate
had been a trauma whose effects were still pulsating, notwithstanding Ford's declaration that "Our long national nightmare
is over." In the meantime, there was Ford, who had never waged
a national campaign and who had never been elected to public
office outside of a congressional district in Michigan.

Reagan was becoming convinced that he should run. He
told Deaver, "I just don't think Jerry can do it." He meant,
Deaver said, tackling the Soviets. "And if I don't do it, I'm going
to be the player who's always been on the bench who never got
into the game." Reagan picked up the phone and put in a call
to Ford at the White House to tell him he would be announcing
his candidacy.

Leading the effort was a new face in the Reagan circle—
thirty-four-year-old John Sears, a Washington campaign strategist who had been behind Nixon in 1968. The Reagans thought
he was incredibly smart, with the aura of a winner, even though
he could be acerbic and difficult and never connected with Reagan on the personal level he preferred. Nancy recalled that Reagan was baffled by Sears's manner. "He doesn't look you in the

eye. He looks you in the tie," he grumbled. Nevertheless, Sears instilled confidence. The Reagans were impressed by his broad knowledge and savvy—and they wanted to win.

On November 20, 1975, a week before Thanksgiving, Reagan declared his intention to run, citing the economy—inflation, unemployment, and interest rates—and the wrongheaded policy of détente, which was compromising the United States' military superiority.

"In my opinion, the root of these problems lies right here—in Washington, D.C.," he said. "Our nation's capital has become the seat of a 'buddy' system that functions for its own benefit—increasingly insensitive to the needs of the American worker who supports it with his taxes."

In spite of its high-minded and optimistic beginnings, Reagan's campaign was almost over before it began when he lost the first five primaries. As he approached the North Carolina primary, the situation was as dire as it could be. Reagan aide Martin Anderson painted the grim picture:

> Okay, so here we are, coming up to the North Carolina primary, he's lost five straight. The Republican Governors have been calling on him to get out. The editorials are calling on him to get out. Nine of ten of the past Republican chairmen of the party are calling on him to get out. Except for George Bush, who was the current chairman of the party, who didn't say anything. And we're out of money. We're about $2 million in debt. . . . We would stop at a campaign site, [and] I remember Michael Deaver would get out and go to the McDonald's and come back—no, sorry, Kentucky Fried Chicken—would come back with a big bucket of Kentucky Fried Chicken. We'd pull out chicken and that was our food.

They wouldn't sell us anything unless we paid cash in advance.

The North Carolina polls were discouraging; they put Reagan ten points behind. But then an angel appeared in the form of a Texas supporter named James Lyon. He made the campaign an offer it couldn't refuse: a loan of $100,000, if it would use the money to put Reagan on TV, just talking to the American people.

When presented with the offer, Reagan considered it for a moment and said, "Okay, you borrow that money and I'm going to run in every blankety-blank primary from here to the convention, even if I lose every single one." It worked. To the astonishment of the Ford campaign and the Republican establishment, Reagan won North Carolina. And he kept winning, so as the convention approached, he was within spitting distance of Ford.

Sears convinced Reagan that it would be a bold move to announce his vice presidential choice a month before the convention. He thought that would force Ford to announce his choice early. Ford was in a bind; he needed a way to appease the conservatives in his party, and the sitting vice president, Nelson Rockefeller, was not going to fill that role. Rockefeller had announced early in the campaign that he wouldn't be a candidate—he had been pushed or had jumped, no one knew for sure, but he had probably been pushed—and Ford had floated a number of names. However, Sears's strategy backfired when Reagan inexplicably chose Pennsylvania senator Richard Schweiker, a liberal-leaning moderate who was anathema to Reagan's conservative supporters. Later, when the delegate count got painfully tight, some of his conservative backers urged him to dump Schweiker, but he adamantly refused. "If you were to stand here right now and tell me that you could guarantee that I'd get the nomination if I did that, there's no way I'm going to do it," he told one of them. Schweiker had been loyal to him, and Reagan was loyal in return.

Leading up to the convention, both camps had showered attention on the wavering delegates, each using their special brand of favors. For Ford that meant invitations to the White House or personal calls from the president. For Reagan it meant access to Hollywood, as delegates received calls from the likes of matinee idols Jimmy Stewart and Pat Boone. When the convention opened on August 16 at the Kemper Arena in Kansas City, the count was tantalizingly close: with 1,130 delegates needed to win, Ford had 1,118 to Reagan's 1,035, with 106 uncommitted. The pendulum could swing either way.

Close conventions are like hurricanes fueled by their own manic energy. A surge can go one way, then explode elsewhere. A puddle can turn into a flood in minutes. And bargaining and persuading continue on a more intense level, with surrogates flooding the delegations, creating dozens of miniconventions on the floor. Minds get changed and then switched back, and it's not certain until the roll call which way the votes are going to go.

The count was so tight that each side fought vigorously for every vote. At one point, a Ford delegate broke her leg stepping off the raised floor of the convention hall, and she was in tremendous pain. The obvious course of action was to get her to a hospital. One problem: her alternate was a Reagan delegate. A doctor was called, who made a hasty splint. She stayed to vote for Ford and was then carried out.

Watching the nominating process from his hotel room, Reagan realized that he was going to be defeated. He could see it before anyone else, and he broke the news to the others, who still didn't want to believe it. The final vote was 1,187 for Ford and 1,070 for Reagan. Reagan fell short by only 117 delegates.

As his aides tried to control their tears—Nofziger was sobbing in the bathroom—Reagan was calm and even contemplative. "You know what I regret the most?" he asked quietly. "I had really looked forward to sitting down at the table with Brezhnev to negotiate on arms control. He would tell me all the things that our side would have to give up. And then, when he was finished, I was planning to stand up, walk around the table, and whisper one little word in his ear: *Nyet.*"

The following morning, Deaver, who admitted that he'd been out drinking and drowning his sorrows with staff until four in the morning, was jarred awake at 7:30 by a group of Reagan's California advisors pounding on the door of the Reagans' suite. They demanded to see Reagan so they could discuss his becoming Ford's running mate.

"I think he's still asleep," Deaver demurred.

"Well, get dressed and go get him."

Deaver got dressed, went into the Reagans' bedroom, and woke them up. He told them about the insistent committee sitting outside. "I don't want to be vice president," Reagan said, burying his face in the pillow. "Go tell them that."

"They don't want to see me. They want to see you."

"Damnit!" Reagan got up and stormed around the room, getting dressed. Just then the telephone rang, and Deaver picked it up. It was Ford. Reagan listened, smiling. "Yes, yes, I think that's terrific . . . just great," he said. "I'll do everything I can."

He hung up. "He just picked Bob Dole," he said, relieved he didn't have to debate the matter further. His supporters were disappointed, but Reagan knew he'd make a lousy vice president. It just wasn't the right role for him. As he told his dejected supporters, "Only the lead dog gets a fresh view."

In a close nomination fight, there is always the urgent question of what to do with the loser's supporters, who are still in their seats and feeling emotional. So when the Reagans entered the hall the final night to enormous applause from their supporters, Ford's people looked on with some chagrin. Overnight, the calculation had changed from winning the nomination to winning the general election, meaning that party unity must be achieved, almost magically. Like any winner, Ford might have wanted to claim the spotlight all on his own, but he had to contend with more than a thousand disillusioned delegates whose hearts were breaking. That is not an uncommon spot for the winner to be in—the 2008 Democratic National Convention, when Barack Obama defeated Hillary Clinton, comes to mind—and the fear of a rogue insurgency is quite real. Throughout the day there had been behind-the-scenes conversations between the Ford and Reagan staffs about whether Reagan should speak that night. The word from the Reagan camp was that he'd consider it only if Ford asked him to come up onto the stage. The word came down that Ford would ask Reagan to join him onstage at the end of his speech. However, when he stood onstage, trying to speak above the clamor, Ford had a moment of truth. As Reagan's delegates rose up in an ovation that showed little sign of abating, Ford raised his hand and beckoned to Reagan.

Reagan wasn't sure what the gesture meant. "Am I being asked to come down?" he asked Deaver as the convention erupted in shouts of "Come on down!"

"I think so," said Deaver as Ford beckoned again. Reagan stood up and adjusted his jacket. "What am I going to say?"

"You'll think of something," Deaver shouted above the din.

He bounded onto the stage, vigorously shook Ford's hand, and waited for the delirious cheering to stop. And then, in a conversational, folksy manner, he began talking about a bicentennial-year assignment he'd received to write a letter for a time capsule that would be opened in Los Angeles in a hundred years. "They suggested I write about the problems and issues of the day," he said. "And I set out to do so, riding down the coast in an automobile, looking at the blue Pacific out on one side and the Santa Ynez Mountains on the other, and I couldn't help but wonder if it was going to be that beautiful a hundred years from now as it was on that summer day." He spoke sincerely of how the experience had convinced him that writing about contemporary domestic problems would be meaningless to that future generation if the great threat of nuclear weapons had not been addressed. In 1976, there was no way to know whether a century later those people would know whether his generation had accepted the challenge to prevent a nuclear future.

> Will they look back with appreciation and say, "Thank God for those people in 1976 who headed off that loss of freedom? Who kept us now a hundred years later free? Who kept our world from nuclear destruction?"
>
> And if we fail they probably won't get to read the letter at all because it spoke of individual freedom and they won't be allowed to talk of that or read of it. This is our challenge and this is why we're here in this hall tonight. . . .
>
> We must go forth from here united, determined, and what a great general [Douglas MacArthur] said a few years ago is true: "There is no substitute for victory."

The delegates, most of whom had remained standing throughout the speech, cheered, and the band played "California, Here I Come." As Ford once again took center stage, more than one delegate said, "We nominated the wrong guy." It was such a dramatic moment and such a riveting speech that the convention felt a bit let down when Ford spoke. Reagan was too much of a gentleman to have intentionally hijacked Ford's big night. But effectively that's what happened.

The next morning, as Reagan thanked his campaign advisors and prepared to head home, he quoted some lines from an English ballad he had learned as a child: "I'll lay me down and bleed awhile . . . although I am wounded, I am not slain. I shall rise and fight again."

Ford never regained momentum during the campaign. The Republican establishment, which had been solidly behind the president, quickly began to see the fissures in his candidacy. The floundering economy was a big factor. The energy crisis, high unemployment, and low economic growth, a bitter cocktail termed "stagflation," had the nation on edge. But the party also had to face a more existential truth: the nation was still recovering from Watergate, and there were lingering doubts about Ford's pardon of Nixon. Since Ford had not been elected, either as vice president or as president—a historic first—there had been none of the natural bonding process between the man and the people that occurs during an election campaign. Instead, he'd been appointed by the person he had replaced and then pardoned. The American people were not happy with that; it stank of a quid pro quo. The 1976 campaign became a cleansing process, a crusade to rid the Oval Office of old ghosts. Unfairly or not, Ford was swept away in the discontent. Jimmy Carter, the little-known governor of Georgia, was able to portray himself as not only competent but *good*—a moralist seeking an office that had been tarnished.

Ford was not a particularly fine campaigner, and as a result his mistakes were magnified. The worst gaffe occurred in a debate with Carter when he defended the Helsinki Accords, saying "There is no Soviet domination of Eastern Europe, and there never will be under a Ford administration." It was blatantly untrue, and the statement made Ford look as if he didn't know what he was talking about. He later clarified that he'd meant he did not *accept* Soviet domination, but it was too late. On November 2, the nation voted to end Ford's presidency after less than two and a half years.

TEN DAYS AFTER JIMMY Carter's inauguration, Reagan had a houseguest in California. Richard Allen was an old Nixon hand who was planning to run for governor of New Jersey. He'd asked Reagan aide Pete Hannaford if he could meet with Reagan and get him to sign some fund-raising letters for him. The appointment was arranged, and Allen showed up at Reagan's house. He told Reagan he'd like him to sign the letters and maybe come to New Jersey to do a campaign appearance.

Reagan looked at him, puzzled. "Why, yes. I'll do that. But you came all the way out here to ask me that?"

"Yes, I did," Allen replied.

"Why didn't you just call me on the telephone? I'd have been happy to say yes."

Allen told him he'd thought he should ask in person, and Reagan appreciated that. Then, to Allen's amazement, he invited him to stay and talk. And they spoke for most of the day, breaking for sandwiches at lunch. At one point Reagan said, "I'd like now to tell you my basic theory about the Cold War."

"What's that?" Allen asked.

"Some people say I'm very simplistic, but there's a difference between being simplistic and simple. A lot of very complex things are very simple if you think them through.

"Yes, sir," Allen nodded.

"Keeping that in mind," Reagan went on, "my theory of the Cold War is, we win and they lose. What do you think about that?"

Allen said he felt as if he'd been hit with a ton of bricks. The hair rose on the back of his neck. "Do you mean that? Do you actually mean that?"

"I said it. Of course, I mean it," Reagan said with a smile.

"Well, Governor, I haven't the faintest idea what you're going to do with the rest of your life, but if you intend to run for president of the United States, you just signed me up right now, because that's been my objective for a long time."

As Allen recalled the meeting, "I came away walking on a cloud." He returned to New Jersey and told his wife, "I'm dissolving my committee, I'm giving back the money, I'm not going to run for governor of New Jersey. I'm going to help make that guy, if I can, president of the United States."

Allen wasn't alone in his enthusiasm. Reagan had that effect on people. But it was early days. Reagan's cadre of advisors was still nominally in place, and they were poised for action. But the wise course was to let things develop organically. No one wanted to push Reagan to make a decision about 1980, because he might have said no. Sears, Meese, and Deaver put it to him this way: Don't decide right now, but let's start a campaign committee and be ready if the time is right. Reagan was satisfied with that plan, and his public exposure through his radio show and newspaper columns remained high.

In 1978, as he was beginning to seriously contemplate a presidential run in 1980, Reagan found his resolve strengthened by a European trip and a visit to the Berlin Wall. He and Nancy were accompanied by his advisors Dick Allen and Peter Hannaford and their wives for the visit. According to Hannaford, Berlin—and the wall—made a lasting impression on Reagan.

He told the US Embassy staff that he wanted to go through Checkpoint Charlie and enter East Berlin, and consular officials accompanied the group through the checkpoint to Alexanderplatz, a large public square half a mile in from the wall.

While Nancy and the other wives ducked into a state-run department store to check out the goods, the men lingered outside. They saw a policeman stop a young man walking through the plaza carrying a shopping bag. As they demanded his papers in a harassing manner, Reagan watched. "It was quite chilling," Hannaford said. "Reagan saw that and he didn't forget it."

Later, back on the western side, they visited the Axel Springer House, the large publishing building overlooking the wall. "And high in the building, you look right down over the Berlin Wall to a place where not long before a young man had tried to go over, and they shot him and left his body hanging there," recalled Hannaford. "It wasn't still there, but it had happened not long before. When Reagan heard this story, his jaw set. You could just tell he had it in mind we would change all this one day. You could see it, hear it, in the things he had to say."

Reagan never forgot the emotional impact of being at the wall. It was incomprehensible that in the decades following the fall of Nazi Germany, such a prison would be erected in the heart of Berlin, with the sole purpose of keeping an entire population of people under guard. The existence of the wall encapsulated his abhorrence of the Communist state. What kind of society, he wondered, can function only by trapping its citizens and forcing them into compliance? There could be no justification in ideology or necessity for such an abomination. Why was the Western world—and the United States!—so complicit in the continuation of this travesty? That wall should come down, he thought. He returned to the United States haunted by what he had experienced.

By the third year of Carter's presidency, it was becoming clear that there was going to be an opening for a strong contender. The professor and historian Andrew E. Busch captured Carter's core dilemma well, writing that not only was he besieged by economic crises, but in his posture toward the Soviets "he became Teddy Roosevelt in reverse, speaking loudly and carrying a twig. An increasing majority of Americans thought Carter too small for the job." If Carter had been elected in a post-Watergate cleansing, his moral authority was diminished by his failures of governance.

The speech that would most symbolize his ineffectual leadership was the so-called malaise speech, delivered on July 15, 1979. Carter believed that an honest appeal to Americans, a form of tough love about their role in the nation's decline, their crisis of confidence, would be well received. And at first it was. But Carter's judgmental tone and harsh words were hard to stomach once they sunk in. Americans felt they were being blamed, chastised rather than inspired. With gas lines lengthening and the economy struggling, the nation needed leadership, not stern lectures.

Like Ford before him, Carter had a strong challenger emerging in his own party. Senator Edward Kennedy was initially coy about his intentions, but the nostalgia brigade was urging him to run against Carter in 1980. Kennedy's baggage could be summed up in one word: Chappaquiddick. In 1969, Kennedy had been involved in an accident on Chappaquiddick Island in Massachusetts. After a night of partying, he had been driving in a car with a young woman, Mary Jo Kopechne, when it had veered off a bridge and plunged into the water. Kennedy had escaped, but Kopechne was trapped in the car and died. Because

Kennedy had left the scene and not reported the accident for ten hours, he'd eventually been charged with negligence. But for more than a decade Chappaquiddick had tarnished him, with endless speculation about whether he had acted from more than negligence and to what extent he was implicated in Kopechne's death. It was an enduring stain on his reputation. However, many Democrats, eager for a reprise of Camelot, chose to ignore it.

Some analysts believe in retrospect that Kennedy's campaign was doomed before it even began, when he gave an interview to the journalist Roger Mudd. Asked to explain his vision and motivations for seeking the presidency, Kennedy was inarticulate and rambling; he gave the impression of not having a cogent reason for running, perhaps other than having been born a Kennedy. He limped into the primary season without a forceful message, and it was only the national disappointment in Carter that gave his campaign any momentum at all.

On November 4, 1979, Islamic radicals in Iran seized the US Embassy and took fifty-two Americans hostage. The hostage crisis was ultimately so devastating for Carter's presidency that it's easy to forget the way it was in the beginning. At first Americans rallied around the president; his approval rating rose to over 60 percent. As the crisis dragged on, however, support for Carter turned to blame, giving Kennedy's campaign a surge. But by the time of the convention, Kennedy's star had also dimmed. He lost badly to Carter, then further split the party by standing aloof on the convention stage and refusing to take Carter's hand in a gesture of party unity. Disharmony among the Democrats, the hostage crisis, and continuing domestic woes teed up the election perfectly for the Republicans.

Reagan announced his candidacy on November 13, 1979,

nine days after the hostages were taken, with a forceful, thoughtful speech that covered both domestic and foreign issues, utilizing the stirring, deeply personal prose he favored:

> To me our country is a living, breathing presence, unimpressed by what others say is impossible, proud of its own success, generous, yes and naïve, sometimes wrong, never mean and always impatient to provide a better life for its people in a framework of a basic fairness and freedom.
>
> Someone once said that the difference between an American and any other kind of person is that an American lives in anticipation of the future because he knows it will be a great place. Other people fear the future as just a repetition of past failures. There's a lot of truth in that. If there is one thing we are sure of it is that history need not be relived; that nothing is impossible, and that man is capable of improving his circumstances beyond what we are told is fact. . . .
>
> We who are privileged to be Americans have had a rendezvous with destiny since the moment in 1630 when John Winthrop, standing on the deck of the tiny *Arbella* off the coast of Massachusetts, told the little band of pilgrims, "We shall be as a city upon a hill. The eyes of all people are upon us so that if we shall deal falsely with our God in this work we have undertaken and so cause Him to withdraw His present help from us, we shall be made a story and a byword throughout the world."
>
> A troubled and afflicted mankind looks to us, pleading for us to keep our rendezvous with destiny; that we will uphold the principles of self-reliance, self-discipline,

morality, and—above all—responsible liberty for every individual that we will become that shining city on a hill. I believe that you and I together can keep this rendezvous with destiny.

REAGAN BEGAN THE PRIMARY season as the front-runner, but he had a strong field of contenders, including George H. W. Bush, John Connally, and Howard Baker. Once more leading the charge for Reagan was John Sears, along with Charles Black and James Lake.

"It was conventional wisdom, even among the press, that Carter was not going to win if he had a strong opponent in the general election," Black said. "Reagan felt good, and he felt like he could win it." But there were internal hurdles to be overcome. The tensions in the campaign that had begun to brew in 1976 were now on full display, with two opposing camps—"the California versus the East Coast guys," as Black put it. Deaver, Nofziger, and Meese had one strategic vision; Sears, Black, and Lake had another—and both sides were vying for control. At first they tried to manage their differences, forming an executive committee that met every Monday in Los Angeles. But as Sears and Deaver continued to butt heads over Reagan's schedule, the atmosphere between the key aides grew tense. Both Deaver and Sears wanted to run the show, and there wasn't room for two alpha males fighting over the candidate. Sears decided that Deaver needed to go. Black didn't think it was a very good idea, given Deaver's close relationship with Reagan, but Sears insisted.

The day after Thanksgiving, Sears, Black, and Lake went to see Reagan, and Sears laid it out for him: if they were to have a chance of winning, Deaver would have to go.

"Are you going to talk about this guy behind his back?" Reagan asked sharply.

"No, not necessarily," Sears replied.

Reagan picked up the phone and asked Deaver to come over.

Nancy was also in the room, and when Deaver arrived, they discussed the problem for a while. Finally Deaver stood up. "Look," he said, "if I'm in the way of you being president, I'm going to quit. I quit." He walked out.

Reagan looked at the others with a tight expression on his face. "The best man in this room just left," he said. He was very unhappy to have been pushed into that spot, and later in the campaign he brought Deaver back and then took him to the White House.

Meanwhile, the campaign had other problems. An early misstep was the decision to all but skip the Iowa caucuses. The Sears team believed it made more sense to focus on New Hampshire, a vital early-voting primary state where Reagan could establish a foothold in the East. Sears showed Reagan a poll that predicted he'd win Iowa without heavy lifting. In his absence, Reagan's opponents stormed the state, and they made hay by calling out Reagan's absence at an Iowa debate. Bush won Iowa, grabbing the front-runner status. The loss had tremendous symbolic significance. Partisans whispered that perhaps Reagan didn't have the stamina, perhaps he wasn't a golden boy after all. So much had been invested in creating the image of his dominance that the loss briefly took the wind out of his sails. Reagan felt blindsided, and his confidence in Sears started to fade, but Sears continued to insist that New Hampshire was the jewel in the crown.

"We made a decision that even if we got run out of the campaign, we had to get a win in New Hampshire," Black said. It didn't lift Reagan's mood when *Newsweek* ran a cover story on Bush with the headline "Bush Breaks Out of the Pack."

Reagan decided that the only way to win was to do it his way. That meant getting out among the people. Reagan biographer Craig Shirley recounts a decidedly Reaganesque move. His sixty-ninth birthday would be on February 6, 1980, three weeks before the New Hampshire primary. He decided to "celebrate" by campaigning like crazy and with tremendous vigor. He'd show them what a sixty-nine-year-old could do! On his birthday, he made a remarkable nine campaign stops.

But his masterstroke was to initiate a one-on-one debate between himself and Bush just three days before the primary, hosted by the *Nashua Telegraph*. Reagan offered to pay for the event himself, and Bush agreed, in spite of the outrage of the other candidates who were excluded. According to Shirley, Sears masterminded a trick: on the day of the debate he invited the other candidates to the debate, and when they showed up on the stage before an audience of 2,500 people, Bush went ballistic. That hadn't been the agreement. The *Telegraph*'s editor, Jon Breen, wasn't happy, either. After arguing with Reagan, Breen ordered that his microphone be shut off. Reagan pulled himself up to his full stature and declared indignantly, "I'm paying for this microphone!"

That delighted the crowd, and the other candidates left the stage to Reagan and Bush. Few people remember what was said during the debate. Reagan stole the show before it even started and regained his momentum.

At about two in the afternoon of primary day, while the polls were still open, Reagan nabbed Black. "Charlie, where's John?"

"He's making telephone calls."

"Could you round up John and Jim and come and see me in the suite?"

Black nodded, and as Reagan walked away, he thought, "I know what this is."

Sure enough, when they arrived at the suite, Reagan, who notoriously hated to sack people, fired them. After that, he was unbeatable. He won New Hampshire decisively with 50 percent of the vote, and he continued to win, sewing up the nomination early, with more than double the votes Bush received.

The Republican National Convention in July didn't have much suspense, except for a certain pressing matter. "One of the most amazing things to me is that we went to that convention without knowing who was going to be vice president," Deaver, who was back by Reagan's side, recalled. "I think that's just fascinating. It didn't seem so odd at the time. I honestly believe Ronald Reagan had thought about this and eliminated people, and that George Bush was the guy who made sense to him." But that wasn't always apparent. Ed Meese and pollster/strategist Richard Wirthlin had suggested that Reagan consider picking Gerald Ford as a unity candidate. He wasn't immediately averse to the idea, and he asked Meese and Wirthlin to test the waters with Ford and his people.

Deaver stayed in the suite with Reagan, and he could see him growing increasingly uneasy as time passed and he hadn't heard back from Meese and Wirthlin. Around six o'clock, he decided to have dinner and turned on the TV. There was Ford talking to Walter Cronkite about a "co-presidency."

"Reagan almost choked on whatever he was eating, and said, 'Co-presidency? Where the hell is that coming from?'" Deaver recalled. "He said, 'We've got to do something about this right now. You go up and tell Ed and Dick that I want them to come down here right now.'"

Deaver raced upstairs and summoned the negotiators away. "Reagan wants to talk to you." Henry Kissinger, who was on Ford's team, walked in at that point, and Deaver said, "You'd better get President Ford down to talk to Reagan. Reagan has just seen this thing on television, and he's livid."

Soon Ford arrived at the suite, and he and Reagan went into the bedroom to speak privately. When they came out and said their good-byes, Reagan told his staff, "Jerry didn't want to do it. Jerry thinks it's a bad idea. Jerry's going to be with us all the way, said he would do whatever it took to help us. Unless somebody's got a better idea, get me George Bush."

Clearly, Bush had not expected to be asked. He told reporters, "Out of a clear blue sky, Governor Reagan called me up and asked if I would be willing to run with him on the ticket. I was surprised, of course, and I was very, very pleased. I feel honored. I did tell him I would do what all Republicans should do—support the platform. And I told him that I would work, work, work."

Judging by the response of the convention, Republicans were also pleased. This was not only a unifying ticket, it was a winning ticket. Bush, who had once jabbed at Reagan's policies as being "voodoo economics," was ready to draw a new alignment. No one was particularly concerned about Illinois congressman John Anderson's decision to mount an independent run. Although he would do relatively well in the general election, with 6.6 percent of the popular vote, the liberal-leaning Anderson drew equally from both parties.

There was no question about who was at the top of the Republican ticket. The election was Reagan's alone to win or lose. He was the anti-Carter, the slayer of mediocrity, and the two men's relationship, bordering on mutual contempt, was reminiscent of the icy standoff between Eisenhower and Truman. In his White House diary, Carter frequently jabbed at Reagan as inept and superficial, saying in one passage that his "life seems to be governed by a few anecdotes and vignettes that he has memorized." He thought Reagan swam in a shallow pool, and he didn't fully appreciate the growing affection and trust many Americans felt for him. Rosalynn Carter shared that view. She recalled being glad when Reagan was nominated by the Republicans to run against her husband, writing in her diary that his politics were so bad it would be no trouble to beat him. Throughout the campaign, the Carters and their team underestimated Reagan's unique appeal.

For his part, Reagan thought Carter was mean-spirited and a poor leader. His lack of clarity and resolve on the subject of nuclear arms especially troubled Reagan, as did his weak response to the Soviet invasion of Afghanistan. But Carter's biggest problem was that he lacked a compelling vision. As Andrew E. Busch put it so cogently, "There was a distinct sense in which Americans were repudiating not just the failures of Carter's stewardship, but the failures of his imagination. Reagan was the only candidate among the three who did not accept the widespread assumption that the United States must simply accept its fate as a power and a society in decline."

When the League of Women Voters scheduled a debate and invited Anderson to participate, Carter refused to attend; he wanted a one-on-one match with Reagan. Reagan cheerfully took advantage of the opportunity to debate Anderson without Carter, and he did very well. Carter's refusal made him look officious and petty—and maybe scared. By the time Carter agreed to a debate with Reagan the week before the election, the stakes were enormous.

Patrick Caddell, Carter's pollster, looked back on the debate as a fatal error. "The only strategic mistake we made in the entire campaign was to debate Reagan," he said. "We had created all these doubts about Reagan. Reagan desperately needed a forum, where he could prove not only that he was more competent than the President, but simply where he could stand up and say, 'Hey listen, I'm not going to blow up the world. Do I look like the kind of guy that will destroy your country and your future?' He is very good at that. That was the reason for that debate."

It worked to Reagan's advantage. He came into the debate slightly ahead of Carter in the polls, with the goal of presenting a picture of strength and moderation. He knew how to do so; he'd been doing it for years, swatting away the "extremist" tag his opponents had tried to pin on him since 1966.

Carter was on the defensive, and he wasn't at his best. Even Reagan was aghast when Carter described his view on the nuclear arms race by saying "I had a discussion with my daughter, Amy, the other day, before I came here, to ask her what the most important issue was. She said she thought nuclear weaponry, and the control of nuclear arms." No stranger to the charming anecdote, Reagan thought that one fell flat, leaving the nation to imagine a weak president taking cues from his twelve-year-old daughter. (After the debate, Deaver had signs made to pass out at rallies, reading, "Amy Carter for Secretary of State.")

In the final moments of the debate, Carter attacked Reagan head-on, listing all the ways he was outside the mainstream. But Reagan dealt him a crushing blow with his closing statement: "It might be well if you would ask yourself, are you better off than you were four years ago?" The question struck a chord. Viewers heard it not only as a pocketbook calculation but as an existential reckoning. It was a clarification of the central question on everyone's minds, and it was so powerful that it continues to be asked in campaigns to this day.

With Reagan's poll numbers rising, Carter's final opportunity came in the form of an "October surprise"—news the weekend before the election that a deal on the hostages was imminent. The media was engaged in nonstop coverage of the drama. After all, Election Day would be the one-year anniversary of their capture. Carter suspended his campaign and returned to Washington as the nation held its collective breath. On Sunday afternoon, looking pale and exhausted, Carter told the country that although the new developments were positive, he could not say when the hostages would be released. On Monday, Caddell delivered the bad news to the Carters: his polling showed they were not going to win the election.

On Tuesday, the Reagans were home in California, where they voted early. They were planning to watch the election returns with friends and were expecting a long night. Reagan was in the shower and Nancy was in the tub, with the TV on in the living room, when Nancy heard John Chancellor announce that Reagan was expected to win in a landslide. In those days, the networks didn't try to wait until the polls closed in the West to announce a winner if the result seemed clear.

The Reagans raced into the living room, wrapping towels around themselves. "And there we stood," Nancy recounted, "dripping wet, wearing nothing but our towels, as we heard that Ronnie had just been elected!"

In the Carter camp, the mood was stoic after Carter called Reagan to concede, but Rosalynn let out her true feelings later in her memoir. "I was bitter at what I had seen on television for weeks that I thought was so unfair to Jimmy; bitter about the hostage situation dominating the news for the last few days before the election as the media 'celebrated' the anniversary of the hostage capture." She was bitter about so many things, and "I was the only one who admitted it."

To no one's surprise, the two wives did not exactly hit it off. When Rosalynn invited Nancy to the White House for the obligatory tour during the transition, Nancy noted that "the chill in her manner matched the chill in the room." Rosalynn refused to show Nancy the bedroom, which she really wanted to see, and turned the tour over to her secretary halfway through, pleading other commitments. Nancy was disappointed, but Rosalynn might have been surprised to know that she was also sympathetic, writing, "It must be painful to have to show the residence to the wife of the man who defeated your husband."

Nancy thought the place looked shabby, in desperate need of an update. That sentiment was probably responsible for fueling a rumor, which she insisted was not true, that she'd asked the Carters to move out early so renovations could get started.

The transition meeting between their husbands was equally cool. Carter lectured Reagan for an hour on the important issues of the day, and Reagan listened attentively. Carter kept asking him if he wanted to take notes, and Reagan said no, he'd just listen. Privately, Carter thought that was ludicrous. How could he remember anything if he didn't take notes? Carter, still smarting from his loss, believed that Reagan wasn't up to the job. But according to an account by the historian Douglas Brinkley, the Reagan camp had a different version:

> "Reagan recalled verbatim everything Carter had told us," Meese remembered, defending his old boss against accusations from the Carter camp that the president-elect had been inattentive. "He didn't take notes because he didn't need to." Meese believed that Reagan had felt sorry for Carter at the White House that day—that the Gipper was just not a good hater. "Though he profoundly disagreed with Carter on policy issues, Reagan harbored no mean-spiritedness toward Carter," Meese insisted. "It's usually the loser that is full of sour grapes."

In describing the meeting to reporters, Carter had his game face on, calling it "enjoyable" and "productive." He even mentioned that their wives had had a "good visit." But the truth was that he felt discouraged and demoralized. Like any president about to see his legacy upended, he thought he'd let the country down. Many years later, it still hurt. "Allowing Ronald Reagan to become president was by far my biggest failure in office," he said.

CHAPTER 4

A REVOLUTION OF IDEAS

Have you got goose bumps?" Reagan asked Deaver. He was sitting behind the Resolute desk in the Oval Office for the first time, at the end of a long Inauguration Day. His hands were spread out in front of him, pressing against the old English oak, gripping the desk, and getting a feel for it. It was a solemn moment, the fullness of his new role settling in on him late at night—the first of many times he would feel wonder at the office.

January 20, 1981, had been full of similar moments of awe, interspersed with the bittersweet and the human. The peaceful transition of power was ceremonial but also intimate, winners and losers standing together: on one side, the weary, demoralized Carters, bruised by their loss and resigned to reality; on the other, the Reagans, bright-eyed and optimistic, entering an exciting new phase of their lives. The scene had been played out on many other occasions. It was the noble tradition of the transitory nature of command in America—the victor and the vanquished, together under one flag.

The day began early at Blair House, where the Reagans were staying, along with all of their family members—Nancy's parents and brother, Richard, with his wife, Patricia, and their children; Reagan's brother, Moon, and his wife, Bess; Maureen and her fiancé, Dennis; Michael and his wife, Colleen, and their son, Cameron; Patti; and Ron and his wife, Dora. When Deaver woke Reagan at 8:00 A.M. and said he had to get up because the inauguration was in four hours, Reagan asked plaintively, "Do I have to?" He was just kidding.

The previous night there had been a star-studded inaugural gala—Hollywood's tribute to its favorite son. It was spearheaded by Frank Sinatra, just as he'd done for Kennedy twenty years earlier to the day. This time the gala was televised by ABC so Americans could vicariously share in the glamour. All the old stars were there, among them Jimmy Stewart, Bob Hope, and Ethel Merman. The emcee, Johnny Carson, joked, "This is the first administration to have a premiere."

As Reagan rose and began to prepare for Inauguration Day, he took a call from President Carter, who told him in a voice made weary by forty-eight hours without sleep that the hostages would be released that day, but he didn't know at what hour they'd be in the air. Reagan sincerely hoped it would come to pass while Carter was president. Surely he deserved that. Reagan decided that if the hostages took off before he took his oath of office, he would open his speech with praise for Carter.

At 9:30, the Reagans joined the Bush family at St. John's Episcopal Church for a brief service before returning to Blair House to make final preparations. Soon afterward they entered the North Portico of the White House across the street, where the Carters were waiting in the Blue Room for the traditional preinaugural coffee. Reagan was dressed in a club coat, striped pants, and a gray vest—no top hat—and Nancy in her signature bright red dress and coat by the designer Adolfo. It was an awkward meeting. The Carters looked exhausted and grim, wincing at the niceties and going through the motions as if they'd have liked to be anywhere else. In the car on the way to the

Capitol, Reagan chatted nervously while Carter stared out the car window in silence. Their wives, in a separate car, barely spoke as they rode.

The capital was swarming with people; the predictions were that the inauguration would boast the largest crowd ever, aided by the unusually balmy weather, overcast with temperatures in the mid-fifties. Yellow ribbons fluttered in the breeze, a symbol of hope that the hostages would come home.

For the first time, the ceremonies would take place at the west front of the Capitol instead of the east front, facing the Washington Monument and looking beyond to the graves at Arlington. The change had been dictated by Congress the previous year as a cost-saving measure, but it perfectly fit the symbolism of the western president-elect. He could take the oath with his gaze set on the nation outside the closed circle of Washington—across the plains to his childhood home and then to the coast, where he had begun his political journey.

Reagan especially appreciated the view of Arlington and wanted to incorporate it into his speech. He wrote most of the speech himself, organizing his thoughts on four-by-six-inch cards, but he had the assistance of Ken Khachigian, a masterful longtime Republican speechwriter who had been with him during the campaign.

In preparing the speech, Reagan gave Khachigian a thick stack of index cards with notes from his past speeches. Those were his themes, the simple, consistent notions he had held for years. In a sense, there was no such thing as a new speech for Reagan. He was content with his principles, and the only question was how to give them a fresh treatment. When Khachigian came back with a draft early in January, Reagan thought it too flowery. Reagan's rhetoric was always personal—poetry, when it was used, was not pretentious. He took out his yellow lined pad and began rewriting the draft in his own words. It was a short speech, only twenty minutes long, and it focused on two primary points—efficiency in government and strength in foreign policy—the familiar ideas of Reagan's political life, going all the way back to 1964.

Spelling out the economic problems he was determined to solve, he presented the firm view that had been a standard of his campaign stump speech:

> In this present crisis, government is not the solution to our problem; government is the problem. From time to time we've been tempted to believe that society has become too complex to be managed by self-rule, that government by an elite group is superior to government for, by, and of the people. Well, if no one among us is capable of governing himself, then who among us has the capacity to govern someone else? All of us together, in and out of government, must bear the burden. The solutions we seek must be equitable, with no one group singled out to pay a higher price.

Second, he signaled that the enemies of freedom would not be given a pass in his administration. Again, this was an old theme, dating back to his initial political awakening:

> As for the enemies of freedom, those who are potential adversaries, they will be reminded that peace is the highest aspiration of the American people. We will negotiate for it, sacrifice for it; we will not surrender for it, now or ever.
>
> Our forbearance should never be misunderstood. Our reluctance for conflict should not be misjudged as a

failure of will. When action is required to preserve our national security, we will act. We will maintain sufficient strength to prevail if need be, knowing that if we do so we have the best chance of never having to use that strength.

Above all, we must realize that no arsenal or no weapon in the arsenals of the world is so formidable as the will and moral courage of free men and women. It is a weapon our adversaries in today's world do not have. It is a weapon that we as Americans do have. Let that be understood by those who practice terrorism and prey upon their neighbors.

Reagan summoned Khachigian and told him he wanted to tell a particular story as homage to all the soldiers resting at nearby Arlington National Cemetery. The story had been related to him by a friend, describing a soldier named Martin Treptow, who had been killed in action during World War I and was buried at Arlington. Treptow had kept a diary with a stirring inscription: "My Pledge: America must win this war. Therefore, I will work, I will save, I will sacrifice, I will endure, I will fight cheerfully and do my utmost, as if the issue of the whole struggle depended on me alone."

Khachigian dutifully checked out the story. No diary could be found, and it turned out that Treptow was buried in his home state of Wisconsin, not Arlington. When he told Reagan, assuming the story wouldn't be used, Reagan didn't care. "Put it in," he said. He was a master of the emotional truth and often didn't sweat the small details. Indeed, the Treptow story would become one of the most memorable moments of his inaugural address. It came at the end, and Reagan used it to make his final point:

The crisis we are facing today does not require of us the kind of sacrifice that Martin Treptow and so many thousands of others were called upon to make. It does require, however, our best effort and our willingness to believe in ourselves and to believe in our capacity to perform great deeds, to believe that together with God's help we can and will resolve the problems which now confront us.

And after all, why shouldn't we believe that? We are Americans.

At 11:57 A.M., moments after Vice President Bush took his oath of office, Reagan rose to stand before Chief Justice Warren Burger, who would be delivering the presidential oath. Nancy was at his side, holding his mother's Bible, old and taped together, opened to Nelle's favorite verse, II Chronicles 7:14:

If my people, who are called by my name, will humble themselves and pray and seek my face and turn from their wicked ways, then I will hear from heaven, and I will forgive their sin and will heal their land.

Nelle had presciently scrawled a note in the margin: "This is a good verse for the healing of nations, too."

At the moment of his oath, the sun broke through, a beam landing on the platform, so when Reagan stepped to the podium to deliver his address, the gray gloom had lifted. Before speaking he glanced at Carter, hoping for a sign that the hostages had taken flight. Carter gave a barely perceptible shake of his head. No, they were still on the ground. The perfect movie ending was not to be.

Reagan gave his speech, and then the Reagans departed to

the traditional luncheon with congressional leaders in the Capitol's Statuary Hall, the columned Greek Revival amphitheater that had been the meeting place of the House of Representatives in the early days of the nation. There they feasted on California cuisine, drinking California wines. At 2:15, Reagan rose to address the guests, grinning happily. "Some thirty minutes ago," he said, "the plane bearing our prisoners left Iranian airspace, and they're now free of Iran." The assembly cheered, and there was a tremendous sense of relief.

It was always speculated that the Iranians had deliberately waited until Carter was no longer president to set the hostages free, a final humiliation for the man they loathed so much—and maybe an appeasing gesture to Reagan. If that were true, the Reagans had nothing but contempt for the evil symbolism. Nancy learned that when the phone rang in the car taking Carter and former vice president Walter Mondale to Andrews Air Force Base with news of the release, they burst into tears. "I've had my differences with the Carters, but they certainly deserved better than that," she wrote.

The long afternoon continued with an inaugural parade, beginning with the Reagans riding in an open limousine down Pennsylvania Avenue, waving to the crowds, before taking their place in the viewing stands. The parade featured eight thousand marchers, including a band from Dixon, and hundreds of equestrian teams. Three hot-air balloons rose above the crowds. The Mormon Tabernacle Choir rode a seventy-foot float and stopped before the presidential viewing stand to sing "The Battle Hymn of the Republic."

"Home" at the White House at last, after the ceremonies and parades, it all sank in for the Reagans. Everything was perfect in the living quarters on the second floor—they were especially amazed to see their own furniture from California, already neatly arranged and waiting for them. They walked through the rooms holding hands, and despite Nancy's earlier opinion that the place was shabby, it had an Inauguration Day glow. There were inaugural balls to get dressed for—eight of them—but they took time to pause and luxuriate for a moment in the wonder.

REAGAN FELT A SENSE of familiarity about going to work the first day and sitting down behind his desk. He had descended from the family quarters at 7:30 A.M., walking along the portico at the Rose Garden and entering his new office.

He was considered an outsider, but he wasn't really. As a former two-term governor of the country's most populous state, he was practiced in the rubrics of the executive branch. Although he shared that governing background with Carter, that's where their similarities ended. California has often been likened to a small country, a diverse and complex state, whose budget is as large as or larger than most nations'. Its culture, politics, and economy reflect the country at large in ways that few states can match.

In particular, Reagan had experience with a vast organizational operation. In his political life, he had collected an impressive cadre of experts and loyalists, but he was bringing a more diverse team on board, including people from past administrations and even Democrats. For that reason, the Reagan transition, run by Meese, was a huge operation, costing more than $3 million, two-thirds appropriated by Congress and the rest from private donations. At the time that was significant cash. According to the historian Carl Brauer, the expenditures galled Reagan's enemies. Arthur Schlesinger, Jr., complained in the *Wall Street Journal*, "The true-hearted conservatives conducting the transition in Washington are staging a bureaucratic orgy that those ancients who recall the transition from Eisenhower to Kennedy in 1960 can only watch with stupefaction and incredulity." Reagan and Meese shrugged off the criticism. How else can you organize such an enormous enterprise?

The most important staffing choice came not from one of Reagan's old hands but from the George H. W. Bush campaign. James Baker had been Bush's campaign manager and had become an advisor for the Reagan campaign in the general election. But he was not part of Reagan's inner circle, which was dominated by Meese, Deaver, and Weinberger. So he was surprised when he got a call from Reagan the day after the election at his hotel in Los Angeles. Reagan asked if he could drop by to talk. To Baker's astonishment, Reagan offered him the position of chief of staff. Reagan realized he needed more than his California team; he needed a Washington insider.

Baker accepted, but he could feel the unwelcoming vibes from the California gang and, indeed, from many Reagan supporters. Even so, Baker was a consummate professional, a skilled organizer, and a loyal aide. His job, he knew, was to serve the president, not to fight with him or undermine him in any way. "The chief of staff truly holds what is potentially the second most powerful job in Washington," he wrote of his role, "but the rule to remember is that the power comes from the position not the person. The chief of staff is what the title says—*staff*."

Meese might have seemed to be the obvious candidate for chief of staff. He'd been at Reagan's right hand for so many years, had led the transition, and shared his ideology in a way that Baker might not. There was some grumbling among conservatives when he was passed over. Reagan appointed him counselor to the president, showing that Meese had his ear, but with two strong men at the helm, there was bound to be some jockeying, and the media took delight in suggesting that there were tensions between Baker and Meese.

Deaver had surprised Reagan after the election by saying he didn't want to go to Washington, mostly because his wife was balking at the move. "Well, if that's the way you feel," Reagan answered unhappily. Deaver returned home after their meeting and was opening a bottle of wine to celebrate with his wife when the phone rang. "Gosh, Mike," the president-elect said. "I've been thinking about this, and I really need you to come back there with me."

"I just don't think I can do that," Deaver said, glancing at his wife.

"I just can't go back without you," Reagan insisted. "So come back for one year."

Deaver said yes and hung up the phone to find his wife in tears. She hadn't heard the full conversation, but she knew.

Deaver would be deputy chief of staff under Baker, but Reagan gave him a plum office, the study right off the Oval Office that usually belonged to the president. "I can't take this," Deaver protested. "Where are you going to go when you want to get out of the Oval?"

Reagan laughed. "Look," he said, "I've tried for twenty-five years to get that round office. Why would I want this little square office?" So, Deaver said, "That's how I got the best real estate in Washington, D.C."

In that way, Baker, Meese, and Deaver became the most powerful troika in modern presidential history. Their role said a lot about Reagan's governing style. As Hedrick Smith wrote in the *New York Times*, "The Meese-Baker-Deaver combination fits Ronald Reagan's concept of the Presidency and his style of leadership just as surely as Sherman Adams suited Dwight Eisenhower. With his chairman-of-the-board approach, Mr. Reagan delegates substantial power to subordinates and deliberately holds himself aloof from a lot of decisions that used to absorb Jimmy Carter. And he seems comfortable with the dispersal of power beneath him."

Thanks to the team of Baker, Meese, and Deaver, the early period of Reagan's presidency was viewed by many as well organized. But it would be wrong to paint an entirely rosy scenario. Lyn Nofziger, who was appointed as assistant to the president for political affairs, was not particularly fond of Baker; he never trusted him—he wasn't a Reagan man. And there were others like that making their way into positions of influence. "We spent a lot of time making sure that Reagan people were getting into government, and that non-Reagan people were being kept out of government," he said. He saw that as his role, the long-time aide turned protector of the vision. But the White House operation was far more complicated than a gang of loyalists in California. In the end, it was a salty mix of true believers and pragmatists.

Caspar Weinberger, who had been Reagan's finance director when he was governor and then chairman of the Federal Trade Commission, was tapped for secretary of defense. It might have seemed odd picking a finance guy for the role, but Reagan respected Weinberger's leadership skills and was confident that he shared his ideals. Weinberger recalled, "He notified me on December 1—which I remember because it was my father's birthday—that he wanted me to be secretary of defense. He started out by saying, 'I know you have a very full and a very rich and a very satisfying and a happy life.' And he said, 'I want to spoil the whole thing.'"

For secretary of state, Reagan looked outside his circle, choosing Alexander Haig. Haig had a strong résumé, having been supreme allied commander under Ford and briefly Carter and chief of staff for a year under Nixon, but he wasn't necessarily an obvious choice. It appears that Reagan was influenced by the pro-Haig entreaties of none other than Richard Nixon, who had begun sending letters of advice during the campaign. No one denied that Haig had talent. However, he was the antithesis of a team player, imperious and full of self-regard, jealous of his turf, and besieged by grievances that he frequently took to the president. In his diary, Reagan complained about Haig's regular threats to quit—he was said to carry a letter of resignation in his pocket.

Haig came out swinging right away. In a meeting in Baker's office the afternoon of the inauguration, Haig was there with a set of demands. "Reagan told me I've got complete control of foreign policy."

"He didn't tell you that you have complete control of foreign policy," Baker countered.

"Oh, no, no," Haig said. "He did." And it continued from there.

Weinberger, who bore the brunt of much of Haig's discontent, observed that "from the beginning he was obsessed with the idea that people were trying to undermine him. He was very worried about perquisites and his own primacy as foreign policy advisor. He disliked intensely anybody else commenting on any foreign policy matters in the presence of the president." Haig's bullish behavior would only get worse during the first year of Reagan's presidency. In retrospect, most people agree that having a rogue character in the role of public diplomat might not have been such a good idea. It's odd that Nixon pushed the appointment in the first place, since few people understood international diplomacy as well as he did.

Filling out the foreign policy team was Richard Allen, another inner-circle choice—remember, he'd been blown away by

Reagan's resolve to win the Cold War years earlier and had given up his own political aspirations to support Reagan's candidacy. Allen was appointed national security advisor. He was quite familiar with the dynamics of the NSC, but one thing he didn't like was the classic conflict between the NSC and secretary of state, which had been in evidence with Henry Kissinger and then with Zbieniew Brzezinski and Cyrus Vance during the Carter administration. He was determined to restore a sense of collaboration, and when he interviewed staff members he told them bluntly, "Look, the NSC is going to be a different place. We're not going to fight for control of policy. Policy is going to be made in a collegial way, in the way it was always made before. . . . If you're looking for the high-voltage action and the big visibility and all the other perks, don't come to this NSC." With Haig at State, that would be a challenge, however.

Allen introduced Reagan to another key foreign policy player, Jeane Kirkpatrick, a professor of government at Georgetown University, whom he selected as ambassador to the United Nations. Allen had first brought Kirkpatrick to Reagan's attention in November 1979 when he showed him an article she'd written for *Commentary* magazine titled "Dictatorships and Double Standards." Reagan liked the article. "Who is he?" he asked.

"Well, first of all, he is a she," Allen said.

When Allen arranged a meeting, Kirkpatrick was concerned. She was a card-carrying Democrat and thought that might be a problem. At the meeting, she put it to Reagan right away, asking him if he minded that she was a Democrat. He reminded her that he'd been a Democrat, too, for much of his life, and it didn't bother him. What he cared about was her ideas—and those he liked. In fact, Kirkpatrick became one of his favorites for her boldness and her refusal to back down to the Soviets.

William Casey, who had managed Reagan's campaign after

the Sears team was fired, was picked to head the CIA. That was part of Reagan's international strategy as well. Reagan believed that the CIA should assert itself more aggressively in international hot spots, including conducting covert actions and supporting anti-Communist organizations abroad. Those efforts would lead to some successes, but also to failures that would plague Reagan's presidency.

On the domestic side, Reagan appointed Donald Regan, the chairman of Merrill Lynch, to be secretary of the Treasury. "Reagan without the A," the president called him. Already accustomed to being the man in charge, Regan took firm control of the economic reins. Regan has received so much press on and analysis of his later role as chief of staff and his famous fallout with Nancy Reagan that many people fail to appreciate his contribution to selling and executing Reagan's economic policy in the early years of his presidency.

Straight out of the gate, President Reagan placed his primary attention on the economy, more than on foreign policy. The voters, in rejecting Carter, had given him a mandate that he was determined to use. Although polls showed that dislike of Carter had been a stronger motivation than an embrace of conservatism, he would show them that they'd chosen wisely. He had one important thing going for him: his unwavering belief in the principles he preached. He knew he had a small window in which to get his legislative goals executed: budget cuts to streamline the federal government and tax cuts, which he believed would spark economic growth. He was determined, as he told his cabinet at an early meeting: "We're going to make history in that no government has before voluntarily reduced itself in size." He instructed his cabinet, "Make sure bureaucracy can't end-run us. Or we'll booby trap their swivel chairs."

Reagan praised Regan for being a great salesman of his pro-

gram, but he also had the boyish David Stockman, a numbers
whiz, laying the groundwork as the director of the Office of
Management and Budget. Feisty and outspoken, the two-term
congressman from Michigan was not initially on board with
Reagan's supply-side philosophy, but he was a bear about cutting waste. Early on he tangled with Weinberger, arguing that
the defense budget was out of control. In this case, Weinberger
knew something about budgets; he also understood how to appeal to Reagan. He took graphics to a cabinet meeting to discuss the defense budget. One showed a slumping, dejected Boy
Scout. "Is this what we want defending our country?" he asked.
The next graphic showed a technological he-man, armed and
ready. "Mr. President," he concluded, "this is your choice." He
won that argument, but Stockman labored on in his mission to
cut government waste, one of Reagan's chief campaign promises.

Stockman's star might have risen farther had it not been for
his foolish decision to give a series of interviews to *The Atlantic*
during the first year. His candid tales of the inside workings of
the White House's legislative efforts were published in a lengthy
December piece, "The Education of David Stockman." In the
article, Stockman was portrayed as a conflicted executor of the
budget strategy, calling Reagan's across-the-board tax cut "a
Trojan horse" and sowing doubts about the core programs of
the White House, which, he said, had been devised in haste and
were flawed.

When Reagan read the article, he was furious. Meese and
Deaver thought Stockman should be fired, although Baker disagreed. In the end, he kept his job but was taken to the wood-
shed by the boss. Trust being the currency of an effective White
House operation, Stockman never recovered his sterling reputation and was gone by Reagan's second term.

THE BIG EGOS OPERATING in Reagan's orbit deferred to the president, if they knew what was good for them, and Reagan was a study in ego demolition. He despised the petty internecine warfare that was typical in administrations and refused to mediate disputes among his staff and cabinet members. "You work it out" was his typical reply when people complained about each other.

Reagan's management style was polite, even-tempered, and personable. He wasn't a screamer; his honeyed voice seemed incapable of rising to that pitch. Famously, he had a big jar of jelly beans on his desk, and he liked it when visitors indulged. Glass jars of jelly beans were also at cabinet and staff meetings, where they were passed down the table, each person pouring out a handful and popping them into his or her mouth. (Reagan's jelly bean habit became such a trademark that the artist Peter Rocha created a portrait of the president, composed of ten thousand Jelly Belly jelly beans, that is on display at the Reagan Library.)

His approach was egalitarian. Martin Anderson, the assistant to the president for policy development, characterized it this way: "See, the thing about Reagan, the assumption is made that everything is divided in neat categories, and he didn't work that way. In fact, at meetings he thought if the domestic people wanted to comment on the foreign policy and the foreign policy on the domestic policy, that was just fine. He wasn't a stickler for you stay in your box and you stay in your box, which upset a lot of people on the staff, because they're used to staying in their boxes." Not only did he mix it up in cabinet meetings, he set up "supercabinet" committees, similar to boards of directors, to focus on key issues. He liked listening to a lot of different opinions, having vigorous debates, and getting input from people outside the cabinet offices. Needless to say, such power sharing was abhorrent to people like Haig, but it suited Reagan's management style.

One of Reagan's most effective weapons was humor. When advisors filed into the Oval Office, the awe and sobriety of the place could put them on their heels. They were there for serious business, often divided into warring camps, ready to fight for their positions. Reagan disarmed them before they could get their hackles up. His personal assistant, Kathleen Osborne, recalled the frequent laughter that emanated from the Oval Office when staff members or visitors were present.

Howard Baker, who served for a time as Reagan's chief of staff in his second term, after retiring from the Senate, noted that "so many of his decisions were hung on the tree of humor," comparing him to Abraham Lincoln in that respect.

That was just one clue to his political success. David Gergen, the White House director of communications during Reagan's first term, wrote of the president's impressive emotional intelligence, noting that his sunny personality, relentless optimism, warm manner, and humor weren't only on the surface; they were who he was at the core. After four years of Carter's puritanical disapproval, which had settled over the White House—and the nation—like a heavy cloak, perhaps people were ready for a little sunshine. The contrast was striking: Carter's message of American malaise versus Reagan's optimism. An aide, when asked "Why do you like Reagan?," responded, "For one simple reason—he seemed to like me." Americans felt it, too.

Deaver recalled that Reagan kept several blank personal checks in the top drawer of his desk, and he would occasionally write checks to people he came across who were in need. One time, he noticed that a check he'd written to a woman hadn't shown up on his bank statement, so he called her.

"You know, you haven't cashed that check," said the president of the United States.

"Oh, no, I framed it," she replied.

"Well, my God, I sent you that money so you'd have some money to eat. I'll send you another check, you keep that one framed and cash this one."

"In my experience, the Reagan you saw in private was just the same as the one you saw in public," Charlie Black said. "He was easygoing, he was very kind and polite. I like to tell the story of how in those days when a lot of people smoked, if you had a meeting in his office, he'd go around and clean up the ashtrays at the end of the meeting before the next crowd came in. He was just a good man, well motivated in all of his intentions and his philosophy. It took a lot to get him mad."

Not that Reagan was one-dimensional. He could get angry, but, as an aide noted, his displeasure was usually about issues, not people. He wasn't known for his temper; quite the opposite. He was unfailingly courteous. The one "tell" that he was annoyed or frustrated was that he'd take off his glasses and throw them on his desk. On one occasion, that aide recalled, the glasses flew off the desk, disappearing onto the floor, and he and the president both got down on their hands and knees to hunt for them. Crawling around under the desk, they looked at each other and burst out laughing.

Reagan could also use sarcasm to biting effect, as he did with his attorney general. William French Smith, an original member of Reagan's California kitchen cabinet, was Reagan's first AG. One day he came to the Oval Office with a big idea. Concerned about illegal immigration, he announced to the president that he had a plan to institute a national identity card. "That was right off the wall," Anderson said. "And we hadn't prepared for it." Recognizing that it could be a disastrously controversial action, Reagan spoke. "He didn't say, 'That's a dumb goddamn idea,' or, 'I don't like that,' or, 'You shouldn't have done that,' or 'I wouldn't do this,'" Anderson remembered. Instead, Reagan said, "Well, we can brand all the babies."

That was the death knell. It never came up again.

He had a Republican Senate and a Democratic House of Representatives, and he immediately set out to woo their members. He had a friendly relationship with Howard Baker, the Senate majority leader. But he also had to contend with Tip O'Neill, the powerful Speaker of the House, whose regard for Reagan was known to be low—he once called him "Herbert Hoover with a smile."

Reagan's assistant for legislative affairs, Max Friedersdorf, had served under Nixon, Ford, and Carter, and it was his job to bring Congress into alignment. First and foremost, that meant courting O'Neill. During the transition, Reagan told Friedersdorf that he wanted to invite O'Neill and his wife to the White House for dinner as soon as he was in office, and it was hastily arranged.

The dinner for eight upstairs in the private residence included the Reagans, O'Neill and his wife, Millie, the Jim Bakers, and the Friedersdorfs. "I was kind of on pins and needles because Tip O'Neill was pretty brusque—he's a strong personality and a gruff old guy, like a big bear of a man," recalled Friedersdorf. "His wife, Millie, was sweet as she can be, but it was kind of a tense situation for me." He met them at the elevator and took them into the president's sitting room. O'Neill and Reagan sat at opposite ends of a couch, where they ordered martinis and began telling each other Irish jokes. So far, so good.

Nancy was rolling her eyes. "I've heard this a million times," she said to the wives. "Would you like to see the Lincoln Bedroom and the sleeping quarters?" They gratefully followed her out of the room.

At dinner, Reagan gave a flattering toast to O'Neill, speaking of how much he admired him and how he was in the tradition of the great Boston politicians. O'Neill loved it. By the time the O'Neills left that night, Friedersdorf was thinking "This is going to be a little easier than I thought. He [Reagan] could charm the socks off of you." The president accompanied the O'Neills down in the elevator and walked them to the car. "Night, Tip," he called warmly.

But after that occasion, Reagan got his first big reality check on Washington politics—that any personal warmth between the two men didn't extend to their legislative battles. Initially, Reagan was baffled when O'Neill came out swinging against him publicly. He called up the Speaker and said he was hurt to read something nasty O'Neill had said about him. "I thought we had a pretty fine relationship going."

"Ol' buddy," O'Neill chortled, "that's politics. After six o'clock we can be friends, but before six, it's politics."

Following that, when Reagan called him, he sometimes said, "Look, Tip, I'm resetting my watch. It's six o'clock."

Much has been made of the bipartisan spirit supposedly created by "Ron and Tip." But their relationship was unquestionably contentious. The myth gained purchase mostly because people liked the visual of two old Irishmen of similar backgrounds and stature working across party lines for the good of the country. But whatever their personal fondness for each other, it stood to reason that they would be legislative enemies. Reagan was leading a revolution against the very principles that O'Neill held most dear. They might have seemed like brothers when they were together privately, but they had different ideas of government.

Kenneth Duberstein, who replaced Friedersdorf at the end of 1981 when he left to take a position as consul general to Bermuda, found that Reagan's temperament was his greatest gift in negotiations. He was a uniter, "always speaking to people's better sides and giving them hope. As he used to say, 'There's a pony in there some place.'"

Duberstein observed that except for being two old Irishmen, Reagan and O'Neill were opposites, always in danger of ending up further apart when they sat down to negotiate. Reagan had to figure out a strategy. "Reagan found the formula," he said, "and the formula was, Let's bring people together. Let's bring people inside the tent. He believed in free trade, he believed we're a nation of immigrants. He believed everyone had a choice to make. He was willing to fight for what he believed in, but he was always optimistic. It attracted people. He inspired people, he inspired the better angels. And he was self-deprecating. You know, he seldom used the word *I*. He always preached to us, 'It's *we*, not *I*. We're all in this together.'"

MANY PRESIDENTS HAVE BEMOANED the claustrophobic nature of being in the White House—Harry Truman referred to it as "the great white jail." Reagan, accustomed to being his own man, found it so, calling it a "bird in a gilded cage sense of isolation." He didn't mind being alone; he minded being protected, coddled, controlled. A month into his presidency, he wanted to perform a ritual that had been sacrosanct in his marriage from its first year: buying his wife a Valentine's card. He informed the Secret Service agents that he'd like to go shopping for a card. They complied, of course, but it was such a complex expedition that he vowed never to repeat it.

He didn't fault the Secret Service. He understood that it had its job to do—and would feel even more strongly about that after a devastating attempt on his life on March 30, 1981.

So much time has passed since the assassination attempt that people often forget or are surprised to realize that it occurred just two months into Reagan's presidency. The timing was stunning; Reagan's presidency might have been over before it got started. Some writers have speculated that the experience cast a cloud over him, weakened him, and made him gun-shy, but that's hardly convincing, considering that virtually everything he accomplished in his eight years occurred afterward.

The day it happened was so ordinary, and the event Reagan was speaking at so mundane, that the Secret Service agents didn't insist he wear a bulletproof vest, as they sometimes did. On that afternoon, he was exiting the Hilton Hotel, where he had given a luncheon speech to the Construction Trades Council, when he heard several loud bangs; he thought they sounded like firecrackers. As he started to turn in surprise, Jerry Parr, the head of his Secret Service detail, tackled him and shoved him into the limousine. He felt a terrible stab of pain and assumed Parr had broken one of his ribs.

In the confusing early moments after the shots were fired, it was clear only that press secretary James Brady; Secret Service agent Tim McCarthy, who had spread out his arms to shield Reagan's body; and police officer Thomas Delahanty were wounded. Reagan was assumed to be unhurt, and his car began to head back to the White House. But then he started coughing up blood, and Parr screamed at the driver to make a U-turn and get to George Washington University Hospital. Reagan still thought a broken rib was impeding his breathing.

Deaver, who had been standing next to Reagan when the shots were fired but didn't know the president had been hit, jumped into a car in the motorcade and was following the president's car. Arriving behind Reagan, Deaver witnessed him stepping out of the limo and entering the hospital. "Reagan had a habit—if he'd been sitting in a plane or car, or even on a podium—when he got out, he would cinch his pants up . . . and then he'd button his coat," Deaver said. "And that's exactly what he did, cinched his pants up and buttoned his coat. He looked all right to me. The minute he crossed the frame of the door, it was like being behind the curtain. He collapsed. He got there and collapsed."

At that point no one knew that Reagan had been shot. They raced him into the emergency room and cut off the brand-new blue pin-striped suit he'd put on that morning. As doctors and nurses filled the room, examining him for injuries, one of the doctors held up his suit jacket to reveal a small bullet hole. Reagan slid in and out of consciousness while he was being prepped for surgery to locate the bullet. At one point he opened his eyes to see Nancy's terrified face coming into view. "Honey, I forgot to duck," he whispered.

As Reagan headed for surgery, an alternate drama was taking place at the White House. With Baker, Meese, and Deaver at the hospital and Vice President Bush stuck on a plane coming back from Texas, Haig marched into the pressroom and announced that he was in charge.

"Constitutionally, gentlemen, you have the president, the vice president and the secretary of state, in that order, and should the president decide he wants to transfer the helm to the vice president, he will do so," he said. "As of now, I am in control here in the White House."

Reporters gaped at him. He'd skipped a couple of lines in the succession order. It was actually the vice president, the Speaker of the House, the president pro tempore of the Senate (Strom

Thurmond), and *then* the secretary of state. What was Haig talking about?

Watching Haig storm around the West Wing barking orders, Weinberger was livid. He challenged Haig's authority.

"You'd better read the Constitution," Haig replied angrily.

"*What?*" shouted Weinberger. Haig was dead wrong about the order of succession but refused to listen to reason. Americans watching Haig's wild-eyed performance on TV might have been alarmed, but most probably didn't realize that he was not technically the person in control.

If the events around the assassination showed Haig in an embarrassing light, they also demonstrated what Vice President Bush was made of. "George Bush struck just the right note," William Safire wrote in the *New York Times*, and it seemed to be so. As the historian Jon Meacham recounted in his superb biography *Destiny and Power: The American Odyssey of George Herbert Walker Bush*, the vice president's instincts on that fateful day demonstrated his faithfulness, his humanity, and his character. On the plane returning to Washington, he was intent on not being overly officious or egotistical, when the true crisis was that Reagan—"my friend," he called him—was in desperate straits. So when John Matheny, his air force aide, suggested he land on the South Lawn instead of at Andrews Air Force Base so he could get to the hospital more quickly, Bush was concerned that it would look like showboating. "John," he said, "only the president lands on the South Lawn."

Meacham wrote that after the assassination attempt, Reagan felt closer to Bush and more confident in him: "The crisis had passed, and Bush emerged from the crucible of the shooting as a sensible and steadying force. . . . Reagan, already disposed to treat Bush with respect, had all the more reason to believe that his vice president's professions of devotion and duty were genuine."

Partisan bickering aside, the nation came together to support its felled leader. Cards, gifts, and flowers poured in. While Reagan was in intensive care after a successful surgery, his staff had to ward off eager visitors from Capitol Hill. More than one of them no doubt imagined the photo op of a lifetime: being beside the president at his hospital bed. Strom Thurmond managed to talk his way past the guards and enter Reagan's room, where he found him lying in bed with a mass of tubes, barely conscious. Nancy was angry about that, so Friedersdorf was delegated to stand guard. Only Tip O'Neill was allowed to pass. He entered the room, got down on his knees next to the bed, and kissed Reagan. "God bless you, Mr. President, we're all praying for you," he said. Together they murmured lines from the Twenty-third Psalm:

The Lord is my shepherd, I shall not want.
He maketh me to lie down in green pastures;
    he leadeth me beside the still waters.

The big, intimidating bull of a Speaker was crying. He sat and held the president's hand for a long time.

HAIG NEVER FULLY RECOVERED from his assassination-day power grab. As Reagan got better and began to plot his focus for the coming months and years, he was growing weary of Haig's antics. It wasn't that Haig was always off the mark. "It's amazing how sound he can be on complex international matters, but how utterly paranoid with regard to the people he must work with," Reagan wrote in his diary.

By his second year in office, Reagan knew if he was going to tackle the Soviet problem, the mission of his life, he would need a steadier hand at State. So, in June 1982, when Haig once more threatened to resign over some office wrangle, Reagan took him up on his threat. Then he instructed the national security advisor to get George Shultz on the phone.

Shultz had been around political and economic circles for decades. As a professor of economics at MIT, he had served on Eisenhower's Council of Economic Advisors. Nixon had tapped him for three different positions: secretary of labor, director of the Office of Management and Budget, and secretary of the Treasury. Now back in private life as executive vice president of Bechtel Group, he was an informal foreign policy advisor to Reagan. Shultz was as unassuming as Haig was bombastic. He was thoughtful and even-keeled, widely respected and admired. Reagan liked him and felt they were on the same page.

Shultz was in London, speaking to a group of Bechtel clients, when someone passed him a note, saying there was a call from the White House. He was told that the president wanted to talk on a secure phone and the US Embassy was prepared to accommodate him.

Shultz went to the embassy and called Reagan. "Al Haig has resigned as secretary of state and I want you to be secretary of state," Reagan said.

Shultz was taken aback. "Are you asking me to accept this offer over the phone?" Yes, Reagan replied, explaining that it was very important that there be no gaps. He needed him now.

Shultz said yes, and finally, after a false start, Reagan had the team he needed to win the Cold War.

PART TWO

SPEAKING TRUTH

CHAPTER 5

THE TRUMPET CALL

May 22, 1982

President Reagan bent over the neat stack of papers, turning the pages, scribbling words, crossing out paragraphs, and adding his own thoughts in longhand with a black felt-tipped pen on a yellow legal pad—"just purring along," as one of his aides described his writing style. The task at hand that day was to compose a speech that would be a first for a US president—to be delivered in London on June 8 before both houses of Parliament at Westminster Palace.

He felt good—strong and healthy barely a year after the assassination attempt. A month earlier, he'd had an opportunity to show the nation just how robust a seventy-one-year-old man could be. It had long been his dream to throw out the first pitch of the baseball season, but he'd been unable to do it in his first year because he had been recovering from his injury. As the season approached in year two, he kept reminding his staff that he wanted to do it, and on April 5 he'd gotten his wish at Memorial Stadium in Baltimore. He went out onto the field, accompanied by Orioles owner Edward Williams and the day's pitcher, Dennis Martinez. The three of them began backing away from home plate, gauging the distance. About halfway to the mound,

Martinez said, "Right about here, Mr. President, is where I'd throw the ball." Reagan kept backing up, smiling all the way. When they reached the mound, Martinez said, "Mr. President, it's a long way from here to home plate." Reagan gazed out at the cheering, waving crowd and gripped the ball. "Well, I think I can do it." He'd been practicing at Camp David with his Secret Service agents, and he wasn't about to compromise. He stared at the catcher, who was crouched in place, wound up just as he'd practiced, and sent the ball sailing over home plate. A strike! The crowd came to its feet with a roar. Reagan was elated. He'd proved a point: he was back in full form, ready to take on anything.

Now he was intent on proving a different point on a global scale. Layers of complexity accompanied the invitation and the venue of the Parliament speech, touching on the sometimes delicate protocols of two friendly nations with a historically complex relationship. It didn't help that Reagan was a controversial figure, widely considered a warmonger by the nuclear freeze crowd or a second-rate actor by the intelligentsia. Surely Parliament was too elevated a platform for such a man, or so they said. Critics might have recalled that Winston Churchill had given three addresses before both houses of the US Congress (a rare invitation), the first on December 26, 1941, nearly three weeks after the United States had entered the war in Europe. Some appalled Brits asked whether Reagan considered himself to be on a par with Churchill. There was also a concern among Reagan's foreign policy advisors that some members of Parliament who were unfriendly to Prime Minister Margaret Thatcher might use Reagan's visit to embarrass her by boycotting his speech or supporting demonstrations. Those concerns were all in the background for Reagan. He focused on one goal: to deliver a hell of a speech that would take a bold stand in a world threatened by Soviet aggression.

Speechwriting in the Reagan White House was a collaborative venture, with Reagan as an active participant. He enjoyed crafting speeches, and had his days not been jam-packed with the nation's business, he would have liked to write them all himself. The common notion that Reagan, the former actor, merely stood on his mark and spoke lines written by others has been dispelled by everyone who worked with him on a speech. Before becoming president, he had often written his own speeches and radio addresses, and he continued to be the chief author of his Saturday-morning addresses while in the White House. He spent a lot of time poring over the drafts, marking them up, adding and deleting. He had an instinct for the way words sounded—"I write for the ear," he said.

His speeches were by turns conversational and idealistic, burnished with stories (some embellished or loosely adapted) about real people in perilous or inspiring circumstances. He wanted audiences to respond emotionally, and he was skilled at imagining the impact words on a page would have when spoken. "Sometimes, speech writers write things that seem very eloquent on paper, but sound convoluted or stilted when you say them to an audience," he observed in his autobiography. He urged his writers to use simple language—shorter sentences and single-syllable words whenever possible—and to keep the length to about twenty minutes. "Remember, there are people out there sitting and listening, they've got to be able to absorb what I'm saying."

The speechwriters in turn had great respect for Reagan's gift for understanding and reaching out to an audience. He could, he told one aide, imagine them as individuals he was talking to one-on-one, as if he were among friends at a barbershop. He always saw himself as having a personal chat with listeners, talking to them as one would to friends, including jokes to break the intensity. In a drawer of the Resolute desk in the Oval

Office, he had stacks of four-by-six and three-by-five cards with inspirational quotes, as well as jokes and one-liners, that would often make their way into the drafts. He had a selection of jokes specifically related to the Soviet Union. He dropped one of them into the Westminster speech: "The Soviet Union would remain a one-party nation even if an opposition party were permitted, because everyone would join the opposition party." A later speech to a Veterans of Foreign Wars gathering included this zinger: "By the way, did you hear that the Communists now have a million-dollar lottery for their people? The winner gets a dollar a year for a million years."

The jokes and one-liners served a higher purpose than merely producing a laugh, however. They created a laser focus on his main points and brought the audience to his side. Reagan's use of humor demonstrated an instinctive grasp of human nature—the desire people have to be in on the joke.

Reagan was a far more complex human being than his critics gave him credit for being or his adoring fans acknowledged. But the one consistent quality of his speeches was that they reached for higher ground, a nobler purpose. "We have every right to dream heroic dreams," he'd said in his inaugural address, and he believed it.

Heroic dreams, it would seem, were required. The world Reagan inherited when he took office was a landscape of failed promise and lost hope. Ever since Eisenhower's unsuccessful effort to bring the Soviets to the table, US presidents had failed to make real progress, even dangerously backtracking during the Vietnam War era. Though Nixon, who was skilled at negotiating with adversarial governments, had tried to work with Soviet leader Leonid Brezhnev, he had ceded the opportunity by choosing to court China. Jimmy Carter had made his position clear when he said, "We no longer suffer from an inordinate fear of communism"—relegating what Reagan believed was the greatest threat of the era to a mere standoff. Carter had mostly played defense with the Soviets after their incursion into Afghanistan in 1979. He had done all the usual posturing, mostly ineffectual, imposing economic sanctions and withdrawing from the 1980 Summer Olympics in Moscow, but his response had been insufficient. Distracted by the Iran hostage crisis, he had missed an opportunity to confront Brezhnev from a position of strength. During the 1980 campaign, Reagan had urged the Carter administration to fight fire with fire by sending antiaircraft missiles to the Afghan rebels fighting the Red Army. Once in office, he continued to speak out about the invasion as a violation of human decency and international law, and he backed up his words with tangible support for the rebels.

On the nuclear front, Reagan was unwavering. Despite heavy criticism, he decided to place intermediate-range missiles in Germany and Great Britain to counter the Soviet placement of missiles in Eastern Europe, aimed at the West. That hardened his critics' contention that he was a warmonger. Almost lost in the outrage was his more nuanced position on the subject of nuclear buildup: he despised nuclear weapons and feared the consequences of a buildup. He considered it one of the highest purposes of his presidency to end the nuclear arms race. But he would do it his way—not by standing down, as the nuclear freeze movement would have him do, but by showing strength. "Peace through strength" was his mantra. It was a core principle, based on the conviction that only by challenging the Soviet Union from a position of power could the United States bring it to the negotiating table. Shultz agreed. "If you don't have any strength, your diplomacy is in the ashcan," he said. "You've got nothing to take to the table. And at the same time, if you don't have any diplomatic process going on, it erodes your strength. A good diplomatic process helps your strength. So our key words were realism, strength, diplomacy."

In a dramatic call for a nuclear abatement quid pro quo, Reagan announced near the end of 1981 that the United States was willing to cancel the deployment of missiles to Europe if the Soviet Union would agree to dismantle its intermediate-range missiles trained on Europe. The Soviets shrugged off the notion. They didn't trust the United States. But Reagan didn't trust them, either. His views on détente had long been clear: "Détente—isn't that what a farmer has with his turkey before Thanksgiving?" he'd asked pointedly during the 1980 campaign. He reasserted that view often after he took office. When he was asked at a press conference whether détente was possible, he replied that the Soviets would lie, cheat, and steal to get what they wanted, so doing business with them was pretty difficult.

When he said that so bluntly, people in the room gasped, their genteel sensibilities offended. Even some of his own staff blanched. But walking back to the Oval Office, he stopped and confronted NSC advisor Richard Allen, who was trailing him.

"Oh, say, Dick."

"Yes, sir."

"The Russians—they *do* lie, cheat, and steal to get everything they want, don't they?"

"They sure do, Mr. President," Allen agreed.

Reagan grinned at him. "I thought so."

What had sounded like an off-the-cuff remark—a gaffe, even—had actually been carefully planned. People could be as shocked as they wanted, Reagan figured; his goal was to make sure the Soviets knew he was onto them.

In mid-May, when he first saw a draft of the Westminster speech, which had been thoroughly whitewashed by State and Defense Department editors, he was disappointed. It pulled so many punches that it felt like a limp handshake. Frustrated, he sent off a copy to *Washington Post* columnist George Will, whose opinion he valued, asking him to take a look at it. Will's reply came back shortly. "It called to mind the old axiom: A camel is a horse designed by a committee," he wrote. "It reflected the State Department, where everyone has interests and no one has ideas."

That was just as Reagan had thought. He was relieved when William Clark, who had replaced Richard Allen as national security advisor in 1982 after a minor scandal had forced Allen's resignation, told him that chief speechwriter Anthony Dolan had been working on the speech for a couple of months. Maybe he had something ready.

Dolan, a bearded thirty-three-year-old wordsmith with a gift for soaring prose and a conscience honed by a lifetime of Catholic faith and conservative ideals, had a gift for channeling the president. Dolan would tell you that he knew Reagan because he'd been an acolyte since he was a thirteen-year-old boy growing up in Connecticut. In particular, the young Dolan was attracted to Reagan's powerful anti-Communist message. "We had a truck that was the Tombstone Float," he recalled of his youthful political adventures. "On it were tombstones of all the countries that had fallen under communism. And the U.S.A. was at the end, with a tombstone that had a big question mark on it. It would go through Bridgeport, and in the Hungarian and Polish neighborhoods people would applaud wildly."

Having been a student of Reagan's words for nearly a lifetime, Dolan felt comfortable writing for him. A speechwriter's job, he believed, was not to put words into a president's mouth but to be in tune with him—to hear his own words and speak them back to him. "They always thought I had some secret way of getting to Reagan, as he'd choose my drafts," Dolan said. "But I was just giving him back what he was saying in the sixties."

When White House reporters would mention his job title, Dolan would say, "Ronald Reagan is his own chief speechwriter."

Dolan knew Reagan would want to see a consensus draft, so he included language from an NSC paper by Richard Pipes, among other sources. But he focused primarily on the context Reagan had been bringing to the Cold War since the 1960s. Rather than harsh anti-Communist rhetoric, Dolan elevated the tone and made it resemble other speeches Reagan had been giving that year, where he said the Cold War contest was just part of the struggle against twentieth-century "statism" and totalitarianism, both Nazism and Communism, a struggle that made the Soviet Union "a sad, bizarre chapter in human history whose last pages even now are being written."

When Reagan saw Dolan's draft, he immediately recognized his familiar content and told his advisors he now had something to work on. Reagan did several revisions, adding and subtracting, rewriting.

The draft Reagan sent out was distinctly Reaganesque and this predictably set off alarm bells with the moderates at the White House and State Department. The ongoing battle between true believers, whose motto was "Let Reagan be Reagan," and the more pragmatic staffers, who sought to guard Reagan against the consequences of using inflammatory rhetoric, was reignited every time he was to make an important speech. But while there would be more back and forth over the Westminster draft, the version Reagan had worked on essentially survived.

The setting and the ceremonial nature of the event were quite dramatic. At the allotted hour, the Reagans arrived at Westminster Palace. The speech would take place in the beautiful Royal Gallery, a large hall lined with royal portraits and lit by the glow of stained-glass windows. Severely damaged by a bomb blast during World War II, the Royal Gallery had been restored to its former splendor and was used for visits of foreign dignitaries and other ceremonies. When the members and guests were seated—as predicted, many members stayed away in protest—Thatcher escorted Nancy to a front-row seat. Then the State Trumpeters played the Royal Fanfare to signal Reagan's entrance into the gallery, accompanied by the lord great chamberlain, the hereditary officer of state and representative of the queen.

Reagan began to speak, firmly and decisively, laying out his view of the stark contrast between repressive powers and free nations.

> We're approaching the end of a bloody century plagued by a terrible political invention—totalitarianism. Optimism comes less easily today, not because democracy is less vigorous, but because democracy's enemies have refined their instruments of repression. Yet optimism is in order, because day by day democracy is proving itself to be a not-at-all-fragile flower. From Stettin on the Baltic to Varna on the Black Sea, the regimes planted by totalitarianism have had more than 30 years to establish their legitimacy. But none—not one regime—has yet been able to risk free elections. Regimes planted by bayonets do not take root.

That was a hard truth, he said, one that many people had trouble facing in their desire to be fair to both sides and seek ways to coexist peacefully. But there were not two sides, he emphasized. There could be only one winner in the fight:

> If history teaches anything it teaches self-delusion in the face of unpleasant facts is folly. We see around us today the marks of our terrible dilemma—predictions of doomsday, antinuclear demonstrations, an arms race in which the West must, for its own protection, be an unwilling participant. At the same time we see totalitar-

ian forces in the world who seek subversion and conflict around the globe to further their barbarous assault on the human spirit. What, then, is our course? Must civilization perish in a hail of fiery atoms? Must freedom wither in a quiet, deadening accommodation with totalitarian evil?

Then he delivered the most memorable and controversial line with a highly charged attack on the entire premise of the Communist state:

What I am describing now is a plan and a hope for the long term—the march of freedom and democracy which will leave Marxism-Leninism on the ash-heap of history as it has left other tyrannies which stifle the freedom and muzzle the self-expression of the people.

Margaret Thatcher smiled approvingly from the front row. The speech, she wrote in her memoir, was "remarkable. . . . It marked a decisive stage in the battle of ideas which he and I wished to wage against socialism, above all the socialism of the Soviet Union." The point, she believed, was not only to defend against communism but to "put freedom on the offensive."

Reagan had recognized a kindred spirit in Thatcher from their first meeting, which had taken place when he and Nancy visited England during the Carter administration. He'd begun contemplating a presidential run in 1980, but it was still in the future. While in England, Justin Dart, one of his old kitchen cabinet advisors, had offered to introduce him to a friend who was the first woman to lead the British Conservative Party. He was very impressed with Thatcher and immediately judged that she would make a wonderful prime minister. "Of course," he wrote, "it never occurred to me that before many years would pass, Margaret and I would be sitting across from each other as the heads of our respective governments." Once in office, he and Thatcher bonded over a shared antipathy to socialism and a commitment to winning the Cold War. That's not to say that their relationship was a lovefest. It was far more complicated and intellectually rigorous than that, and they didn't always agree.

For example, at the time of the Westminster speech Great Britain was embroiled in a war in the Falkland Islands. Reagan's advisors thought the invasion smacked of colonialism, and Reagan debated the proper course to take with Thatcher. In one late-night phone call, he urged her to offer a more even-handed cease-fire deal that would give the Argentinians a role to play—a suggestion she vociferously challenged. Reagan lost that argument, but when he hung up the phone, he was smiling. "Isn't she marvelous?" he asked Deaver, who had not liked her aggressive tone with the president. "Shows such spunk. Just marvelous." On the subject of the Soviet Union, however, they had no debate. The "Iron Lady" would be Reagan's most powerful and effective counterpart in the fight he was determined to win.

The takeaway from Reagan's speech to Parliament was that it was a robust defense of democratic principles on behalf of the United States and Europe, based on Reagan's philosophy of "peace through strength." It also offered hope that the Cold War would end and that freedom would reign. Reagan believed that words were among the greatest weapons in an arsenal, and his were fighting words, although only about one-third of the members attended to hear them. Among those who did, the TV cameras captured smirks of disapproval. The general media reaction ranged from apathy to disdain. "Unmemorable," judged the *Guardian*. "Vintage Reagan," journalist Sam Donaldson said, not meaning it as a compliment. Many thought Reagan's prose was naive, not fully grasping his strategy.

The Westminster speech was a firm opening salvo in a battle whose ultimate aim was peace. But before peace could happen, Reagan believed, we needed to stop beating around the bush and pretending that the Soviet way had legitimacy on a par with that of the United States. That was a substantially different posture from the one held by Soviet experts at the time and indeed by some members of Reagan's own foreign policy team. The standard belief was that the United States and the Soviet Union were of relatively equal strength and competing philosophies. Reagan didn't see it that way. He devised a simple test for legitimacy, one the Soviets didn't pass: a nation could not survive without freedom, without human rights, without a religious spirit, and with the force of its power directed at keeping its citizens under the gun. Standing on the wrong side of history, isolated, it would inevitably fail. The free world didn't have to bring the Soviet Union to its knees; it would collapse of its own weight.

That was a point he'd been making repeatedly over the years. Furthermore, an aggressive arms race was decimating the Soviet economy and sending the government on the hunt for loans to prop up its system. Shultz had seen the decline firsthand as secretary of the Treasury under Nixon. "One of my jobs there was economic relations with the Soviet Union," he said. "So I went back and forth, and I saw their agricultural program was a total failure. Their health system was no good. Their own people—you would talk to them privately on the side, and they were very worried about their economy. So I could see all these weaknesses."

Things hadn't improved. Writing in his diary after a briefing on the Soviet economy, Reagan noted, "They are in very bad shape and if we can cut off their credit they'll have to yell 'Uncle' or starve." It bears mentioning that Reagan's position on the matter had been virtually unchanged for twenty years. In the early 1960s, he had written about his frustration with US efforts to accommodate the Soviet Union. "If we truly believe that our way of life is best aren't the Russians more likely to recognize that fact and modify their stand if we let their economy come unhinged so that the contrast is apparent?" he asked. "Inhuman though it may sound, shouldn't we throw the whole burden of feeding the satellites on their slave masters who are having trouble feeding themselves?"

According to Kenneth Adelman, who directed the Arms Control and Disarmament Agency for five years during Reagan's presidency, Reagan wasn't just introducing a new strategy but a new paradigm. "Reagan's view was, 'We're legitimate, they're illegitimate. We have to deal with them on issues because they're here, but that doesn't mean that they're legitimate to deal with.' That attitude really came through, and that was a gigantic change. That somehow you're on the ass-end of history, you're curtains." That, of course, drove the diplomats and moderates crazy and seemed at first blush totally contrary to the goal of rapprochement.

The esteemed writer and commentator Charles Krauthammer saw it in an intriguing light. In a panel discussion at the Heritage Foundation, he said that what he found most striking about the speech was its

psychological optimism. The idea that communism was a passing phase was the truly revolutionary point. It took us from containment and at a time when it was a question of whether containment itself could be sustained and began speaking about rollback. That was revolutionary, that was shocking, and it spoke not only of rollback in the periphery, not only of rollback as understood in the Dulles years, meaning Eastern Europe, but Reagan essentially was saying that the rollback would go all the way to Moscow and it would end in Moscow itself.

It was a sophisticated argument, and many people failed to expand their minds beyond the simple, more familiar debate about nuclear weaponry. On the streets, the cry for a nuclear freeze was growing louder as the president's position remained firm. Only days after Reagan's Westminster speech, one million people gathered in Central Park in New York City in an antinuclear rally (the largest protest in US history), and similar demonstrations spread across Europe. They were opposed to Reagan's program of strategic nuclear arms buildup. The movement leaders were arguing persuasively that the world already had so many nuclear weapons that it would be immoral to deploy more.

Reagan was not opposed to a nuclear freeze. Like his predecessors, he believed that "a nuclear war cannot be won and must never be fought." But as long as the United States remained in an inferior position in the arms race, he thought it would be madness to withdraw further.

Then, in November, Reagan faced a shift in the tectonic plates of global diplomacy with the death of Leonid Brezhnev and the elevation of the former KGB head Yuri Andropov to Soviet premier. Brezhnev had been in power since the beginning of Reagan's political career; he was the only Soviet leader most modern statesmen had ever known. But in spite of the excessive overtures that US presidents had made to Brezhnev (Nixon had even invited him to Camp David and given him a Cadillac as a gift), little had been accomplished.

Anatoly Dobrynin, the longtime Soviet ambassador, informed National Security Advisor Bill Clark that they expected the president to attend Brezhnev's funeral in Moscow. But Reagan balked. "Bill, I never met the man. It would be hypocritical to fly to Moscow for his funeral, never having been there before."

Clark explained that Shultz, Weinberger, and Kirkpatrick all thought he should go, but Reagan held firm. "No, I've thought about it. When I meet my first Soviet leader, I want it to be for something other than death. We'll send George."

However, Reagan arranged to visit the Soviet Embassy in Washington and sign the condolence book. After signing, he leaned over to whisper to Clark and Nancy, "Do you think these people in here would mind if we just said a little prayer for the man?" He smiled when he said it, but he wasn't joking, and he did say a prayer.

There was a great deal of discussion about whether Reagan should immediately set up a summit meeting with Andropov. His instinct was to wait, especially after he received a very convincing letter from Richard Nixon to that point. "I strongly feel that you should avoid a quickie get-acquainted meeting," Nixon wrote. "The first time the two of you meet will be the major news event of your first term, dwarfing everything else that has happened before or since." Nixon went on to caution Reagan that such feel-good meetings could reassure people and create briefly positive headlines, but without substantive results, the positive feelings would not last—"Where a summit produces spirit, not substance, the spirit evaporates very fast."

Reagan appreciated Nixon's advice and was intent on avoiding the appearance of anything short of a strong position. The summit could wait a year or so. He was certain that the Soviet Union was directly involved in efforts to undermine his goals by cynically encouraging the nuclear freeze movement and even infiltrating peace groups in the United States and Europe. A classified congressional hearing found no direct evidence of this from the FBI or CIA, but Reagan was unconvinced. In a November 1982 press conference, which he opened by speaking of the death of Brezhnev, he accused the Soviet Union of trying to manipulate the American peace movement for its own purposes. "There was no question but that the Soviet Union saw an advantage in a peace movement built around the idea of a nuclear freeze, since they are out ahead," he said. "And I want to emphasize again that the overwhelming majority of the people involved in that, I am sure, are sincere and well intentioned and, as a matter of fact, are saying the same thing I'm saying. And that is, we must have a reduction of those nuclear weapons, and that's what we're trying to negotiate now in Geneva. But to put the freeze first and then believe that we have not weakened our [case] for getting a reduction, when the other side is so far ahead, doesn't make sense."

He could read the skepticism in reporters' eyes. "The d—n media has propagandized our defense plans more than the Russians have," he wrote in his diary.

THE STEADY CADENCE OF thousands of nuclear freeze supporters rallying at the Capitol and a chill rain were the backdrop of the morning as Ronald Reagan prepared to leave the White House for a trip to Orlando, Florida, on March 8, 1983.

It would be only a one-day trip, but it was the kind of respite presidents treasure: a quick visit with foreign exchange students at Epcot Center followed by a speech to an adoring "base" audience, in this case a gathering of the National Association of Evangelicals.

It wasn't supposed to be a major speech; Reagan's staff viewed it as strictly B-list, not A-list. In the third year of his administration, it was just one of many domestic outings, only to be noted in passing. Robert P. Dugan, Jr., the director of the National Association of Evangelicals, who sent the request to Reagan, was thrilled when Reagan accepted, expecting the president to please the crowd with a moral boilerplate, hitting all the favorite themes of evangelicals. But members of the association also hoped that Reagan would address a topic very much on his mind: the fight against communism. Some of the more pacifist members of the NAE had recently been wandering outside the fold, joining the nuclear freeze movement, and this had raised some concerns among the conservative members. Reagan could be counted on to use his seasoned mix of warmth and fire to persuade the doubters.

In preparing for the event, the White House director of speechwriting, Aram Bakshian, assigned Dolan to work on the speech. Dolan labored away at the evangelical speech, crafting it around important themes for the audience—an attack on abortion on demand, the need for prayer in schools, and the ongoing battle against modern-day secularism—rising to a crescendo to pose the question of sin and evil in the world, as characterized by the Soviet Union. Here Dolan saw a chance to repurpose some lines that had been deleted from his Westminster speech draft the previous year. Recycling was a habit of Dolan's. As Bakshian would recall later, "Long after I left, I remember an ending which I thought was rather hokey that had been rejected several times, including by the president, in some State of the Union drafts and other items. Well, it finally showed up in a speech. I guess the lesson was, if you wait long enough you can recycle your rejects. Tony must have kept this thing in a refrigerator, in a freezer or something, for years."

Among the lines excised as too inflammatory for the Westminster speech but repurposed by Dolan for the evangelicals: a reference to the Soviet Union as a "militaristic empire" whose ideology justified any wrongdoing; the line that "Communism is another sad, bizarre chapter in human history whose last pages even now are being written"; and a scathing quote from C. S. Lewis's *Screwtape Letters*: "The greatest evil is not done now in those sordid 'dens of crime' that Dickens loved to paint. It is not even done in concentration camps and labor camps. In those we see its final result. But it is conceived and ordered . . . in clear, carpeted, warmed, and well-lighted offices, by quiet men with white collars and cut fingernails and smooth-shaven cheeks who do not need to raise their voice."

The rhetoric of good and evil, deemed too incendiary for Parliament, found its way into Dolan's Orlando draft and included some dramatic embellishments.

When Bakshian saw the draft, his eyes lit on one phrase in particular: "Evil Empire." He paused and considered it, already hearing the protests of the pragmatists in his head. He thought, *Now, if I flag this in any way, it's going to get pulled.* But he didn't want it pulled because, simply, he thought it was true. So, he decided to leave it. "First of all, it *is* an evil empire, what the hell, and if someone up there disagrees or is nervous about it, it's up to them to notice it."

Communications director David Gergen wasn't so sanguine. In *Eyewitness to Power* he wrote of studying the draft, which attacked the Soviets in "terms so strong it rattled the windows." He began to slice with his editing pen, then called in Robert "Bud" McFarlane, the deputy national security advisor, to take a stab at it as well. By the time the draft got back to Dolan, it was covered with green ink, and the "Evil Empire" reference and surrounding text had been crossed out.

Dolan didn't sit still for that. He fought back, urging them to let the president weigh in. "Just send him the draft as it is," he insisted. "Let him decide." Gergen was torn, feeling that the draft was strong even without the inflammatory prose. "I kept wondering: Was it okay to leave in that phrase calling the Soviets the Evil Empire? Were we going to upset U.S. diplomacy?" He finally relented.

Just returned from a five-day trip to California during which he had met with Queen Elizabeth and Prince Philip, Reagan received the draft on March 5 with most of the disputed text intact. Over the next couple of days he did his usual editing, crossing out some passages and adding several paragraphs of his own.

Reagan tinkered, the pragmatists worried, and Dolan waited nervously for the president's verdict. When Reagan's version arrived, Dolan was elated to find the rescued gems of his recycling bin restored. The Evil Empire was back. The Soviet Union as "the focus of evil" was back. C. S. Lewis's stirring challenge was back.

No one protested. "Once he [the president] saw it and signed off on it, it proved impossible to back up on," Bakshian said. "The media wasn't looking for anything though, because as far as they were concerned, 'Oh, this is one of these dumb right-wing things and who cares about preachers.'"

But Reagan knew exactly what he was doing—sending a message to Andropov: *I know what you are, and I'm going to make sure the American people know it, too.* The handwringers at the White House who were so afraid of upsetting the delicate diplomatic balance with strong words would have to step aside on this one. There are times, he believed, when the truth has to be starkly stated. Later, some of those who had feared that the speech was too confrontational would admit that Dolan had been right to lobby for it and Reagan had been right to give it. As Gergen wrote, "I hate to admit it, but it's true: history has shown that Tony Dolan was right and I was wrong. That phrase, the Evil Empire, allowed Reagan to speak truth to totalitarianism." But in the moment, that outcome was far from clear. It was the president's call, and he didn't hesitate.

A crowd of 1,200 evangelicals welcomed Reagan enthusiastically when he stepped up to the podium in the Citrus Crown Ballroom at the Sheraton Twin Towers Hotel in Orlando at 3:00 P.M. on March 8. Flanked by the beaming leadership and standing in front of a royal-blue backdrop, he began to speak in a conversational tone about prayer.

"The other day in the East Room of the White House at a meeting there, someone asked me whether I was aware of all the people out there who were praying for the President," he told the crowd. "And I had to say, 'Yes, I am. I've felt it. I believe in intercessionary prayer.' But I couldn't help but say to that questioner after he'd asked the question that . . . if sometimes when he was praying he got a busy signal, it was just me in there ahead of him."

There were laughs and some cheers. He went on through the script and finally came to the centerpiece. He told the crowd that some years earlier he'd heard a young father, who happened to be very prominent in the entertainment world, tell a large gathering, "I would rather see my little girls die now, still believing in God, than have them grow up under communism and one day die no longer believing in God." He recalled that the thousands of young people in the audience "came to their feet with shouts of joy."

He went on:

Yes, let us pray for the salvation of all of those who live in that totalitarian darkness—pray they will discover the joy of knowing God. But until they do, let us be aware that while they preach the supremacy of the state, declare its omnipotence over individual man, and predict its eventual domination of all peoples on the Earth, they are the focus of evil in the modern world. . . .

So, in your discussions of the nuclear freeze proposals, I urge you to beware the temptation of pride—the temptation of blithely declaring yourselves above it all and label both sides equally at fault, to ignore the facts of history and the aggressive impulses of an evil empire, to simply call the arms race a giant misunderstanding and thereby remove yourself from the struggle between right and wrong and good and evil.

The audience interrupted Reagan thirty-two times with applause and calls of "Amen." Although not everyone present supported Reagan's nuclear policy, they cheered his moral clarity. Meanwhile, outside the hotel, a group of about 150 protesters chanted, "Hey, hey, Uncle Ron, we don't want your neutron bomb" and "Ronald Reagan, he's no good. Send him back to Hollywood."

What Bakshian called a "stealth" speech shot out into the atmosphere like a flare. Reagan's fighting words thrilled some and shocked others. Nancy Reagan, who frequently urged her husband to tone down the rhetoric so that people would stop calling him a warmonger, didn't think it was particularly helpful to say that the Soviet Union was an Evil Empire. In the *New York Times*, Anthony Lewis judged the speech "dangerous," and worried about a Soviet response. There was so much fear of upsetting diplomatic efforts that we had forgotten how to define the terms, or so Reagan thought.

Caspar Weinberger recalled one of the critics saying to Reagan " 'You've destroyed twenty years of patient diplomatic effort.' And he said, 'But what did patient diplomatic effort for twenty years get us? It got us an expanding Soviet Union and a continual expansion of their ability to enslave peoples and deny freedom. And it left us so vulnerable we couldn't do anything when Afghanistan was invaded. That's not much of an accomplishment.' "

Weinberger, who was a Soviet hard-liner in Reagan's mold, agreed that Reagan's policy signaled a dramatic change from "a passive containment, get-along, two-systems-that-can-work-together and all that, to the determination that you couldn't work with them. They were not just two systems. They were diametrically and antithetically opposed to each other in every way."

There was also the symbolism of choosing a religious venue and including remarks about faith and prayer in the speech. In the *Wall Street Journal*, Arthur Schlesinger, Jr., no fan of Reagan, complained that the speech "marks a revival of the Cold War as a holy war. . . . This conception of the Cold War, unless the president is kidding, raises problems." Kidding? A strange suggestion. Reagan could not have been more clear.

Reagan was a man of faith who did not hesitate to talk about God's role in the world and the nation or the power of prayer. Even though he rarely attended church as president, not wanting to disrupt the services, he was very religious and prayerful. One of his favorite quotes about prayer and the presidency was purported to have been said by Abraham Lincoln: "I'm driven to my knees today in the overwhelming conviction that I don't have any place else to go."

The religious tone of his Orlando speech made many people uneasy. But others were more supportive. The *Richmond Times-Dispatch* called the speech "the unadorned truth," and the *Washington Times* approved of the president's fiery rhetoric. In a letter to William Willoughby of the *Washington Times*, thanking him for his positive article, Reagan expressed frustration that some people didn't think it was proper or acceptable for the president to talk about faith.

Dear Mr. Willoughby,

I want you to know how deeply I appreciate your article about my recent speech in Orlando. You do put things in perspective, and that is reassuring. I get the idea from reading some of the other comments that there are a lot of people in the media who are very "broad-minded" except when it comes to tolerating people with religious convictions.

I wonder what Teddy Roosevelt would think if he could survey the current scene. He called the Presidency a "bully pulpit," but nowadays if one uses words like *God* and *Prayer* from the "pulpit" the alarm bells go off.

Reagan had a firm belief that the existential difference between the United States and the Soviet Union went well beyond political philosophy to the very ground of their moral being. He often wondered how a nation could be great or a social system could endure without faith in God and respect for religious freedom. He'd return to that theme again and again.

The Orlando speech was only the first act of a larger drama. Weeks later, in a televised speech to the nation, Reagan introduced the Strategic Defense Initiative, an antimissile defense system designed to neutralize an attack by strategic nuclear weapons. It was to be a defensive, not an offensive, system. He wanted to underscore the fact that he was focused on peace, not angling for war.

Even Reagan's advisors were stunned by that bold new notion. "He didn't share that with anybody before that," Adelman said. "I know that Shultz was kind of blindsided by it. . . . Weinberger . . . may have had two days' notice. But it was stunning, stunning." Adelman's own reaction was "Oh, my God, this is really something new and terrific. It's going to be a whole new ball game. I didn't realize the extent of how new it was going to be. I didn't realize that the Soviets were going to go ape shit about it. I didn't realize how big a deal it was."

In truth, Reagan had been thinking about it for years. As he told Edward Rowny, an arms control expert, in 1979, the idea that "we've got a pistol at the Soviets' head, and they've got a pistol at our head"—in other words, mutual assured destruction, was, to use the apt acronym, MAD. "Why don't we put on a helmet and protect ourselves?" he asked. Rowny warned him that the science was a long way away. But Reagan wasn't deterred. Strategic defense, he felt, was just common sense.

The public criticism was swift and fierce, especially from Democrats.

Senator Ted Kennedy was said to have coined the term "Star Wars," a mockery of the program that stuck. The characterization infuriated Reagan, for good reason. It was a trivialization of his proposal that made him look foolish and impulsive. The Star Wars comparison was also inaccurate. Reagan wasn't talking about futuristic weapons systems zooming through outer space, obliterating enemy attackers. Nor was he describing an Obi-Wan Kenobi–style mystical shield, which scientists affirmed was in the realm of science fiction. But "Star Wars" caught on, and once the public imagination was captured, the media did little to dispel the notion. Reagan often complained about how much he hated the term Star Wars. He repeatedly demanded that the press call the program by its proper name, the Strategic Defense Initiative. But his pleas went unheeded. Star Wars it was and remains to this day. And if American politicians and press were calling the program Star Wars, Moscow was happy to join in.

For those who thought Reagan was a lightweight thinker whose ideas came more from movie scripts than from reality, SDI was so much pie in the sky. Reagan was angry that the program was misunderstood and misrepresented, and he resented the press's refusal to tell the truth about it.

Once again, the practical realities of nuclear warfare were often ignored. The pro-freeze crowd had an unrealistic idea that everyone could just lay down their arms and go home. The pro–arms race crowd thought more was better—an idea that had long ago been shown as folly by no lesser men than Dwight D. Eisenhower and Nikita Khrushchev. Did it matter, Ike had wondered, whether a nation was able to destroy the world once over or a dozen times? Khrushchev had seemed to agree that the arms race was pointless, telling Eisenhower that in the event of a nuclear encounter, "We get your dust, you get our dust, the winds blow around the world and nobody's safe." But if anything, weapons expenditures were greater than ever, and the futile arms race was robbing weak economies—a factor that was especially urgent for the Soviet Union in the 1980s.

What was needed was ways of shaking loose the inertia. Everyone knew intellectually that a nuclear attack would be an incalculable disaster. But for most Americans the threat seemed abstract. To make the reality more visceral to Americans sitting at home in their living rooms, ABC aired a film on November 20, 1983, called *The Day After*, which was watched by 100 million people. It was about as real as it comes, focusing on the lives of the people of Lawrence, Kansas, after a nuclear attack obliterates their small college town. When Reagan viewed a copy of the movie before its airing, he wrote in his diary, "it left me greatly depressed. . . . My own reaction was one of our having to do all we can to have a deterrent & to see there is never a nuclear war."

The Friday before the film aired, he once again expressed his heartache and frustration, writing "I feel the Soviets are so defense-minded, so paranoid about being attacked that without being in any way soft on them we ought to tell them no one here has any intention of doing anything like that. What the h—l have they got that anyone would want." But he added, "We know it's 'anti-nuke' propaganda but we're going to take it over & say it shows why we must keep on doing what we're doing."

CHAPTER 6

RON AND MIKHAIL

A large grizzly bear lumbered through the woods as a sober announcer's voice intoned, "There is a bear in the woods. For some people, the bear is easy to see. Others don't see it at all. Some people say the bear is tame. Others say it's vicious and dangerous. Since no one can really be sure who's right, isn't it smart to be as strong as the bear? If there is a bear."

The 1984 campaign was in full swing, and the Soviet Union was in Reagan's sights. "Through this whole period of time, the only thing that was really on Reagan's mind was the Russian situation, the cold war, nuclear holocaust," campaign advisor Stuart Spencer said. Reagan's opponent, Walter Mondale, who had been vice president under Carter, represented, in Reagan's view, the ineffectual leadership of the past. Reagan understood that if he lost to Mondale, it would be a repudiation of all he believed and lead to a dangerous weakening of the United States' position in the world.

The year 1984 dawned with a standoff between the Soviet Union and the United States, captured in *Time* magazine's "Men of the Year" cover on January 2, which showed a somber—even angry—illustration of Reagan and Andropov facing away from each other. "In the beginning were the words," the cover story began, describing the growing antagonism between the men.

"At the top, verbal missiles fired in magisterial wrath: Ronald Reagan denouncing the Soviet Union as an 'evil empire' that had committed 'a crime against humanity' when its fighters shot down a Korean jetliner; Yuri Andropov responding that the Reagan Administration had 'finally dispelled' all 'illusions' that it could be dealt with. At a baser level, crude vilification: American caricatures of Andropov as a 'mutant from outer space.'"

In Washington, Reagan wasn't buying into the dismay. Instead, he was laying the groundwork for the centerpiece of his campaign, doing what he could to inspire and reassure Americans who feared that he was bent on war. In a live address to the nation from the East Room on January 16, he offered an olive branch to the Soviets—the first of his presidency—stating, "I believe that 1984 finds the United States in the strongest position in years to establish a constructive and realistic working relationship with the Soviet Union. We've come a long way since the decade of the seventies, years when the United States seemed filled with self-doubt and neglected its defenses, while the Soviet Union increased its military might and sought to expand its influence by armed forces and threat." But he cautioned that it wasn't enough for the two sides to whittle away at their differences. And with the Soviet Union breaking off negotiations on intermediate-range missiles, even the small signs of progress were not in evidence. Yet in calling for new initiatives, he struck a conciliatory tone reminiscent of the one Eisenhower had employed early in his presidency, following the death of Stalin. "We can't predict how the Soviet leaders will respond to our challenge," Reagan said, his voice softening for effect. "But the people of our two countries share with all mankind the dream of eliminating the risk of nuclear war. It's not an impossible dream, because eliminating these risks are so clearly a vital interest for all of us. Our two countries have never fought each other. There's no reason why we ever should. Indeed, we fought common enemies in World War II. Today our common enemies are poverty, disease, and above all, war."

Summoning an image of common humanity, he asked people to consider a scenario:

Just suppose with me for a moment that an Ivan and an Anya could find themselves, oh, say, in a waiting room, or sharing a shelter from the rain or a storm with a Jim and Sally, and there was no language barrier to keep them from getting acquainted. Would they then debate the differences between their respective governments? Or would they find themselves comparing notes about their children and what each other did for a living?

Before they parted company, they would probably have touched on ambitions and hobbies and what they wanted for their children and problems of making ends meet. And as they went their separate ways, maybe Anya would be saying to Ivan, "Wasn't she nice? She also teaches music." Or Jim would be telling Sally what Ivan did or didn't like about his boss. They might even have decided they were all going to get together for dinner some evening soon. Above all, they would have proven that people don't make wars.

Reagan's storytelling was aimed not only at Americans but at the Soviet people. He wanted them to know that the United States meant them no harm, despite what their leaders might have been telling them. But within weeks, the scene would change again with the death of Andropov on February 10. Once more Reagan refused to attend the funeral, telling NSC advisor and Soviet expert Jack Matlock, "I don't want to honor that prick." He sent Bush and Shultz, and they delivered a personal letter to the new Soviet leader, Konstantin Chernenko, expressing a hope that they could work together to establish a "stable and constructive" relationship. Chernenko was an aging Soviet functionary who was in such poor health that he struggled to read the eulogy at Andropov's funeral. But he set the tone for his regime by announcing a Soviet boycott of the Summer Olympics in Los Angeles that year—a peevish gesture that undoubtedly caused more pain in the Soviet Union than in America and was likely payback for Jimmy Carter's decision to do the same thing with the Moscow Olympics in 1980.

Even though Mondale tried to shake up the presidential race by choosing Geraldine Ferraro, the first woman to join a major party ticket, as his running mate, his campaign was plagued by inertia and indifference as the initial exhilaration about having a woman on the ticket was dashed by a scandal involving Ferraro's husband, John Zaccaro. Democrats, who might have preferred a new face, even the flawed Gary Hart or Jesse Jackson, the two other contenders for the nomination, never felt inspired by Mondale, an old-school Hubert Humphrey acolyte who reminded them too much of the malaise they were trying to escape. Meanwhile, Reagan benefited from improvements in the economy and a forceful foreign policy—not to mention the raw appeal of his persona. After the political conventions, the contest was never even close, although Mondale got a slight boost from a lackluster Reagan performance in their first debate.

By the second debate Reagan rebounded, and more. The climax came when the debate moderator, Hank Trewhitt of the *Baltimore Sun*, raised the issue of his age. "You already are the oldest president in history, and some of your staff say you were tired after your most recent encounter with Mr. Mondale,"

Trewhitt said to Reagan. "I recall, yes, that President Kennedy had to go for days on end with very little sleep during the Cuba missile crisis. Is there any doubt in your mind that you would be able to function in such circumstances?"

"Not at all, Mr. Trewhitt," Reagan replied with a confident smile. "And I want you to know that also I will not make age an issue of this campaign. I am not going to exploit for political purposes my opponent's youth and inexperience."

Looking impressed by the way Reagan had turned the question around, Trewhitt joked, "Mr. President, I'd like to head for the fence and try to catch that one before it goes over."

Later, reflecting back on the campaign, Mondale made this admission: "If TV can tell the truth . . . you'll see that I was smiling. But I think if you come in close, you'll see some tears coming down because I knew he had gotten me there. That was really the end of my campaign that night, I think."

The question of Reagan's age and stamina, frequently raised, was often deftly shut down by the man himself. Sure, he might have dozed off on occasion during long meetings, but he was hardly alone in that; younger heads had nodded at the endless drone of economic figures or national security details. More impactful were his presence of mind, his calm demeanor, and his near serenity, even in crises. Peter Robinson, a young speechwriter during Reagan's second term, recalled such a moment, which others would say was typical. A last-minute flurry of rewrites had been made for a State of the Union address, and an hour before Reagan was set to speak, the final speech had not been delivered. Robinson imagined that if he were in Reagan's shoes, "I'd have been having a panic attack—sweaty palms, dry mouth, heart palpitations. By the time I received the text, I'd have been in no condition to deliver it." But, he said, Reagan was calm as he reviewed the text during the limo ride to the Hill, and he delivered the speech flawlessly. "The next morning he arrived at the Oval Office looking just the way he always did, which is to say as fresh and at ease as if he had just put in a couple of hours at a health club."

To be sure, Reagan had his share of age-related health problems, but when the American people saw him, it was his erect posture and youthful optimism they noticed. "He was a Californian," Weinberger quipped. "Our constitution requires us to be optimistic." When Reagan's critics argued that his appearance was just an actor's pose, it didn't seem credible. Some things you just can't fake.

He had a sense of humor about it. Kathleen Osborne, his personal secretary, recalled that occasionally reporters would call saying they'd heard rumors that Reagan had suffered a heart attack. Her take was that some troublemaker had started the rumors in order to affect the stock market. She devised a strategy that would put any doubts to rest: "I'd lay my phone on the desk, prop open the door, if the president was in there alone, and I'd say, 'Mr. President, have you had a heart attack today?' And he'd say, 'No.' I'd say, 'Okay, thank you.' I'd go back to the phone, and of course they had him on speakerphone in the press office, so they heard the president's voice, they knew."

In the months leading up to the election, Nancy continued to press Reagan to soften his tone with the Soviets, and at her urging he agreed to schedule a meeting with Soviet foreign minister Andrei Gromyko when he was in the United States for the UN General Assembly in September. Encountering Nancy at a reception there, Gromyko said, "Whisper peace in your husband's ear every night." She responded tartly, "I will, and I'll also whisper it in your ear."

Soon after, in a three-and-a-half-hour conversation at the

White House, Reagan repeatedly suggested ways of opening up a new dialogue between the nations, but Gromyko maintained a posture of distrust. His verdict on the meeting, in a statement released by the Soviet news agency TASS, was damning: "There were no visible signs of the United States being ready to take realistic positions on the substance of acute problems of war and peace." His rigid stance frustrated Reagan and seemed to justify his rhetoric about the Soviets. He didn't expect to accomplish much with the current regime.

If "Bear in the Woods" was Reagan's dramatic reminder of the Soviet threat, the end-of-campaign ad "Morning in America" was his appeal to the better angels of the nation. That was the Reagan people responded to most viscerally: the positive visionary who reached out with a message of strength, prosperity, and even happiness. It worked. On Election Day, Reagan scored an overwhelming victory over Mondale, winning forty-nine states and 525 electoral votes. Standing before a large crowd of supporters on election night, Reagan promised them, "You ain't seen nothing yet."

In the months before the inauguration, Reagan's focus was on the Soviets. On December 22, he welcomed Margaret Thatcher for lunch at Camp David. He was eager to hear about Thatcher's meeting with Mikhail Gorbachev, the Soviet second in command, who was considered the heir apparent to Chernenko, a significant position given Chernenko's poor health. He met Thatcher's helicopter in his Camp David golf cart, dubbed "Golf Cart One"—the preferred means of transport on the ground—and drove her along the winding paths to Aspen, the president's cabin. Over lunch, Thatcher related that Gorbachev was surprisingly charming but added that she'd always found that the more charming the adversary, the more dangerous. (The truth of that notion was not lost on Reagan, who had crushed his own political opposition with a charm offensive directed at the American people.) But she cautiously liked Gorbachev, whose personality lacked the "wooden ventriloquism of the average Soviet apparatchik."

Thatcher told Reagan she had assured Gorbachev that Reagan was an honorable man. She reminded him that Reagan had sent a personal handwritten letter to Brezhnev shortly after taking office, while he was recovering from the assassination attempt, and she had been surprised that Gorbachev knew nothing of the letter. The president, she told him reproachfully, had poured his heart and soul into that message and received only the barest acknowledgment from Brezhnev. In other words, Reagan had tried to reach out but had been rebuffed. As for the Soviet fears that the warmonger president would consider a first strike, she reminded Gorbachev that the United States, a nation of great power, had used that power sparingly and was more interested in achieving political goals.

Once again, Reagan felt heartened by Thatcher's collaboration and willingness to speak firmly to the Soviets about the West's shared aims. After lunch, as the two leaders took a walk along the bucolic pathways of Camp David, they spoke, as old friends do, about the issues that united and sometimes divided them. Thatcher had her own reservations about SDI, which she vigorously debated with the president. She believed that the strongest deterrent to the use of nuclear weapons was the very standoff—mutually assured destruction—that Reagan despised. But in the main, she emphasized the warmth and endurance of their friendship.

Reagan's second inaugural was barely an event, as if nature itself were impatient to keep powering forward. For one thing, January 20, 1985, fell on a Sunday, so there was a private ceremony in the Grand Foyer of the White House, with the oath being given by Chief Justice Warren Burger, to fulfill the constitutional mandate. The public inaugural was scheduled for Monday, but nature intervened.

Reagan rose on Monday morning prepared for a traditional inaugural and parade, only to be told by his medical advisors that with temperatures hovering near 4 degrees Fahrenheit and a wind chill factor of 30 degrees below zero, it would be dangerous for anyone to be outside for more than a few minutes, especially a seventy-three-year-old president. (Perhaps they were recalling the fate of William Henry Harrison, who had caught a cold at his bitterly frigid 1841 inauguration and died of pneumonia a month later.)

The anticipated crowd of 350,000 was left to find TV sets or sit in their hotel rooms, where they could watch the oath-taking—a second time—in the Capitol Rotunda, the large circular hall beneath the Capitol dome. There, below *Apotheosis of Washington*, a fresco depicting George Washington sitting among heavenly beings, Reagan took the oath on his mother's Bible.

"Today, we utter no prayer more fervently than the ancient prayer for peace on Earth," he said in his inaugural speech. "Yet history has shown that peace does not come, nor will our freedom be preserved, by good will alone." Speaking of the SDI program, he said it would render nuclear weapons obsolete, describing the folly of mutually assured destruction, which was the dangerous status quo. And in a striking diplomatic appeal, he promised, "We will meet with the Soviets, hoping that we can agree on a way to rid the world of the threat of nuclear destruction."

But he had a warning for the forces of oppression, which he laid out in his State of the Union address on February 6: "We cannot play innocents abroad in a world that's not innocent; nor can we be passive when freedom is under siege. Without resources, diplomacy cannot succeed. Our security assistance programs help friendly governments defend themselves and give them confidence to work for peace. And I hope that you in the Congress will understand that, dollar for dollar, security assistance contributes as much to global security as our own defense budget."

And, in what Charles Krauthammer called the "Reagan Doctrine," he voiced support for "freedom fighters" in nations around the world, promising that the United States would be in their corner:

> Harry Truman once said that, ultimately, our security and the world's hopes for peace and human progress "lie not in measures of defense or in the control of weapons, but in the growth and expansion of freedom and self-government." And tonight, we declare anew to our fellow citizens of the world: Freedom is not the sole prerogative of a chosen few; it is the universal right of all God's children. Look to where peace and prosperity flourish today. It is in homes that freedom built. Victories against poverty are greatest and peace most secure where people live by laws that ensure free press, free speech, and freedom to worship, vote, and create wealth. Our mission is to nourish and defend freedom and democracy, and to communicate these ideals everywhere we can.

The growing list of "freedom fighters" who were receiving covert US support included the Afghan rebels fighting the Soviet occupation, Angolans fighting communism in a bitter civil war, and the Contras in Nicaragua, fighting the socialist Sandinista government. But Reagan was also committed to supporting the movements for freedom in Poland, East Germany, and other Soviet bloc nations.

With the beginning of a new term, the White House team was undergoing a major shift. Within months, the old troika had dissolved—Baker switched jobs with Donald Regan and became secretary of the Treasury, with Regan as chief of staff; Ed Meese was confirmed by the Senate as attorney general; and Deaver was gone—the one year he'd originally promised to serve having lasted four.

As chief of staff, Regan was powerful but plagued by controversy and difficult relationships from day one, particularly with Nancy, which was ultimately his undoing. What bugged Nancy, and others, about Regan was that he seemed to think he was on an equal footing with the president. To him the chief of staff position was akin to being the CEO of a large corporation called America. He marched around, running the show, while relationships on the Hill and in the West Wing faltered. A frequent grumble was that Don Regan was so vain he thought "Hail to the Chief" was about him.

Returning as the assistant to the president for legislative affairs, after a three-year absence, it was Max Friedersdorf's job to take Regan up to the Hill to meet the leadership. Friedersdorf reported that it was a disaster: "Regan spends an hour lecturing these guys. You do not lecture members of the United States Senate. I was aghast. It was so embarrassing. I mean, he'd sit there like he's a CEO telling these guys how it's going to be. You imagine telling Bob Dole how it's going to be, or Howard Baker how it's going to be."

The White House was in for a bumpy ride, but when it came to the Soviets, Reagan never faltered.

"THEY KEEP DYING ON me," Reagan complained. It seemed to be true. On March 10, he received word that Chernenko had passed away. Once again he declined to attend the funeral, sending Bush and Shultz in his stead. But after his conversation with Thatcher, he had reason to hope that the Soviet Union's new general secretary, Mikhail Gorbachev, was different, even as Gorbachev publicly cautioned the United States, "Do not rush to toss us on the 'ash heap of history.' The idea only makes Soviet people smile."

Like Reagan, Gorbachev could be an enigma—unpredictable and innovative, while remaining steadfastly loyal to the Party. He also shared the humble roots that had made his rise to power all the more remarkable. Born on March 2, 1931, in the rural farming village of Privolnoe, the first decade of Gorbachev's life was one of extreme hardship and oppression. When Stalin launched his Great Terror in 1936, designed to weed out opposition, both of Gorbachev's grandfathers were arrested; miraculously, they survived and were later released, but the incident was a trauma for the family. Privolnoe also endured a brief Nazi occupation during World War II, and Gorbachev's father was drafted to fight in the war.

Poverty and near famine were constants, even after the war, but none of that got Gorbachev down. "We were poor, practically beggars," he said of his childhood, "but in general I felt wonderful." That comment echoes one that Reagan made about his own childhood. Thus, two men of humble roots and optimistic dispositions were fated to change the world.

Also like Reagan, Gorbachev came from a family that was not well educated, but he craved learning and achieved the seemingly impossible goal of acceptance to Moscow State University. There he joined the Communist Party but distinguished himself as something of an outsider and independent thinker. He was occasionally outspoken—dangerously so, given the times—but managed to couch his doubts about the rigidities of the Soviet system in more philosophical arguments. His agile mind could simply not accept all Stalinist dictates without challenge, but he was far from being a troublemaker. He strove to remain his own man internally in the midst of collective thinking, and he had a great love of the socialist promise, even as he saw its flaws. Those, he believed, could be fixed. He was loyal with a twist, a key to his ability to rise steadily through the ranks and reach the top.

Reagan often spoke from the heart about the crucial role Nancy played in his success, and we can see the truth of this sentiment in her undying devotion and the way she mastered politics and garnered support on his behalf. Gorbachev's wife did the same for him. Raisa Titarenko was a year ahead of Gorbachev at Moscow State University, studying philosophy, and Gorbachev said it was love at first sight when they met at a dance. She was cooler about their prospects, but Gorbachev persisted. "She bewitched me," he remembered. He set out to woo her, and when she finally agreed to marry him, he was ecstatic. Their long, happy marriage was built not only on love but on the highest form of mutual respect. Like Nancy, Raisa became her husband's most trusted advisor. In a comment Nancy might have made, Raisa once said, "We have a division of labor. He's working and I'm looking around. Then I tell him everything I see."

How did Gorbachev view his mandate on taking office? That wasn't so easy to determine at the time. But later, reflecting back on the challenges he had faced, he would cite the conditions in Russia before perestroika: "A dead-end political situation, economic stagnation, a build-up of unresolved social problems, violation of the rights and dignity of citizens." He wrote those words in a 2011 book entitled *The New Russia*, which was very critical of Vladimir Putin. But clearly those were the problems he saw when he took office.

In particular, the collapsing economy, which Reagan frequently poked at, was a desperate reality for the fifty-four-year-old general secretary. He believed that nothing short of an economic transformation was necessary and that it would require a political one as well. In this aim he was bucking a rigid establishment that was resistant to progress and modernization. He had to convince it that change must happen if the Soviet Union were to survive. To accomplish that, he proposed a two-part program: perestroika, a reform of the political structure and a gradual shift from a centrally controlled economy to one that was responsive to market forces; and glasnost, greater openness to diverse ideas and more media freedom. He anticipated resistance from the top, but in travels around the Soviet Union, from Leningrad to Ukraine and through Siberia, he found a welcoming response from citizens who felt crushed by economic problems and powerless against policies that made little sense to them. "Keep it up!" they cried in Leningrad. In a town in west Siberia, every resident came out to the street to greet him. "The people were happy that the 'chief' had finally come to visit them—the talk was direct and unsparing," he wrote. "They asked, 'How is it that we live in slums or old railway carriages? There is a shortage of everything. Here, beyond the Arctic Circle, we cannot get regular flights to the capital or other cities. The Soviet Union and Europe need gas, but it turns out that no one needs us.'"

Andrei Grachev, a close advisor of Gorbachev, in his personal and insightful book *Gorbachev's Gamble: Soviet Foreign Policy and the End of the Cold War*, wrote, "One of the most crucial factors paving the way for future changes in Soviet foreign policy at the end of Brezhnev's reign was a growing feeling within Soviet society that the civilization project initiated at the time of the 1917 October Revolution had reached a stage of general exhaustion, if not fiasco." Ironically, one reason for that demise was the government's homage to its own version of the military-industrial complex that Eisenhower had warned Americans of in 1961.

Brezhnev had gone full steam ahead, his mind-set being that having more missiles than the United States would give the Soviets the winning hand in a war. But the military buildup was bleeding the economy. By Reagan's second term, when the United States was spending around 5.8 percent of its GDP on the military (considered by many to be too high), the Soviets were spending 15 to 17 percent in an economy that was less than half the size of the United States'. So although some Soviets believed that the United States was losing the arms race, it hardly mattered. Furthermore, the USSR's stampede around the globe aimed at spreading communism, such as the Afghanistan invasion (which Weinberger once referred to as "their Vietnam"), was bleeding the country's coffers, as was the rise of insurgencies supported by the United States that had to be countered, an expensive prospect.

Insurgents around the world considered Reagan their hero. That was vividly clear in Poland with Reagan's support of Solidarity, the independent labor movement begun in the shipyards of Gdańsk, led by Lech Wałęsa. A secret poll of six hundred Poles taken by *Paris Match* in 1983 found that they identified Poland's last hope as being, in order, the pope, the Virgin Mary, and Ronald Reagan. Wałęsa came in fourth. To Reagan, the soldiers and insurgents struggling against communism on battlefields throughout the world were "freedom fighters," a description he particularly applied to the Contras opposing the Sandinista government in Nicaragua. "Those old verities, those truths of the heart—human freedom under God—are on the march everywhere in the world," he said in a speech to the Irish Parliament. "All across the world today—in the shipyards of Gdansk, the hills of Nicaragua, the rice paddies of Kampuchea, the mountains of Afghanistan—the cry again is liberty." More specifically, he declared that "We must stand by our democratic allies. And we must not break faith with those who are risking their lives—on every continent, from Afghanistan to Nicaragua—to defy Soviet-supported aggression and secure rights which have been ours from birth." He concluded, "Support for freedom fighters is self-defense."

US support for insurgents around the globe was taking a heavy toll on the Soviet mission. Nations that could ill afford to be in the crosshairs of US might were reeling from the fight.

Many Soviet leaders and foreign policy advisors misunderstood Reagan. They were convinced that he was dedicated to the total destruction of the Soviet Union. But they weren't listening. What Reagan was saying was that the Soviet system was orchestrating its own doom.

One of the most public faces of the old Soviet order was Andrei Gromyko, who had served as minister of foreign affairs since 1957. Whatever his intentions, he had not been able to ease the tensions with the West and was unprepared for a shift in focus by the US president. Before Gorbachev, any diplomatic advances had been strictly incremental and often subject to backtracking. According to Grachev, when Reagan gave his important speech in January 1984, calling on the Soviet Union to join the United States in a quest for peace, Gromyko never circulated the text of the speech to the Soviet leadership, including Andropov, who was ill. And it appears they had no other way of knowing about it. "However strange it may seem today, they did not read the Western press and had no source of information other than the news bulletins that had been carefully distilled and edited by TASS and Soviet Embassy cables," he wrote. It's notable that one of Gorbachev's first acts in office was to reassign and replace Gromyko, in the process completely disregarding Gromyko's recommendation for a successor in favor of Eduard Shevardnadze, a friend and loyalist who would not undercut him on the world stage. Shevardnadze lacked diplomatic experience, but he had the advantage of signaling a fresh start. US diplomats were initially surprised by his openness and even friendliness; they did not miss the cold, humorless face of Gromyko, whom they'd nicknamed "Grim Grom."

Finally, in his fifth year in office, Reagan was ready to try something he had not done before: meet a Soviet leader face-to-face. He asked Bush to deliver a personal letter to Gorbachev at Chernenko's funeral. In it he wrote, "You can be assured of my personal commitment to work with you and the rest of the Soviet leadership in serious negotiations. In that spirit, I would like to invite you to visit me in Washington at your earliest convenient opportunity."

Gorbachev responded with a lengthy letter that was just short of warmly accommodating, with some subtle jabs. He did not directly confront Reagan about his "Evil Empire" rhetoric, but he did write of his desire that a mutual trust be established between them. "It is not an easy task," he wrote, "and I would say, a delicate one. For trust is an especially sensitive thing, keenly receptive to both deeds and words. It will not be enhanced if, for example, one were to talk as if in two languages: one—for private contacts, and the other, as they say—for the audience." In other words, he expected Reagan to tone down his public rhetoric if he wanted to make progress on a relationship. Reagan surely understood that. He was quite willing to shift gears if he were dealing with a more honest broker. Perhaps Gorbachev would be that person. Certainly, his predecessors had not been.

Gorbachev wrote that he would be pleased to plan for a

personal meeting between the two of them, though he asked that they revisit the question of its location. Such a meeting, he said, should not be about signing some major agreements but a "search for mutual understanding on the basis of equality."

No one really expected Gorbachev to come to Washington for his first summit with Reagan; it would have made him look like a supplicant. Nor did Reagan have any intention of going to Moscow. They finally compromised on a neutral site, Geneva, Switzerland, and agreed to meet for the first time in November. There was an interesting historical precedent for a Geneva summit. It was in Geneva in 1955 that Eisenhower first met Khrushchev and formed an initial connection with him. Khrushchev was not yet in power, Nikolai Bulganin was, but he so dominated the summit that everyone had seen the handwriting on the wall. It was in Geneva that Eisenhower first proposed his "Open Skies" concept—a system of mutual accountability that would reduce the threat of nuclear war. After the summit, Bulganin spoke positively about the "spirit of Geneva," but then the complexities of rapprochement settled in. Now the two countries' leaders were heading to Geneva once again, thirty years later.

REAGAN DIDN'T ALWAYS IMMERSE himself in the nitty-gritty details of government—"That's why I have staff," he'd say. He was a big-picture president who was motivated by a broad vision of expanding freedom and justice. When those principles were at stake, he could be daring when others were cautious. It could get him into hot water on occasion, but he rarely backed down. He had confidence in his own sense of right and wrong. "His strongest suit was in knowing what he believed and why he believed it and standing there," Shultz once observed. "The thing that got him in trouble was his intense concern about Americans being held hostage abroad and his desire to do something about it. You have to be happy that a president feels that way, but it turned out it got him into trouble because he didn't get a handle on it. He could let the wish be the father to the thought on some occasions."

Iran-Contra, as it was known, grew out of this sense of calling, which filtered down to his staff. When seven US diplomats and private contractors were taken hostage in Lebanon by the Islamic paramilitary group Hezbollah, the Reagan administration struggled to find a solution. Given the United States' firm policy that it would never negotiate with terrorists, there seemed little to be done. But when an opening appeared to negotiate with moderate Iranians to work out a deal that would secure the release of hostages without directly giving aid to the terrorists, it seemed like a roundabout solution.

Reagan, who felt emotionally devastated by his meetings with the families of the hostages, thought it was up to him to find a way out for them. The idea of selling arms to Tehran in exchange for their influence over the hostage takers seemed promising—in spite of the reservations of his advisors. "I was strongly opposed to the idea of giving arms to the Iranians, or to anybody over there, because we'd spent a lot of time and expended a huge amount of effort to persuade other countries not to sell them anything," Caspar Weinberger said.

> The proposal was that we'd sell them arms ourselves in return for their helping to get our hostages back. It was said, "We have to deal with these moderate elements in Iran." I said, "There aren't any moderate elements. All the moderates were killed long ago, and what you're dealing with are a bunch of unreliable and thoroughly

dishonest and corrupt arms dealers." But the President's idea of trying to get the hostages back overweighed almost everything—including, as he said later, all his own lifetime teachings and doctrines. But he was so unhappy about the idea of Americans being held against their will and our being unable to pull them out that he was willing to try even this, which, he said later, was a great mistake.

The operation would not start to come to light until the following year, and it is unlikely that Reagan himself devoted much time to it. Others in the administration took on the project and did not always share the operational facts. For example, the Contra piece would be revealed only after Attorney General Ed Meese issued a Department of Justice report tracing money missing from the arms sale to a covert project to arm the Nicaraguan Contras. Although supporting the Contras had been a passion of Reagan's throughout his presidency, there was never any evidence that he knew of that particular plot. However, in a sense, he was damned if he knew and damned if he didn't. It would ultimately be a stain on his legacy.

THE VILLA FLEUR D'EAU, a twenty-room nineteenth-century château in a lakeside town outside Geneva with a stunning view of the Alps, was the site of the first summit between Reagan and Gorbachev on November 19, 1985. It was a neutral space to which they could retreat to get to know each other.

For their personal use during the summit, His Highness Aga Khan lent the Reagans another spectacular château, the eighteenth-century Maison de Saussure, also on the lake. There was only one condition for their stay: that they feed Aga Khan's eleven-year-old son's goldfish. Reagan was very conscientious about that, but according to Don Regan, the president came to him the second day and said, "I've got a problem . . . the fish died." An aide was immediately dispatched to find a replacement fish, and he brought back two. Reagan wrote a charming note of apology to the boy—just an example of the way mundane life intrudes on grand events.

With all the sensitive preparations for Geneva, the Reagans were appalled when Don Regan put his foot in it in an interview with the *Washington Post* a week before the summit. Discussing public interest in events in Geneva, he said that women would mostly be paying attention to what Nancy Reagan and Raisa Gorbachev were up to, not the meetings between the principals. "They're not going to understand throw-weights [how much weight a missile can carry] or what is happening in Afghanistan or what is happening in human rights," he said pompously. "Some women will. But most women . . . believe me, your readers for the most part, if you took a poll, would rather read the human interest stuff." His remarks prompted Eleanor Smeal, the president of the National Organization for Women, to snipe that she was glad that Reagan was taking Bonzo to Geneva with him. The outcry distracted attention from the serious intent of the summit, and it further embarrassed Reagan when reporters asked him and Gorbachev about it at a press conference the second day of the summit. Gorbachev must have relished the opportunity to share his conviction that both men *and* women were interested in the peace process. And surely his wife, a serious student of Soviet culture and politics and a former teacher at Moscow State University, would have agreed.

The Reagans arrived in Geneva for the summit a day early, and the president was excited. This had been his dream—to go one-on-one with a Soviet leader—and he felt confident of his ability to communicate, without his intentions being mangled by bureaucrats.

His staff felt less assured. God knows, they appreciated Reagan's communication skills, but some were worried that Gorbachev, a generation younger, a master of Soviet and world history, and an exceptionally canny strategist, might show Reagan up. That was not a concern Reagan shared. In a sense, he'd been preparing for such a meeting for most of his adult life. He couldn't wait. He barely slept the night before the meetings commenced, but he didn't feel tired. "The juices were flowing," he wrote. "I wanted to get started."

No one knew better than Reagan that when the two men met, the flashbulbs would be clicking with images viewed by millions, and the first impression would be all about style. His advisors worriedly contemplated a scenario in which an "aging lion," bundled against the Geneva cold, would meet face-to-face with an energized "young tiger." It wasn't the picture anyone wanted. The day before the meetings started, as they briefed the president, they had reason to be concerned. "Reagan was tired, cranky, and uncharacteristically out of it," Adelman recalled. "So, I thought, *Oh God, this is going to be pretty bad. He's an old man*. When all was said and done, he'd been through amazing stuff, but boy, he's out of his league here."

The question of stamina was once again on everyone's minds. Although Reagan seemed generally healthy, he'd gone through two cancer surgeries that year, for a cancerous polyp on his colon and a basal-cell carcinoma on his nose. During his colon cancer surgery, he'd officially turned over the presidency to Bush, raising concerns that at seventy-four, he was growing weaker. But as usual, he showed the doubters just how wrong they were.

On Tuesday morning, Reagan arrived early at the château and was talking to his aides when word came that Gorbachev's limousine was pulling up. It was bitterly cold that day, and Reagan considered putting on a coat, but his personal assistant, James Kuhn, argued against it, thinking the coatless look would make him appear more vigorous. Reagan ultimately decided to greet Gorbachev coatless, though he didn't quite grasp what all the fuss was about.

"He comes down the stairs of the chateau and Gorbachev gets out of the car," Adelman said, clearly relishing the retelling. "Gorbachev has a hat on, Gorbachev has a gigantic scarf on, Gorbachev has a Soviet-like, Russian-like big coat on. He looks like an absolute old man huddled up to keep warm and just seems decrepit and old. He gets out of the car, comes and takes off his hat, and reaches for Reagan. Reagan comes down the stairs like he's a Labrador retriever."

Gorbachev motioned to his coat and Reagan's lack of one, and everyone could see the difference as plain as could be. Then Reagan pointed to the house and gestured for Gorbachev to join him inside, as if he were the owner. "As Gorbachev is going up the stairs," said Adelman, "Reagan slides his hand under Gorbachev's arm in a gesture of kindness, but it came across as *We hope you make it up these stairs, and if you can't I'm here to help you.* The visual of it was this young, frisky, growing leader who had all of tomorrow ahead of him in Ronald Reagan, who is helping this decrepit man from the fallen empire get up the stairs. It was just an amazing sight."

The optics of it were not lost on the Soviets. Sergei Tarasenko, a Gorbachev aide, later recalled the scene: "We came to the porch and I saw President Reagan coming out to greet Gorbachev in a well-tailored suit, looking young with a good haircut, you know. Maybe he was made up a little bit, but skillfully. He projected an image of a young, dynamic leader. And Gorbachev came out of this tank-like limo, black limo, in an autumn overcoat, a heavy overcoat, looking like an old guy."

Once inside, Reagan told Gorbachev a joke to break the ice. "An American and a Russian meet," he began with a twinkle in his eye. " 'My country is the best,' says the American, 'because I can walk into the White House and tell the president he's doing a lousy job.' 'Big deal,' says the Russian. 'My country is just as good. I can go to the Kremlin and tell Gorbachev the same thing—Reagan is doing a lousy job.' " Reagan grinned; Gorbachev smiled tentatively. The joke was unexpected. "He used to drive Gorbachev nuts with his jokes—including Russian jokes," said Frank Carlucci, who would become national security advisor and then secretary of defense later in Reagan's administration.

Reagan found Gorbachev instantly likable. There was a warmth in his face that had not been present in other Soviet representatives during the icy winter of the Cold War years. They retreated for a personal meeting, which was scheduled to run fifteen minutes but lasted more than an hour. Outside, Don Regan began getting nervous at the half-hour mark, and he started pressuring Kuhn to break in. That was the last thing Kuhn wanted to do, but as the minutes ticked on, Regan kept asking him. Then McFarlane joined in. Kuhn was feeling the heat, and he kept sidestepping the request. Finally, McFarlane suggested that Kuhn ask Shultz, which he did.

"Are you out of your mind?" Shultz barked. "If you're dumb enough to do that, you shouldn't be in your job. This is what it's about. The longer they talk, the better it is." (Kuhn was understandably wounded by Shultz's sharp reply, since he was only the messenger, not the instigator.)

Finally Reagan and Gorbachev emerged and walked into

a plenary session, where their expert teams were in place. Through interpreters, they went through the laborious process of stating their views and recounting history from their different perspectives, breaking for lunch around 12:30 P.M.

Reagan's twenty-seven-year-old son, Ron, was at the summit, covering it for *Playboy* magazine. Ron, who was opposed to most of his father's policies, always believed he was a "good, decent and kind man," and he took that fundamental respect with him to the summit. Of course, other reporters grumbled about his special access, and although the White House denied it, Ron happened to be at a tea his mother gave for Raisa Gorbachev and was seen chatting alone with his father. He was also standing among the US contingent waiting for the first session to break up so they could have lunch.

"Dad, you're late," he said when Reagan finally strode in. Reagan explained that everything had taken longer because of the interpreters and then excused himself to go to the men's room. All the others took their places around the table and remained standing, waiting for the president.

"When he came out, Reagan stood at his place and had a grin like a cat who had just swallowed a canary," Adelman recalled. "He was just so beaming. Then one by one all of us realized that one of his arms was in his suit coat, the other arm was just hanging down right there and Reagan was holding the arm in back of it so it would be clear it was hanging down. Then the whole room started laughing, I was one of the last to catch on. Finally, someone next to me says, 'Where's your arm?' And Reagan burst out laughing and said, 'Well, it was here before I met Gorbachev. I don't know where it is now.' He just got the biggest kick out of it, all of us laughed. It was just a great tension lowerer at the time because it really put all of us at ease."

They sat down to lunch, and when someone finally dared to ask, "How was Gorbachev?" he said, "Well, he's a new kind of Soviet leader."

During the morning session Reagan had outlined the incidences of Soviet aggression in defense of the West's countermeasures. In reply, Gorbachev opened the afternoon session in a defensive posture. The Soviet people were peace loving, he argued. Reagan countered: Where were the free elections? Where was the freedom to go where they pleased or do what they liked? Where was the evidence?

When the topic of Afghanistan came up, the debate was vigorous. Adelman felt that Reagan cleaned Gorbachev's clock on the issue of interventionism. "It's just genocide . . . they don't want you there . . . you're killing kids . . . you're butchering the country," he recalled Reagan saying. "Here's Gorbachev in his earphones, cannot imagine what he's hearing. I've often said that the only person there who was more shocked in the room was the State Department note taker; his pants were never dry. But the fact is that Reagan would tell it directly because that was his way. He didn't care that much about the briefing book. He wanted to have these views and he was very frank about that."

As the afternoon wore on, with arms control experts battling back and forth, Reagan asked Gorbachev if he would like to get a breath of fresh air. There was a boathouse down by the lake, and Reagan had arranged to have a fire lit, with comfortable chairs positioned in front of it. His idea had been that the two leaders could have a "fireside chat," away from the summit, with only a translator present.

Warming by the fire, Reagan made a personal appeal that put the conflict into perspective. He quietly told Gorbachev that they were the only two men in the world who could start World War III—or prevent it. Wasn't it their obligation, didn't they owe it to the world and to their own people, to do whatever was necessary for peace?

Gorbachev was listening carefully, and Reagan thought he agreed. But he told Reagan he'd have to address the justified fear his people had of the United States launching a nuclear attack. That brought them to SDI, the most contentious item on the agenda. To Gorbachev, SDI did not seem defensive at all; the Soviet Union believed its true aim was offensive, an effort to neutralize any Soviet weapons and thus render them helpless against a US attack. Reagan reasserted that this was not SDI's purpose at all—in fact, at that point it was little more than a research project, and if it worked, the United States was willing to share its research with other countries so the whole world would be closer to peace. Gorbachev was not convinced.

As they walked back to join the meeting, Reagan paused and asked Gorbachev if he would come to Washington for a second summit. Gorbachev not only agreed but invited Reagan to Moscow for a third meeting. Shultz observed that when the two men rejoined the conference, they were both smiling and seemed at ease with each other.

As Reagan and Gorbachev were carefully leaning in toward a mutual understanding of sorts, their wives were having a tenser summit, beginning with a private tea hosted by Nancy. Sipping almond tea in front of a cozy fire, their hour-long conversation was stiff and unpleasant. Raisa, who was fifteen minutes late to the tea—which Nancy took as a sign of disrespect—lectured the first lady about communism, and, to Nancy's chagrin, the subject of their children never came up. Later, when Reagan asked how her day had gone, Nancy retorted, "That Raisa Gorbachev is one cold cookie."

The discomfort was repeated the next day, when Raisa invited Nancy to tea at the Soviet Embassy. Again, Raisa lectured, as if Nancy didn't understand the missile program. Perhaps Raisa was channeling Don Regan.

Tuesday evening the Gorbachevs hosted a dinner at the Soviet Embassy, and for the first time, Americans saw another side of the couple. They were warm and gracious, and the evening had its share of humor. The first course was caviar, accompanied by shot glasses of vodka. Raising his glass, Shevardnadze joked, "Mr. President, I have to come all the way to Geneva to get this." Even Gorbachev laughed. "Suddenly everyone was talking about visiting California, visiting Moscow," Shultz said. "It was wonderful in a way, but there was little real movement yet on key issues of substance."

On Wednesday, in a private meeting with Gorbachev, Reagan decided to press the matter of human rights. It was a topic the Soviets did not want to pursue, but Gorbachev was prepared. He argued fiercely that Americans had no right to criticize the Soviets when in their country blacks were treated poorly and women did not have equal rights. "The most basic human right," he said, "is everyone's right to a job." He pointed out that in the Soviet system, there was full employment.

Even if that were true, he did not mention that there was little freedom to choose one's job, nor did the socialist economy have lasting potential. Both individual and common growth were stunted. Although he acknowledged that changes needed to be made in his system, he believed in communism and was ready to defend its principles.

In the plenary session, Gorbachev returned to his worries about SDI, and the debate was loud and contentious, the leaders frequently interrupting each other and giving the translators heartburn.

"We'll share SDI with you," Reagan finally said, surprising his own diplomats as well as the Soviets. "Gorbachev thought it was whacko," Adelman said, and he countered angrily, "Mr. President, the United States doesn't even share cow-milking equipment with us." (Later Reagan would ask his aides, "Why don't we share cow-milking equipment with the Soviets?")

Reagan was particularly passionate and eloquent during that debate, Shultz said. "He was intense as he expressed his abhorrence at having to rely on the ability to 'wipe each other out' as the means of keeping the peace. 'We must do better, and we can.' The depth of the president's belief in SDI was vividly apparent. Ronald Reagan was talking from the inside out. Translation was simultaneous. Gorbachev could connect what the president said with his facial expression and body language."

Gorbachev seemed stunned by the emotion in Reagan's presentation and was newly aware that SDI would remain a sticking point. "Mr. President, I don't agree with you," he said, "but I can see that you really mean it." Shultz saw that as a victory for Reagan. "I just thought, *Well, Reagan just nailed down one of our planks. He knows we mean it. That's good.*"

On Wednesday night, the Reagans played host to the Gorbachevs at an intimate dinner at Maison de Saussure. The menu was exquisite—soufflé of lobster, supreme of chicken perigourdine, endive salad, mousse de fromage with avocado, and hot lemon soufflé with raspberry sauce. The three wines served were from California—Silverado Chardonnay 1983, Stag's Leap Cabernet Sauvignon 1974, and Iron Horse Blanc de Blanc 1982.

Once again Reagan saw another side of Gorbachev, the charming, social side. He even told jokes. Reagan concluded that "maybe there was a little of Tip O'Neill in him." Raisa, too, was relaxed and smiling. The dinner ended with warm toasts from both sides, and that evening they decided to issue a joint statement on the conference before they left Geneva the following day. There was a general sense that the first summit had been a success.

About that stamina issue. Reagan flew home on Thursday and immediately headed for Capitol Hill to appear before a joint session of Congress, which was televised nationwide. It was 9:20 P.M. Washington time—3:00 A.M. in Geneva—and he'd been awake for twenty-four hours. Reagan's Air Force One (now on display at the Reagan Library) was half the size of the current model and had no beds or shower facility. But Reagan showed little evidence of exhaustion, just resolve. He spoke of the true accomplishment of the summit: the effort to "reduce the mistrust and suspicions between us." He reported that Gorbachev was in agreement with that goal. In the end, he returned eloquently to the theme of the American spirit:

> As I flew back this evening, I had many thoughts. In just a few days families across America will gather to celebrate Thanksgiving. And again, as our forefathers who voyaged to America, we traveled to Geneva with peace as our goal and freedom as our guide. For there can be no greater good than the quest for peace and no finer purpose than the preservation of freedom. It is 350 years since the first Thanksgiving, when Pilgrims and Indians huddled together on the edge of an unknown continent. And now here we are gathered together on the edge of an unknown future, but, like our forefathers, really not so much afraid, but full of hope and trusting in God, as ever.

In retrospect, Gorbachev's ascension in 1985 allowed Reagan to exploit the strategic weaponry of relationship building—

an iron-fisted, velvet-gloved approach. The American people knew Reagan was as tough on the Soviets as he needed to be. At the same time, the close relationship that developed between Reagan and Gorbachev was utterly authentic. By 1987, they would be calling each other "Ron" and "Mikhail." It was a study in relationship building across ideologies, both seeking a way out of the Cold War. But Reagan's patience would be sorely tested in 1986, when negotiations nearly collapsed.

CHAPTER 7

ICELAND FREEZE

Letters flew back and forth between Reagan and Gorbachev. It was their favorite way of communicating. Long, thoughtful, and sometimes deeply personal, the texts are a study of two men with the world on their shoulders grappling with the big issues. After Geneva, the communications felt more like a dialogue than an argument, written in, as Gorbachev put it, the "spirit of frankness" that had been established between them. After receiving a letter that Reagan had written by hand, using his black felt-tip pen, Gorbachev replied, "I consider your letter important and also value the form you used in writing to me."

Often the letters were lengthy, going into the details of their many areas of disagreement. But there were always reminders of their higher goals and their unique place in history. "Both of us have advisors & assistants," Reagan wrote, "but, you know, in the final analysis, the responsibility to preserve peace & increase cooperation is ours. Our people look to us for leadership, and nobody can provide it if we don't."

Gorbachev agreed that in Geneva they had achieved an unexpected milestone, writing "I attach special significance to the fact that we have been able to overcome the serious psychological barrier which for a long time has hindered a dialogue worthy of the leaders of the USSR and the USA. I have the feeling that now you and I can set formalities aside and can get down to the heart of the matter."

Reagan, accustomed to the biting boilerplate letters of previous leaders, was moved by Gorbachev's expressed interest in getting to "the heart of the matter." He had come away from Geneva appreciating that Gorbachev was a real person, not a ventriloquist's dummy—someone he could speak frankly with. And despite his reluctance, Gorbachev found himself liking Reagan.

The year 1986 began with a remarkable display of unity—an exchange of televised New Year's messages to their respective populations. When Gorbachev's face appeared on their television screens, Americans saw with their own eyes a Soviet leader who seemed to be putting aside the old grievances. They liked his demeanor; it was unlike that of the stern and unbending Soviets of recent memory. "I see a good augury in the way we are beginning the New Year, which has been declared the Year of Peace," Gorbachev said.

We are starting it with an exchange of direct messages, President Reagan's to the Soviet people and mine to you. This, I believe, is a hopeful sign of change which, though small, is nonetheless a change for the better in our relations. The few minutes that I will be speaking to you strike me as a meaningful symbol of our mutual willingness to go on moving toward each other, which is what your president and I began doing at Geneva. For a discussion along those lines, we had the mandate of our peoples. They want the constructive Soviet-American dialog to continue uninterrupted and to yield tangible results.

Likewise, Reagan reassured the Soviet people, who were treated to his genial disposition for the first time:

> Just over a month ago, General Secretary Gorbachev and I met for the first time in Geneva. Our purpose was to begin a fresh chapter in the relations between our two countries and to try to reduce the suspicions and mistrust between us. I think we made a good beginning. Mr. Gorbachev and I spent many hours together, speaking frankly and seriously about the most important issues of our time: reducing the massive nuclear arsenals on both sides, resolving regional conflicts, ensuring respect for human rights as guaranteed under international agreements, and other questions of mutual interest. As the elected representative of the American people, I told Mr. Gorbachev of our deep desire for peace and that the American people do not wish the Soviet people any harm.

It couldn't have been a better start to the year. But in the two-steps-forward-one-step-back manner of peacemaking, 1986 would actually prove to be one of the most difficult years in the relationship between Reagan and Gorbachev, frequently calling into question the whole premise that their two nations were any closer to peace than they had been before Geneva.

In January, Gorbachev grabbed the momentum by sending out a public message calling for the elimination of nuclear weapons by the year 2000. Reagan's national security advisors were worried and suspicious. What was he up to? They suggested that it was a manipulative ploy, not backed by any real intent. They thought that Reagan should reject it outright. But Reagan didn't want to do that. He wasn't going to be the one who put the kibosh on an honest proposal to end the threat of nuclear war. So he publicly stated that the proposal was at first glance constructive, although he had reservations. Thatcher was less conciliatory. She called the proposal "pie in the sky."

One clear subtext of Gorbachev's proposal was his desire to see SDI ended. If there were no more nuclear weapons, why would the United States need a massive nuclear defense system? More than any other sticking point, SDI was the one that gave Gorbachev the most agita. Despite Reagan's many assurances that it was a defensive system, not an offensive one, in spite of Reagan's offer to share US technology with the Soviets, Gorbachev remained unpersuaded. Perhaps he was concerned that any furtherance of American scientific prowess would not be good for the Soviets. But Reagan felt that SDI was essential as a hedge against cheating—or, for that matter, against other nations that might develop missile programs.

A deeper motivation was to keep the Soviets engaged in an expensive quest. "I think President Reagan saw SDI as being yet another pressure on the Soviets, as something that they could not withstand, and I think he was right," James Baker reflected in 1998. "Whether it would work or not, it was a heck of a challenge to the Soviet Empire, which was having a very difficult time competing economically and otherwise."

If there seemed to be little progress on Soviet-American relations early in the year, it could be understood in the context of Gorbachev's larger position. Less than a year in office, he might have been a new thinker, personally committed to a transformation of Soviet society and an end to the arms race. But he also had one foot in the old order. He could not get away with wholesale change. And he could not ever allow the United States to seem to have the upper hand in the propaganda war.

The Soviets continued to be spooked by the United States'

potential space prowess, even as the United States was grieving a catastrophic space disaster. The mission of the space shuttle *Challenger* had captured the public imagination, thanks in large part to the presence on board of a civilian, New Hampshire teacher Christa McAuliffe, who had joined six astronauts as part of NASA's Teacher in Space program. McAuliffe made the event of the launch special to schoolchildren all over the country; millions of them gathered in classrooms and auditoriums on January 28 to watch the takeoff. The inspiring, hopeful moment turned into a nightmare as they watched the *Challenger* explode.

When Pat Buchanan, then the director of communications, burst into the Oval Office to cry, "The *Challenger* has exploded," Reagan was stunned. He rushed to his study, where he watched the replay, over and over again, on his TV. He was brokenhearted by the loss of life. "There is no way to describe our shock & horror," he wrote in his diary.

He'd been scheduled to deliver the State of the Union address that night, and he scrapped it in favor of an address to the nation at 5:00 P.M. about the disaster. He summoned speechwriter Peggy Noonan to work on his brief remarks, and she instinctively grasped the necessary tone: heartache salved by a glorious optimism that was totally authentic to Reagan's nature. Many would say that giving that address was among Reagan's finest moments as president.

Haunted by the image of millions of schoolchildren who had witnessed the explosion, he spoke directly to them:

And I want to say something to the schoolchildren of America who were watching the live coverage of the shuttle's takeoff. I know it is hard to understand, but sometimes painful things like this happen. It's all part of the process of exploration and discovery. It's all part of taking a chance and expanding man's horizons. The future doesn't belong to the fainthearted; it belongs to the brave. The Challenger crew was pulling us into the future, and we'll continue to follow them.

But the most memorable lines, both poignant and poetic, came at the end of the speech:

The crew of the space shuttle Challenger honored us by the manner in which they lived their lives. We will never forget them, nor the last time we saw them, this morning, as they prepared for their journey and waved goodbye and "slipped the surly bonds of earth" to "touch the face of God."

That lasting image was from a poem by John Gillespie Magee, Jr., an American airman and poet who had died in a midair collision during World War II. Americans could find comfort in the words, in the reminder of Earth's temporal nature, and the higher aims that transcend one life or a single endeavor. The space program, Reagan promised, would go on.

But grief was a momentary emotion in light of the urgent pressures on the world stage. Rogue regimes, with terrorist impulses, were becoming bolder. It had long been Reagan's belief that the Soviet Union was supporting terrorist activities in the Middle East, and that was particularly true in Libya under the violent dictatorship of Muammar Gaddafi—whom Reagan referred to as "that crackpot in Tripoli." The bombing of a West Berlin discotheque in March, killing an American soldier and a Turkish woman and wounding hundreds of others, was tied to Gaddafi, and Reagan was warned by intelligence experts that more acts of terrorism could be expected. In a press conference after the attack, Reagan was asked why Gaddafi would target the West. "Well, we know that this mad dog of the Middle East has a goal of a world revolution, Muslim fundamentalist revolution, which is targeted on many of his own Arab compatriots," he replied. "And where we figure in that, I don't know. Maybe we're just the enemy because—it's a little like climbing Mount Everest—because we're here."

Even as Gaddafi rained terror on the region and backed terrorist acts in Europe, Gorbachev continued to support Libya's defense industry. That baffled and disturbed Reagan, who wrote to Gorbachev, "What are we to make of your sharply increased military support of a local dictator who has declared a war of terrorism against much of the rest of the world and against the United States in particular? How can one take Soviet declarations of opposition to terrorism seriously when confronted with such action?"

Reagan decided to send Gaddafi a message in a manner the terrorist dictator would understand. On April 14, US bombers attacked Gaddafi's headquarters, terrorist facilities, and military assets. Reagan felt justified, but the Soviets were angered that the Americans had struck one of their closest Arab allies. From the Kremlin came an official statement that the attack had been an "aggressive criminal action." An important meeting between Shultz and Shevardnadze to begin organizing a Reagan-Gorbachev summit in Washington, DC, was abruptly canceled.

Images of the warm hand-holding across borders only months earlier receded into memory. Reagan could not resist poking at his adversary. At the White House Correspondents Dinner on April 17, he joked, "This is also the night of the Kremlin Correspondents Dinner in Moscow. That's when the members of the Soviet media gather to laugh at Gorbachev's jokes—or else."

Then a new crisis occurred—this time in the Soviet Union. When the nuclear power plant in Chernobyl in the Ukrainian Soviet Socialist Republic exploded on April 26, Reagan immediately reached out, offering support. "The offer was rejected," wrote Jack Matlock, Reagan's invaluable national security advisor on Soviet affairs. "Moscow said everything was under control and they were quite capable of dealing with whatever emergency might exist. The tone was actually accusatory, as if, in offering to help, we had insulted them." Reagan had told his people to resist criticizing the Soviets, but Gorbachev thought the Americans were engaged in a propaganda campaign to make the Soviet Union look bad. "They launched an unrestrained anti-Soviet campaign," Gorbachev complained of the Americans. "It is difficult to imagine what was said and written these days—'thousands of casualties,' 'mass graves of the dead,' 'desolate Kiev,' that 'the entire land of the Ukraine has been poisoned,' and so on and so forth." A war of words, as the temperature began to creep back up.

At the same time, according to Grachev, Chernobyl had a deep effect on Gorbachev's view of the nuclear race, becoming for him what Grachev dubbed "his personal Cuban missile crisis." Grachev wrote, "Before 26 April his intention to propose a curb on the arms race along with a radical reduction of nuclear weapons was mostly based on economic and security concerns, while after Chernobyl his attitude towards nuclear weapons transformed into a psychological aversion, a moral rejection (bringing him in this respect closer to Reagan)."

"Look at the Chernobyl catastrophe," Gorbachev said in a speech before the Politburo. "Just a puff and we can all feel what nuclear war would be like."

Yet as spring faded into summer with no date set for a summit or any agreement on the issues that divided them, it began to seem to the demoralized US national security team that the opportunity for a new beginning had slipped through their fingers. History provided discouraging precedents. Had not Eisenhower and Khrushchev walked a path to understanding before the two countries' relationship collapsed after a US U-2 spy plane was shot down over Soviet airspace? Had not Nixon and Brezhnev held Moscow and Washington summits that had produced the SALT I treaty, only to have progress stalled? Had not even Ford and Carter fully engaged in détente, which, despite its flaws, had at least brought the vying nations to the same table? And where had it led? To decade after decade of disappointment. When the light had broken through during the Geneva summit, it had finally seemed that we were on the right track. Now Reagan was left to wonder, as his predecessors had, if the bedrock of the two countries' disagreements was too solid to be broken with the tools of diplomacy.

With relations already frayed, the fate of two men further complicated the chance for peace. On August 23, the United States arrested Gennady Zakharov, an official at the UN Secretariat, as a spy. Zakharov had been caught in the act of paying an employee of a defense contractor to spy for the Soviets, not knowing that the "spy" was working undercover for the FBI. A week later, the KGB arrested Nicholas Daniloff, an American journalist, in Moscow, accusing him of espionage.

Gorbachev ignored Reagan's assurances that Daniloff was not a spy, which made Reagan "mad as h—l." Was his word not good enough? Or did it not matter? He doubted that the Soviets really believed Daniloff was engaged in espionage. As far as Reagan was concerned, it was pretty obvious what was going on: the Americans arrested a spy, and the Soviets randomly grabbed an American and accused him of spying. The setup was on for a prisoner exchange. The Soviets wanted their man back, and Daniloff was a hostage.

In the midst of those crises and impasses, the progress assumed at Geneva was stagnating. And Gorbachev continued to stubbornly resist setting a date for the promised summit in Washington, DC.

Then, on September 15, Shevardnadze, on a visit to Washington, delivered a surprising letter to Reagan from Gorbachev. The Soviet leader wrote that he was disturbed that their relationship seemed to be faltering, that proposals remained unexplored, and that "in almost a year since Geneva there has been no movement on these issues." Something would have to happen to shake things loose. He wrote, "That is why an idea has come to my mind to suggest to you, Mr. President, that in the very near future and setting aside all other matters, we have a quick one-on-one meeting, let us say in Iceland or London, maybe just for one day, to engage in a strictly confidential private and frank conversation possibly with only our foreign ministers present."

Gorbachev seemed sincere in his desire to break the ice once again. "I could see we were just going around in circles," he told Grachev many years later, when they discussed his state of mind at the time. "That might suit them [the United States] but not us. At the same time, I understood that we were the only ones who could change gear and speed up the process."

Reagan was willing, with a caveat. "I opted for Iceland," he wrote in his diary. "This would be preparatory to a Summit. I'm agreeable to that but made it plain we wanted Daniloff returned to us before anything took place. I let the F.M. [foreign minister] know I was angry and that I resented their charges that Daniloff was a spy after I had personally given my word that he wasn't. I gave him a little run down on the difference between our two systems and told him they couldn't understand the importance we place on the individual because they don't have any such feeling. I enjoyed being angry."

Reagan was firm: no plans for an Iceland meeting would be announced until Daniloff was released.

When Shevardnadze informed Gorbachev that Reagan had agreed to the meeting pending the release of Daniloff, Gorbachev replied, "They will get Daniloff," but then he added that the Soviet government must stand firm so as not to lose face. He wanted to play it out, see how far the United States would go. In the end, the exchange was made—Daniloff for Zakharov. Reagan received some backlash at home for appearing to cave in to the Soviets, but for him the stakes were much higher than the fate of one spy.

With a meeting in Reykjavík, Iceland, scheduled to begin on October 11, both sides went into action to carve out their strategies. Earlier that year, Gorbachev had made a key appointment that would prove to be valuable to the process: Anatoly Chernyaev, a World War II veteran and senior analyst with the Central Committee, as his foreign policy advisor. Chernyaev shared Gorbachev's fondest hopes for perestroika; indeed, the day Gorbachev became general secretary, Chernyaev wrote in his journal, "A new era has begun." He had his work cut out for him.

In Moscow, Chernyaev met with Gorbachev to outline an approach. He told him, "In order to move Reagan, we have to give him something. Something with pressure and breakthrough potential has to be done. We have to decide for ourselves what is realistic, in what the USA is bluffing and what they are ready to do, what we can get out of them right now."

The Soviets seemed willing to go far beyond any previous agreements to further the goal of complete nuclear disarmament. But clearly they were concerned about what they viewed as Reagan's new "space weapons." Trying out his approach, Gorbachev said to Chernyaev, "As far as the SDI is concerned . . . I will look him [Reagan] in the eye as I say this. If you do not meet us halfway, well, then, my conscience will be clear before you and before myself. Now I have to explain to my people and to the whole world why nothing worked out between us. I regret very much that we wasted the time."

At the same time, Gorbachev said that the Soviets "should concentrate all our resources on the development of our own anti-SDI"—showing just how concerned he really was. A defense system to combat a defense system—it made no sense unless you believed, as Gorbachev surely did, that SDI was a wolf in sheep's clothing.

In Washington, Shultz warned the president that Gorbachev was likely to arrive with a set of proposals and the United States should be prepared with its own positions. He thought Reagan had the upper hand. "The American people are all for it [the meeting], so we should not seem to be playing it down or disparaging the chance for solid progress," he wrote in a classified memo to Reagan. The meeting didn't have to have big results to be viewed as successful, but two areas, arms control and human rights, needed to be at the forefront of the US plan. "Gorbachev must go home with a clear sense that Moscow's continuing insensitivity to the humanitarian dimension of the relationship will assume greater significance as prospects open up in areas of mutual concern."

Shultz was not above a little ego polishing: "The policies you set in motion six years ago have put us in the strong position we are in today. . . . We are now entering the crucial phase in the effort to achieve real reductions in the nuclear forces—an historic achievement in itself, and a major step toward your vision of a safer world for the future."

In an intriguing addendum to the summit plans, Richard Solomon, the director of policy planning for the State Department, sent Reagan a memo, marked "Classified" and "SUPER SENSITIVE." In it he detailed the differences in Reagan's and Gorbachev's operating styles that would give Reagan an advantage in negotiations.

GORBACHEV	REAGAN
—highly provocative; and, at times, willing to publicly embarrass political opponents, especially subordinates	—non-provocative; even-tempered
—high political risk-taker	—high political risk-taker
—demanding of his subordinates; requires immediate and detailed responses to significant operational questions	—not demanding of his subordinates; delegates authority and decisions to appropriate individuals
—seeks confrontation	—avoids confrontation
—when he doesn't feel in control of a situation he becomes anxious, forceful, and demanding	—strong self-discipline; rarely appears anxious, flustered, or out of control
—depends very heavily on detailed information to negotiate a subject	—prefers to familiarize himself with general points and leaves the detailed work to subordinates
—an experienced and effective apparatchik who tries to emulate Reagan's polished political style	—seasoned politician
—limited exposure to world media	—highly experienced media personality
—highly reasoned and logical in his approach to arguments	—intuitive and conceptual in his approach to arguments
—good sense of humor	—good sense of humor
—highly charismatic	—highly charismatic

"Despite the contrasting personal styles of the two leaders, Gorbachev and Reagan should be able to work well together because of the complementary nature of their respective operational approaches," Solomon wrote. However, he cautioned that Gorbachev needed a concrete win from the summit, and if it didn't look as though he were getting one, he would pursue it aggressively so he could show the folks back home that he was tough. "Reagan is a far more comfortable, self-assured leader who has very little to prove to the world or himself without compromising his need for a political legacy."

The difficulty of managing strategies and expectations was the impromptu nature of the summit and its undefined goals. Gorbachev had originally proposed it to break the impasse that had set in over the year. Technically, it wasn't even a summit, virtually without the protocols that normally surrounded those high-level meetings; just a face-to-face between two men at the end of the world.

REYKJAVÍK, ICELAND, WAS REMOTE and chilly in October, the sun fighting to peek through before each new burst of driving rain. Darkness fell earlier each day, moving toward the winter gloom when there would be only about five hours of light. The scene was desolate and vaguely ominous, "something out of an Agatha Christie novel," Adelman said. The meeting site was Höfði House, a stark, whitewashed estate overlooking the waterfront. It had an eerie aura and was rumored to be home to a ghost, whose frequent outbursts had disturbed its British owners so much that they had sold the place in 1952. There Reagan and Gorbachev would be confronting their own ghosts from the past.

"If observers sometimes regard the everyday practice of diplomacy as cold and bloodless," Shultz wrote in his memoir, "no one could possibly miss the drama of a summit. There the decision makers face each other. No safety screen stands between the issues and the highest authorities. But what produces drama can also lead to problems and risks."

The Reykjavík meeting would be different from any other summit. There would be no ceremonies or elaborate dinners, and the media would be held at a remove. Only Shultz and Shevardnadze would be at the table with the principals. That suited Reagan just fine. He always felt at his best in eyeball-to-eyeball settings, where he could exert his personal power and persuasiveness. He wasn't even bothered, though his aides were, by how quickly the meeting had come together. He knew his position.

On the first day, Reagan and Gorbachev met alone for a half hour before inviting Shultz and Shevardnadze into the room. Gorbachev told the president he wanted to focus on Soviet proposals for disarmament.

Reagan replied, "There is a Russian saying: *doveryai no proveryai*—trust but verify. How will we know that you'll get rid of your missiles as you say you will?" That was the central question, the one that would resonate throughout those talks and beyond: How could they trust each other? When the others joined them, Shultz was struck by the differences in the two men's demeanors. As Solomon had accurately analyzed, Gorbachev was strong and forceful, attempting from the start to take control of the agenda. Reagan was relaxed and easygoing. "He could well afford to be," Shultz wrote, "since Gorbachev's proposals all moved toward U.S. positions in significant ways."

Gorbachev seemed to agree with Reagan on a goal to eliminate all ballistic missiles over the coming decade, but SDI continued to be a point of contention. He insisted that the program be shelved as part of the agreement.

Reagan replied, "I've given you the ten-year period you wanted, and, with no ballistic missiles, you cannot fear a first strike or any harm from SDI. We should be free to develop and test during the ten years and to deploy at the end. Who knows when the world will see another Hitler. We need to be able to defend ourselves." It was obvious to him. First, SDI was not, to reiterate the point, an offensive system, despite Gorbachev's suspicions. Second, the United States had an obligation to develop scientific means to protect itself, not only against the Soviet Union but against other bad actors in the world that might pose a threat.

The debate led to one of the most intriguing back-and-forths at the meeting, recounted by Shultz, who was in the room:

Reagan: If we both eliminate nuclear weapons, why would there be a concern if one side wants to build defensive systems just in case? Are you considering starting up again with weapons after ten years? I have a different picture. I have a picture that after ten years you and I come to Iceland and bring the last two missiles in the world and we have the biggest damn party in celebration of it!

Gorbachev: Mr. President, we are close to a mutually acceptable formula. Don't think we have evil designs. We don't.

Reagan [persisting]: A meeting in Iceland in ten years: I'll be so old you won't recognize me. I'll say, "Mikhail?" You'll say, "Ron?" And we'll destroy the last two.

Gorbachev: I may not be living after these next ten.

Reagan: I'll count on it.

Gorbachev: Now you can go smoothly to age 100. You have already passed through the danger period. I'm just entering it. Beyond that, I'll have the burden of having gone through all these meetings with a president who doesn't like concessions. He wants to be a winner. We must both be winners.

Reagan: I can't live to 100 worrying that you'll shoot one of those missiles at me. Fifty percent. We both got it. You told your people ten years and you got it. I told my people I wouldn't give up SDI; so I have to go home saying I haven't. Our people would cheer if we got rid of the missiles.

Perhaps because the sparring seemed so amiable, Reagan didn't fully appreciate that Gorbachev was drawing a line in the sand. Setting aside their dispute, they continued to talk, and in the next day and a half they achieved unprecedented agreements on the ten-year program to reduce missiles on a tight schedule "so that by the end of 1996, all offensive ballistic missiles of the USSR and the United States will have been totally eliminated."

Reagan was beginning to let a sense of elation come over him. It was finally happening, a real agreement to end the arms race. Sitting across from America's greatest foe, he could glimpse the fulfillment of his long-held dream.

Then Gorbachev smiled. "This all depends, of course, on you giving up SDI," he said.

Reagan's elation turned to rage. He couldn't believe that with all they'd accomplished, Gorbachev would throw it away. He felt blindsided as Gorbachev assured him that he meant it. He was deadly serious. Agonizing, Reagan experienced a rare moment of self-doubt. He scribbled a note to Shultz: "Am I wrong?"

Shultz whispered, "No, you are right."

That was it, then. Silence fell over the room as Reagan and Gorbachev pushed back their chairs and rose to their feet. They walked out of Höfði House into an early darkness shot through with light from a phalanx of press cameras. Their faces told the story.

"I'd just never seen Ronald Reagan that way before," Kuhn said, "—had never seen him with such a look. I mean, he looked distraught to me, very upset, extremely, very taken aback, upset, borderline distraught. Gorbachev was kind of like, *So be it.* You could tell, just to me you could tell who really wanted this more than the other one. It was like Gorbachev thought, *Well, we can live with the world the way it is.* Reagan wanted to end that and wasn't able to pull that off there."

It must have seemed like madness that the Soviets would halt progress on real disarmament plans based on the speculative, unrealized, and probably unlikely prospect of the Americans creating a strategic defense system. And from the Soviet perspective, Reagan's stubbornness seemed equally mad. Why would he not accept a gift in hand in exchange for a moratorium on his pursuit of a defense system? What was going on here? They'd been so close. Shevardnadze speculated that perhaps "the two leaders just could not handle the ball that they had thrown too high."

At the bottom of the stairs Reagan and Gorbachev turned to say good-bye, cameras capturing their grim faces.

"I still feel we can find a deal," Reagan said.

"I don't think you want a deal," Gorbachev said. "I don't know what more I could have done."

Reagan fought back his anger. "You could have said yes."

Gorbachev turned away, and there was a moment of uncertainty among Reagan's staff. What now? There had been earlier plans to visit the embassy and greet the staff there, as well as a trip to Keflavik Naval Air Station, where there were five thousand navy and air force personnel. But Kuhn wondered if the president still had the heart for it or if he'd want to board the plane and just go home.

He approached Reagan. "Mr. President," he said deferentially, "I know you've got a tremendous amount on your mind, but we don't know what you want to do now. We don't know where you want to go . . . here are your options. You're scheduled to go to the embassy, greet staff, speak to the Navy and Air Force personnel at Keflavik, get on the plane and go. You could just go to the plane and go, you could go right out to Keflavik, speak to the troops, which I think is very important. We can have the embassy staff go out there and you could greet them out there. We could work around it, we could make this adjustment, but you've got to tell us what you want to do." By the end, Kuhn was practically pleading.

Reagan stared at him thoughtfully for a long moment, and then said quietly, "Why don't we just stay with the schedule and do what we're supposed to do."

But it was not an easy task. "We got back to the embassy, we were outside, it was warm, and we were going to greet everybody outside," Kuhn said. "He's just standing there, just looking with this forlorn look on his face. Everybody stayed away from him. They knew. Everybody could tell he was very upset." By the time they reached the air base, Reagan had recovered somewhat, and the event went well, although Shultz, stung by the abrupt end of the negotiations, told reporters that the meeting had been a failure. Boarding the plane back to Washington, everyone held back, wanting to leave the president alone with his thoughts. But halfway across the ocean, he emerged, smiling. "I'm okay now. I gave it a lot of thought. I know I made the right decision back there. We couldn't give up SDI, not for America's future. I made the right decision. I wasn't sure, but I know now I did."

He was furious, though, angrier than he'd ever been. The two days in Reykjavík seemed to have destroyed all hope of disarmament, at least for the time being. "He [Gorbachev] tried to act jovial but I was mad and I showed it," he wrote in his diary. "Well, the ball is now in his court and I'm convinced he'll come around when he sees how the world is reacting."

He didn't yet know of the very different spin Gorbachev had put on the meeting. After Reagan drove away from Höfði House, Gorbachev remained behind to give a press conference to more than a thousand waiting reporters. As he walked back, his mind was in turmoil. He wrote in his memoir, "My first, overwhelming intention had been to blow the unyielding American position to smithereens, carrying out the plan we had decided in Moscow: if the Americans rejected the agreement, a compromise in the name of peace, we would denounce the U.S. administration and its dangerous policies as a threat to everyone throughout the world."

But then a realization hit him: "Had we not reached an agreement on both strategic and intermediate-range missiles, was it not an entirely new situation, and should it be sacrificed for a momentary propaganda advantage?" By the time he reached the waiting reporters, he had made up his mind. He stepped up and told the media, "In spite of its drama, Reykjavik is not a failure—it is a breakthrough, which allowed us for the first time to look over the horizon."

Back in Washington, Shultz was coming around to a similar point of view.

Sensing Reagan's discouragement, he sought to reassure him, reminding him that Christopher Columbus had initially been considered a failure because he had landed on only a couple of islands and hadn't brought back any gold to Spain. But after a while people realized that he had come upon a new world. "In a way, you found a new world," Shultz told him, noting that he had "smoked the Soviets out and they are stuck with their concessions."

CHAPTER 8

"TEAR DOWN THIS WALL!"

February 1987

Howard Baker was at the zoo in Miami with his six-year-old grandson, so his wife, Joy, took the call from President Reagan.

"Joy, where is Howard?" he asked.

"Mr. President, Howard's at the zoo."

He chuckled. "Wait until he sees the zoo I have in mind for him."

Two years out of the Senate, where he had been majority leader, the sixty-one-year-old Baker hadn't yet settled on a new role for himself. Returning to Washington certainly hadn't been in his plan, but when Reagan asked him to be his chief of staff, he couldn't refuse. It was a changing of the guard that had been a long time coming.

In early 1987, Don Regan was on the ropes, and relations had deteriorated such that the president had had no choice but to ask for his resignation. In the months after Reykjavík, Regan had continued to alienate everyone with his imperious grip on power. The thing that bothered Reagan loyalists most was the way Regan's manner was contaminating the president's optimistic, open image and damaging his relationships with members of Congress. Worse, he didn't seem to care about protecting the president, and he was recklessly burnishing his own image at the president's expense. Aides were horrified when a *New York Times* article quoted Regan saying after Reykjavík, "Some of us are like a shovel brigade that follow a parade down Main Street cleaning up."

What was he talking about? Was he saying he'd had to clean up Reagan's messes? It sure sounded like it.

Aides thought that Regan took advantage of the president's even-tempered leadership style by being a brutal enforcer behind his back, setting up a cabal of his own loyalists and cutting others off from access to Reagan. He was mean and abusive, in a way that was so different from Reagan that it left aides feeling gobsmacked.

"He chewed me out all the time," Friedersdorf said. "He hung up the telephone, slammed the receiver down when I'd give him a vote count. I was honest with him, 'I don't have the votes on that'—*bam*. So I knew right then. I've agreed to stay for a year, I'm going to do it, I'm not going to walk out. I've never walked out of any job in my life, but this administration is not going to work." Similar stories abounded, leaking out to the press, whose reporters were delighted to play up the anti–Don Regan narrative.

With two years remaining in office, Soviet relations on life support, Democrats winning both houses of Congress in the 1986 election, the growing pressure of Iran-Contra, and a physical setback from prostate surgery in January, it was the most critical period of Reagan's presidency. His grand agenda seemed to be in a holding pattern, yet the White House was a daily pressure cooker. Reagan struggled to stay above the fray and keep his spirits high and his agenda moving, but he was bruised by the daily hammering he was taking in the press over Iran-Contra. And when he learned that his own staff was in a near mutiny over Regan, he was stunned.

There was no shortage of people angling for Don Regan's ouster, but his biggest mistake may have been alienating Nancy. Some people have portrayed Nancy as having a personal grievance against him—and yes, he did once hang up the phone on her—but according to the first lady, she wasn't the only one with a problem. In fact, when staffers first started coming to Nancy with their complaints about Regan, she had repeatedly demurred, saying "What are you telling *me* for? You ought to be telling my husband." But staffers were afraid to tell Reagan, even if they could get in to see him, so Nancy got an earful. "In spite of what's been said or written, I did not mastermind a plot to get rid of Don Regan," she wrote, trying to set the record straight in her memoir. "There was no cabal. I wasn't in cahoots with anybody to bring about his downfall. By the end of 1986, half of Washington wanted him out."

Reagan was resistant—Nancy thought it was because he never saw the "other" side of his chief of staff; Regan was always jovial and complimentary around the president, a fellow Irishman who connected personally. But Nancy kept up the pressure, and other advisors soon joined her. If there was one thing Reagan couldn't abide, it was the idea that the people working for him suffered from abuse and low morale. Eventually, he came to see that Regan had to go, and he put in the call to Baker.

At the end, it was messy. Frank Carlucci, who was now national security advisor (having replaced John Poindexter, who had been forced to resign because of his role in Iran-Contra), was surprised to see a news report on CNN that Regan was out and was being replaced by Baker. Someone had prematurely leaked it to the media. He picked up the phone and called the president at the residence.

"Mr. President, this is all out on TV," he said.

"Oh, oh."

"Have you said anything to Don Regan?"

"No," admitted Reagan. "I have not."

"Let me see what I can do." Carlucci went to Regan's office and delivered the news, receiving the expected eruption. "Don Regan just exploded," Carlucci said. " 'God damn it! I've been his chief of staff, I've been loyal'—I can't remember all the things he said. I went scurrying back to my office. I told the president, 'You're going to have to call him.' "

But when Carlucci went back to Regan's office in time for the call, Regan was threatening not to take it. "For God's sake, Don," Carlucci cried. "He's the president. You've got to take the call." So he did—"Yes, Mr. President. Yes, Mr. President. Goodbye, Mr. President." He hung up the phone and scribbled a terse note: "I resign as Chief of Staff to the President of the United States."

Reagan was kinder and more gracious. In a lovely note to Regan he thanked him for his service and wished him the best. "Whether on the deck of your beloved boat or on the fairway; in the spirit of our forefathers, may the sun shine warm upon your face, the wind be always at your back and may God hold you in the hollow of his hand."

After Baker agreed to step in, he started to sweat. He'd never "managed" anything in his life—he'd only been a US senator. He called Ken Duberstein, who'd run legislative affairs early in Reagan's administration but had returned to private life. "Help," he pleaded. "Will you come back to the White House as my deputy?"

Duberstein hesitated. "Howard, if you do a White House tour once, it's an honor. If you do it a second time, you're a glutton for punishment." He wasn't eager to return. He'd just bought a new house and was making money for the first time in his life. Reagan's poll numbers were terrible. "He was viewed not simply as a lame duck with two years to go but as a virtual dead duck," Duberstein recalled. So he said no.

Two days later, while Duberstein was giving a speech, he was handed a note. Reagan's assistant, Kathy Osborne, was holding on the line. When he got to the phone, she said, "The president would like to see you at 2:00 this afternoon."

When he walked into the Oval Office, Reagan got up from behind his desk, greeted him, and said, "Howard has told me all the reasons why you can't come back. I just want you to know one thing. Nancy and I want you to come home for the last two years of the administration."

"Of course I said yes," Duberstein said. "And it was the best two years of my professional life."

Reagan's new press spokesman, Marlin Fitzwater, had been Regan's spokesman at the Treasury in the first year of the administration—happier times for Regan. Fitzwater had gone on to fill that role for Vice President Bush. It had been Regan's idea to appoint him to replace Larry Speakes at the White House early in 1987. Speakes had been the White House spokesman since James Brady was shot in the assassination attempt. Many reporters disliked Speakes, calling him a bully who would not hesitate to cut a reporter's access if he was displeased. Reporters such as Chris Wallace found themselves being told, "You're out of business." Fitzwater was a welcome relief. With his deprecating sense of humor, sharp mind, and relative openness, he had a much better relationship with the press. "I liked everybody, and I didn't have any trouble," he said. "I found it easy to work with the press if they thought I was a straight shooter and honest. It didn't seem like a very high standard to me."

An interesting note: as a sign of his abiding respect for James Brady, who had been critically injured in the assassination attempt, along with hoping that he would one day return, Reagan allowed him to retain his title of press secretary; Speakes was acting press secretary for almost six years, and when Fitzwater came on board, he told the president he was fine with that designation as well.

Fitzwater had a kinder take on Don Regan's troubles: "Regan just could not be a staff person. He spent too long in charge of Merrill Lynch and the Treasury Department. He couldn't be number two." Actually, Fitzwater almost lost his job just as he was getting started because Baker wanted to bring in his longtime press secretary, Thomas Griscom. Reagan balked—he wanted to keep Fitzwater. So Griscom became communications director.

But it was a bumpy first year for Fitzwater because he landed right in the Iran-Contra mess. In late 1986, Reagan had appointed a commission, led by former senator John Tower, along with former secretary of state Ed Muskie, and former national security advisor Brent Scowcroft, to get to the bottom of what had happened. The Tower Commission published its report on February 26. Its criticism of Regan was scathing, and perhaps it wasn't pure coincidence that Regan's ouster occurred the following day. Although the president was exonerated from having played a direct role, his lax managerial style was criticized. The report portrayed him as being distant from the center of decision making, neatly fitting into the opposition's narrative about Reagan—that he wasn't running the store.

The press was out for blood, and Reagan needed to address the matter head-on. At 9:00 P.M. on March 4, he spoke from the Oval Office, accepting full responsibility for Iran-Contra, trying to be as frank as he could be, knowing it would not be enough for some people—knowing, too, that his explanation was awkward and did not put him in the best light: "A few months ago I told the American people I did not trade arms for hostages.

My heart and my best intentions still tell me that's true, but the facts and the evidence tell me it is not." With that, the story became not what Reagan had known but why he hadn't known it. It was an embarrassing reckoning, but he was determined to be strong and reinforce a key principle that he had lived by for most of his life:

> Now, what should happen when you make a mistake is this: You take your knocks, you learn your lessons, and then you move on. That's the healthiest way to deal with a problem. This in no way diminishes the importance of the other continuing investigations, but the business of our country and our people must proceed. I've gotten this message from Republicans and Democrats in Congress, from allies around the world, and—if we're reading the signals right—even from the Soviets. And of course, I've heard the message from you, the American people. You know, by the time you reach my age, you've made plenty of mistakes. And if you've lived your life properly—so, you learn. You put things in perspective. You pull your energies together. You change. You go forward.

Reagan needed a way to regain his momentum, to show the nation that he was still the man they knew and trusted. And he needed to get back on track with the Soviets. Despite the stigma of defeat that had surrounded Reykjavík, a critical foundation had been laid on the agreements the two sides *were* willing to make, and those were substantial.

Gorbachev knew it, too. "As difficult as it is to do business with the United States, we are doomed to do it. We have no choice," he told the Politburo in February as he sought their agreement on his latest proposal: a plan to eliminate all intermediate-range missiles. This newly crafted Intermediate-Range Nuclear Forces (INF) Treaty would table the discussions at Reykjavík and allow for a fresh start. In the coming months, Shultz would shuttle back and forth, immersing himself in the effort to come to a common framework for an INF Treaty that could be the basis for the Washington summit, still unscheduled.

Like Reagan in America, Gorbachev was plagued by his own burdens, which had little to do with the peace process. His ambition was nothing less than a complete reorganization of the Soviet system. That meant implementing perestroika, easing the grip of a dominating central control in favor of a more flexible, market-driven economy; loosening Soviet control of Eastern Europe; and introducing glasnost, a policy of openness and freedom of expression. All those policies were met with savage opposition, and even those who nominally supported Gorbachev's efforts were worried that he was moving too far too fast.

By the spring, as their representatives labored on the INF Treaty, Reagan and Gorbachev had started reaching out to each other again, resuming their correspondence. On April 10, Reagan wrote Gorbachev that "it has been a long time since you and I last communicated directly," reminding him, "Together we can make the difference in the future course of world events. Let us pray that you and I can continue our dialogue so that the future will be one of peace and prosperity for both our nations and for the world."

Gorbachev responded in a similar spirit, even noting that the Soviet position on SDI had become less rigid. Unfortunately, he complained, the Americans were not being at all flexible, and that would be necessary in order to reach a final agreement.

For the time being, Reagan was relying on the diplomats to pave the way to a Washington summit. Meanwhile, he would continue to keep the dialogue with Gorbachev going. But if anyone were to accuse him of softening his stance on the Soviets, he had another act in store: in the summer he would challenge Gorbachev on the most symbolic platform of all.

REAGAN WAS STILL HAUNTED by the specter of the Berlin Wall, which he had visited almost a decade earlier. Throughout all of his conversations with Gorbachev, the wall had been a silent backdrop, a proof of the error of Communist ways. The previous year, at a news conference following the twenty-fifth anniversary of the construction of the wall, he said it was clearly an issue he wanted to raise with Gorbachev. "Isn't it strange," he mused to reporters, "that all of these situations where other people build walls to keep an enemy out, and there's only one part of the world and one philosophy where they have to build walls to keep their people in? Maybe they're going to realize that there's something wrong with that soon."

In June 1987, he had an opportunity when he was invited to visit West Berlin as one leg of a ten-day trip to Europe. The visit, which would follow an economic summit in Venice and an audience with the pope, would mark the occasion of Berlin's 750th anniversary. It was squeezed into a tight schedule, an in-and-out landing that would last only a couple of hours. Reagan proposed to use the occasion to give a speech at the Branden-burg Gate, a highly symbolic location. The gate stood in East Berlin at the wall, cut off from the West but rising above the graffiti-splattered wall. There was some debate about Reagan giving his speech there. West German officials were worried that it might seem overly provocative, might anger Gorbachev.

The West German Foreign Ministry made a direct appeal to the White House, arguing against it.

Here again was that old complicity, grounded in fear, that had kept the wall standing for more than twenty-five years. German chancellor Helmut Kohl might speak oratorically about the wall, as he did on the twenty-fifth anniversary, stating that "we will never and can never get used to this monument of inhumanity," but his criticism was muted by the desire to avoid conflict with the Soviet Union. His administration, it seemed, had learned to live with the wall. Reagan felt differently. A speech at the Brandenburg Gate was just the kind of powerful visual he loved. And the speech would be a golden opportunity to articulate on a world stage the violation of human rights that the wall represented.

Assigned to work on the speech was Peter Robinson, a young speechwriter who was a dedicated worker in the vineyard of presidential prose. He'd penned dozens of speeches for all occasions, but he didn't yet have any "major" speeches under his belt—that is, speeches that would make it into the history books. All speechwriters dream of hitting this mark, although it isn't always clear when an everyday speech might suddenly soar, as evidenced by Anthony Dolan's "Evil Empire" address. In April, Dolan, now the head of speechwriting, assigned the Brandenburg Gate speech to Robinson.

Robinson didn't know much about what the speech should contain. He'd received only the vaguest of instructions. To get a personal sense of the atmospherics, he joined an advance team visiting Berlin in April. There he found himself quickly steeped in the strange aura of freedom versus bondage. In his book about his White House service, *How Ronald Reagan Changed My Life*, he recounted his first impression of the wall in a flyover of the city: "From the air, the wall seemed less to cut one city in two than to separate two different modes of existence. On one side lay movement, color, modern architecture, crowded sidewalks, traffic. On the other lay a kind of void." The East Berlin side of the wall, he wrote, "was lined with guard posts, dog runs, and row upon row of barbed wire." He was struck by the ugliness of it.

However, when he met with John Kornblum, the top US diplomat in Berlin, he found the official attitude negative and suspicious. Kornblum lectured Robinson about the tone of the speech. He was anxious not to ruffle feathers, and most of all, he cautioned, don't say anything about the wall! He implied that the wall wasn't a big deal anymore, just a fact of life that everyone was quite accustomed to. Why draw attention to it and risk inflaming people?

But wandering around the city, Robinson found the truth to be quite different. People were upset by the wall. He heard stories of families separated for two decades, of the ominous specter of the armed soldiers planted atop the barrier every day, their orders being to "shoot to kill" anyone who attempted to cross. He heard people say that if Gorbachev were really so interested in glasnost and perestroika, he should do away with the wall. The image took root in Robinson's imagination—it was "a sudden illumination, almost a detonation," he said. He knew he'd found the core idea for his speech: an end to the wall.

When he returned to Washington, Robinson told Dolan about his idea of centering the speech around taking down the wall. Dolan liked it. They then presented it to Tom Griscom. Robinson recalled Griscom saying "The two of you thought you'd have to work real hard to keep me from saying no. But when you told me about the trip, particularly this point of learning from some Germans just how much they hate the wall,

I thought to myself, 'You know, calling for the wall to be torn down—it just might work.'"

Robinson set to work on drafts, fighting a resistant NSC and State Department, which showered him with edits. Finally, a draft was ready to show the president.

Dolan was enthusiastic about the direction of the speech, but before it was circulated, he told Robinson he had to attend a meeting in the Oval Office. He hoped to get a chance to ask Reagan for input on the speech. At the end of the meeting he managed to pop the question. "Mr. President, it's still very early but we were just wondering if you had any thoughts at all yet on the Berlin speech."

In a piece for the *Wall Street Journal* titled "Four Little Words," Dolan described what happened next. "Pausing for only a moment, Reagan slipped into his imitation of impressionist Rich Little doing his imitation of Ronald Reagan—he made the well-known nod of the head, said the equally familiar 'well,' and then added in his soft but resonant intonation while lifting his hand and letting it fall: 'Tear down the wall.'"

Dolan was elated. Back in his office he summoned Robinson. "Can you believe it? He said just what you were thinking. He said it himself."

"So, it was the president's line now," Dolan wrote.

Baker, who had been doubtful about the phrase, which he thought might sound unpresidential, gave in when he realized that it had come from Reagan. Baker said:

Those were Reagan's words, as it turns out. He did that. Those were what we called yellow pad words. He really worked his yellow pad. Did you ever see a presidential yellow pad? It looks just like a regular yellow pad but it has secret watermarks on it. If you hold it up the right way you can see those identifying marks in there. The reason is obvious. Yellow pads are everywhere and the President was using yellow pads, but we needed to be able to tell—was this, sure enough, Ronald Reagan's yellow pad? That's why I called them yellow pad words. If they were written down on Ronald Reagan's yellow pad, we used them.

Richard Allen, who had been with Reagan on his first trip to the wall, remembered that when they were in Berlin, Reagan had said to him, "You know, Dick, we've got to find a way to knock this thing down." So when, nine years later, Reagan gave the speech, Allen recognized Reagan's voice.

However, it's an old custom for great presidential speeches to be subject to debates over authorship. Frederick Ryan, a White House aide to Reagan who later became the publisher of the *Washington Post*, said, "It's funny; there are probably a hundred people out there who have told me that they're the ones who wrote 'tear down this wall.' " That's an exaggeration, but it makes the point. And as Eisenhower speechwriter Malcolm Moos once put it, "When the President of the United States delivers a talk, we've got to assume it's his speech, and we're carpenters but not architects."

As the speech draft began to take shape and make the rounds of the State Department and NSC, the speechwriters encountered fierce resistance. To further complicate matters, Kornblum had sent his own draft of a speech, which was predictably designed to avoid all controversy or direct accusation: "One day, this ugly wall will disappear." The US Embassy in Bonn thought the speech was far too confrontational. Perhaps the Germans were intimidated by Gorbachev; they feared upsetting him. But the situation was complicated. Many West Germans had come to admire Gorbachev as a man of peace, while Reagan still had the reputation of being a warmonger.

The NSC's Peter Rodman, the point man for the speech, challenged the ensuing drafts vigorously. Here we go again, thought Dolan as Rodman returned with yet more changes, trying to tone down the president.

Rodman enlisted Deputy National Security Advisor Colin Powell (soon to become national security advisor when Frank Carlucci replaced Caspar Weinberger at Defense) in the debate; he, too, took issue with key passages and wrote that he was "uneasy at the negative undertone near the end." In one late memo to Powell, Rodman wrote, "The Brandenburg gate speech is better than before, but the staff is still unanimous that it's a mediocre speech and a missed opportunity."

Right up to the day of the speech, the NSC and State Department were submitting corrections. Mostly, they wanted Reagan to ditch "the line." But driving to the Berlin Wall with Duberstein, Reagan was serene. He smiled at Duberstein. "The boys at State are going to kill me," he said, "but it's the right thing to do."

The diplomatic handwringers had their say, but Reagan's was the final verdict. Those who cringed at Reagan-being-Reagan didn't understand the strength of his convictions. He would give the speech he believed in and let the world respond as it would.

Standing before the Brandenburg Gate, whose base was cruelly blocked from view by the wall, Reagan was deeply affected by the scene. Recalling the debate about where to hold the speech, he could feel in his bones that this was the only location that fit. The podium from which he would speak was set on a dais draped in black, red, and gold bunting, the colors of the West German flag. His aides had told him that East Berliners would be able to hear his speech across the wall, although police in East Berlin did their best to block off the area near the wall and push back the crowds. Learning that the police were push-

"For such a little bit of a fat Dutchman, he makes a hell of a lot of noise, doesn't he?" Reagan's father, Jack, said, thus giving him a nickname—Dutch—that would stick. *Courtesy of the Ronald Reagan Foundation.*

Jack and Nelle Reagan taught Reagan and his brother, Moon, the simple heartland values that transcended poverty and struggle. Christmases were hardscrabble, homemade affairs, but Reagan cherished those memories all his life. *Courtesy of the Reagan Library.*

Reagan loved to talk about his years as a lifeguard in Dixon, and tell stories about the people he saved. As president, he once said it was the best job he ever had. *Courtesy of the Reagan Library.*

In 1947, as president of the Screen Actors Guild, Reagan was called to testify before the House Un-American Activities Committee. He hated communism, but expressed concern that innocent people were being denied their constitutional rights and wrongly blacklisted. And unlike some others in Hollywood, he refused to name names at the hearing. *Courtesy of the Reagan Library.*

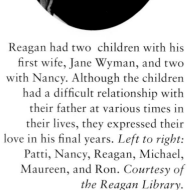

Nelle was a constant inspiration and a positive role model for her son. She taught him he could be anything he set out to be. *Courtesy of the Reagan Library.*

Reagan had two children with his first wife, Jane Wyman, and two with Nancy. Although the children had a difficult relationship with their father at various times in their lives, they expressed their love in his final years. *Left to right:* Patti, Nancy, Reagan, Michael, Maureen, and Ron. *Courtesy of the Reagan Library.*

Nancy was the love of his life, his most trusted friend and advisor, the one who never let him down. He often spoke about how much he needed her by his side. Away from her on the road, he wrote, "I'm all hollow without you." *Courtesy of the Reagan Library.*

Although he often told people, "I'm an actor, not a politician," his election in 1966 as governor of California launched the most important journey of his life. *Courtesy of the Reagan Library.*

In 1980, Reagan represented a new spirit of optimism—a remedy for the sense of malaise the nation was experiencing. His was a revolution of ideas and style. He was swept into office in a landslide, with 489 electoral votes. *Courtesy of the Reagan Library.*

On Inauguration Day, January 20, 1981, Reagan told the American people, "We will again be the exemplar of freedom and a beacon of hope for those who do not now have freedom." *Courtesy of the Reagan Library.*

Three men defined the management style of the early Reagan White House. The troika (*left to right*): James Baker, chief of staff; Ed Meese, counselor to the president; and Mike Deaver, deputy chief of staff. *Courtesy of the Reagan Library.*

Reagan and Speaker Tip O'Neill developed a warm personal relationship, based on their Irish roots and complementary personalities, but it did not extend to legislative matters, where they were fierce combatants. *Courtesy of the Reagan Library.*

Reagan was a prolific writer, always penning his thoughts and speech notes on the familiar yellow lined pad. *Courtesy of the Reagan Library.*

Just five months after almost losing his life in an assassination attempt, Reagan looked remarkably fit as he cleared the brush at his beloved California ranch, Rancho del Cielo. *Courtesy of the Reagan Library.*

Addressing the British parliament in 1982, Reagan announced that the Soviet Union was destined for "the ash heap of history." *Courtesy of the Reagan Library.*

Reagan's speech before the National Association of Evangelicals on March 8, 1983, was not expected to get much press, but when he declared the Soviet Union an "evil empire," the world took note. *Courtesy of the Reagan Library.*

Reagan's closest partner on the world stage was the Iron Lady, Prime Minister Margaret Thatcher. They didn't always agree, but they were united in their determination to rid the world of communism. Here Reagan welcomes Thatcher to Camp David on December 28, 1984. *Courtesy of the Reagan Library.*

Reagan and Gorbachev met for the first time on November 19, 1985 in Geneva. Separated by a chasm of ideology and history, they could not have imagined how far they would travel together. *Courtesy of the Reagan Library.*

Their faces tell the story. Reagan and Gorbachev left the Reykjavík Summit in 1986 angry and disappointed by their failure to reach an agreement. Some people worried they would never meet again, but they were able to rise above their conflicts and continue their negotiations. *Courtesy of the Reagan Library.*

When Reagan stood before the Brandenburg Gate and cried, "Mr. Gorbachev, tear down this wall!" his words were a call to action that rattled the world order. Less than two and a half years later, the wall fell. *Courtesy of the Reagan Library.*

Standing with Mikhail Gorbachev in Red Square, Reagan declared that the "evil empire" was a thing of the past. He recognized before many others that the Soviet Union was dying under the weight of its ideology. *Courtesy of the Reagan Library.*

At the Moscow Summit, the Reagans wanted to meet ordinary people. On a spontaneous walk in the Arbat, they jumped onto a cart and eagerly threw themselves into the moment. *Courtesy of the Reagan Library.*

Reagan's aides were initially worried about the president giving a speech under the glowering visage of Lenin, but it was Reagan who seemed larger than life on the Moscow State University stage as he spoke of the promise of democracy. *Courtesy of the Reagan Library.*

Reagan's final meeting with Gorbachev as president, joined by president-elect George H. W. Bush, occurred on Governors Island, a fitting site, with the Statue of Liberty in the background. *Courtesy of the Reagan Library.*

It was an emotional farewell on January 20, 1989, as the Reagans prepared to fly home to California. "We weren't just marking time; we made a difference," Reagan told the nation in his farewell address. *Courtesy of the Reagan Library.*

"Visitors to this mountaintop will see a great jagged chunk of the Berlin Wall," Reagan announced at his library dedication in 1991. Over nine feet tall, marked with colorful graffiti, the piece is a relic of a conquered state and a reminder of the lasting possibility of freedom. Here Reagan poses with Polish president Lech Wał sa. *Courtesy of the Ronald Reagan Foundation.*

Reagan was intimately involved in his speeches. He loved the writing and editing process, and he was always in control of his message. Reviewing the transcripts at the Reagan Library, the author recognized the frequent scrawl of his Sharpie pen. *Photo by Mark Laing.*

Visitors to the Reagan Library have an irresistible impulse to grasp the well-worn bronze hand of the statue at the entrance— as did this author. *Photo by Mark Laing.*

The author is inspired by Reagan's burial site on the grounds of the Ronald Reagan Presidential Library and Museum. The inscription, which Reagan chose himself, is the signature of his character: "I know in my heart that man is good, that what is right will always eventually triumph and there is purpose and worth to each and every life." *Photo by Mark Laing.*

ing people back made Reagan angry enough to speak louder so he could be heard over the barrier that divided them. Painting a vivid picture of the global meaning of the wall, he said:

Behind me stands a wall that encircles the free sectors of this city, part of a vast system of barriers that divides the entire continent of Europe. From the Baltic, south, those barriers cut across Germany in a gash of barbed wire, concrete, dog runs, and guard towers. Farther south, there may be no visible, no obvious wall. But there remain armed guards and checkpoints all the same—still a restriction on the right to travel, still an instrument to impose upon ordinary men and women the will of a totalitarian state. Yet it is here in Berlin where the wall emerges most clearly; here, cutting across your city, where the news photo and the television screen have imprinted this brutal division of a continent upon the mind of the world. Standing before the Brandenburg Gate, every man is a German separated from his fellow men. Every man is a Berliner, forced to look upon a scar.

In the speech, Reagan returned to an old theme of the decrepit state of communism, and the impossibility of such a vision surviving:

In the 1950's Khrushchev predicted: "We will bury you." But in the West today, we see a free world that has achieved a level of prosperity and well-being unprecedented in all human history. In the Communist world, we see failure, technological backwardness, declining standards of health, even want of the most basic kind— too little food. Even today, the Soviet Union still cannot feed itself. After these four decades, then, there stands

before the entire world one great and inescapable conclusion: Freedom leads to prosperity. Freedom replaces
the ancient hatreds among nations with comity and
peace. Freedom is the victor.

Yet there was reason to hope, he said, detailing new signs
that the Soviets were becoming more open to freedom. He spoke
of some of the advances that were taking place, deeming them
small steps toward openness and freedom. But then he delivered
the punch line:

> There is one sign the Soviets can make that would be un-
> mistakable, that would advance dramatically the cause
> of freedom and peace. General Secretary Gorbachev,
> if you seek peace, if you seek prosperity for the Soviet
> Union and Eastern Europe, if you seek liberalization:
> Come here to this gate! Mr. Gorbachev, open this gate!
> Mr. Gorbachev, tear down this wall!

A thrill shot through the audience when he said those words:
perfect, unadorned, righteous. The spectators erupted in loud
applause, and Reagan liked to think that there were many silent
cheers emanating from the hopeful hearts of those on the other
side of the wall. The speech would take its place in history,
though few remarked on it at the time. Yet, watching the speech
at home in Washington, Robinson might have thought he heard
the sound of a trumpet.

REAGAN WAS NERVOUS. IT had been the hardest year of his presidency, weighted down by scandals and staff upheavals. His poll
numbers had dipped by more than twenty points, and he was feel-

ing a rare uncertainty about his ability to advance his agenda. It had seemed as though the damnable year would never end. Now, on December 8, he had one more important mission, a third summit with Gorbachev—the one that almost didn't happen after the stall in Reykjavík. The one, finally, on American soil.

As he waited in the Diplomatic Reception Room of the White House, preparing to go outside and greet Mikhail and Raisa Gorbachev when they drove up, Reagan was bundled in a coat and scarf and feeling a little bit on edge. Nancy walked in, also in a coat, and went up to him. She was nervous, too, Fitzwater recalled. "I think she was afraid the American people would love Raisa more than they loved Nancy." She leaned in for a tight hug. "You'll be great, Ronnie," she murmured.

The summit had been difficult to schedule—remember, it had first been proposed at Geneva—and in September 1987 there still had not been an agreement on the date. At one point, the Soviets suggested dates around Thanksgiving, seeming not to appreciate the significance of the holiday or the fact that the Reagans were planning to be at their California ranch. Reagan scrawled an annoyed note in his diary wondering if he'd have to cancel Thanksgiving. A California summit was briefly considered. "She's already bought the groceries for Thanksgiving," Powell warned Shultz about Nancy, laughing. "Gorbachev's going to the ranch whether he wants to or not." But the meeting was soon cleared for December 8 to 10 in Washington.

Meanwhile Shultz and Shevardnadze had been shuttling back and forth—Shultz to Moscow in April and October, Shevardnadze to DC in September and October—trying to iron out what they wanted to achieve at the summit. Everyone was looking for a decisive moment, which meant signing the INF Treaty and making enough headway on the Strategic Arms Reduction Treaty (START) so that a treaty could be signed at the next summit.

START was a long game, subject to endless failed negotiations, especially once Reagan had proposed SDI, but if signed it would become the crowning achievement of nuclear disarmament.

The Washington summit was different from all the others, not only because a treaty would be signed but because it was taking place in Washington, DC. This was not neutral territory; it was a home-field advantage for Reagan, although no one could have guessed how adoring the public response to the Gorbachevs would be.

In spite of his air of confidence and command, Gorbachev came to Washington during a troubled time in his own administration. As popular as he was in the United States, he was facing intense blowback at home. "We were gradually freeing ourselves of stereotyped thinking and the habit of blaming everything on the 'imperialist Western states,'" he wrote of that period. But the process was understandably controversial. He was constantly put on the defensive about his radical program of perestroika and his penchant for negotiating with old enemies. On one hand, establishment Soviets were urging him to slow down. On the other, radical opponents, such as Boris Yeltsin, were saying he wasn't moving fast enough. Yeltsin, a blustering, hard-drinking Russian stereotype of a man, was the outspoken populist to Gorbachev's cautious reformer. The first secretary of the Moscow City Committee of the Communist Party, who had been brought into the Politburo by Gorbachev, tasked with managing political and economic reforms, Yeltsin had grown increasingly angered by the slow course of change. He believed that Gorbachev had been corrupted by his political associations and was more loyal to the Party than to the people. In a devastating attack on Gorbachev and the system at an October 21, 1987, Central Committee meeting, Yeltsin criticized the "cult of personality" around Gorbachev and the glacial pace of perestroika. Gorbachev thought that ironic, as Yeltsin himself was a master of personality politics in Moscow, where he was frequently seen in photo ops siding with the common man against the powerful state. "He would suddenly appear at a factory, take the manager and lead him to the workers' cafeteria to give him a public dressing-down, acting as if he were the protector of the people and the manager a monster of cruelty," Gorbachev wrote. "To the enraptured applause of Muscovites he promised that problems of housing, medical care and services would be resolved in record time." Those public displays, Gorbachev saw, were mostly for public relations purposes. But Yeltsin's grandstanding had little effect. As he raged in front of the Central Committee that day, Gorbachev saw the outpourings of a man whose ambitions had outpaced his influence. To the shock of many, Yeltsin concluded with a dramatic announcement of his resignation.

On November 9, Gorbachev learned that Yeltsin had been found covered in blood and rushed to the hospital. The initial report was that he had attempted suicide. But when doctors examined his wounds, they found them superficial; he had apparently used office scissors to simulate a suicide attempt. Rumors ran wild, fueled in part by Yeltsin, who at one point claimed to have been attacked by a mob on the street and at another point to have accidentally fallen on his scissors. Gorbachev, eager to save face for Yeltsin, quietly appealed to the committee to release him from his duties.

Now Gorbachev was headed for Washington for what he hoped would be a signature achievement: the signing of the INF Treaty. Reagan had to deal with his own share of opposition to the treaty. Conservatives in Congress called him an appeaser and warned that the agreement would put the United States at a disadvantage. "President Reagan is little more than the speech reader-in-chief for the pro-appeasement triumvirate of Howard H. Baker Jr., George P. Shultz and Frank C. Carlucci," steamed Howard Phillips, the chairman of the Conservative Caucus, in a *New York Times* op-ed. In the *Los Angeles Times* he was quoted as calling the president "a useful idiot."

But Shultz believed that Reagan still had the upper hand, and he told him so. "Gorbachev comes to Washington to address an agenda *you* have defined, against a background of American strength and consistency *you* have created," he wrote in a memo to the president before the summit. "As such, his visit reflects a qualitative change in the nature of the U.S.-Soviet relationship you inherited in 1981." Not only would the INF Treaty be signed, but Shultz was confident they would lay the groundwork for a broader START treaty the following year.

Meanwhile, Fitzwater, busy managing the press for the major event, had initiated a collaboration that was something of a breakthrough. Imagining the embarrassing specter of Gennadi Gerasimov, Gorbachev's press secretary, holding competing press conferences across town, he came up with an interesting idea: to ask Gerasimov if he would be willing to do joint briefings, starting with one the day before the summit. Gerasimov agreed. That afternoon, reporters packed into a hall at the Marriott, where they were treated to a good-natured back-and-forth by the two press secretaries. Fitzwater had expected the idea to be a hit with the media, and he was right. He also had a sense of humor about it. "I knew Gennadi Gerasimov had been with Gorbachev for a while and he spoke great English and he was really bright and good-looking. I remember after the series of briefings *Time* magazine said, 'Who would have guessed that the Soviet spokesman would look like Cary Grant and the American spokesman look like Nikita Khrushchev?'"

As the Russian limo carrying the Gorbachevs pulled up at the south entrance of the White House, the Reagans walked briskly to the car to greet them. Everyone was smiling, but the smiles between Reagan and Gorbachev seemed friendlier than in the past—more intimate.

"I have often felt that our people should have been better friends long ago," Reagan said as they stood together for a twenty-one-gun salute by the military honor guards. Gorbachev nodded in agreement.

Once inside, the two men met privately in the Oval Office. Reagan began by giving Gorbachev a gift, a pair of cuff links with the symbol from Isaiah 2:4 referencing the phrase "They shall beat their swords into ploughshares, and their spears into pruning hooks." Gorbachev smiled with appreciation. It was an appropriate symbol, he told Reagan, given the treaty that they hoped to sign later that day.

Then the president once again took the opportunity of a private moment to press the issue of human rights. He gave Gorbachev a card containing the names of Soviet citizens who were petitioning to be granted exit visas. It was a personal request, he stressed.

Gorbachev agreed that human rights was a high priority for the Soviet government—in itself a remarkable admission—but said that the matter of exit visas was complicated. He denied Reagan's assertion that more than half a million Jews wanted to leave the Soviet Union, and returned to a favorite theme: a repetition of America's own human rights ills, including incidences of anti-Semitism. They sparred back and forth.

Reagan and Gorbachev had different ideas about the importance of human rights. Gorbachev saw it as a side issue, while Reagan thought it was just as important as everything else they were discussing. Days earlier, in a speech before human rights groups, he had placed human rights improvement on a par with arms reduction. He had said, however, that a window was opening, if only a crack. Not that long before, the Soviets had refused to discuss human rights, calling them an internal affair. But now the matter was being openly discussed.

That was Reagan's way when addressing communism: he always dug deeper, considering the true nature of the chasm between the two systems. Arms control was essential, he believed, but he also thought that such a change meant little if people were not free to live and worship as they chose.

Gorbachev finally said he was open to discussing the matter—but not that day. He did, however, invite Reagan to visit his country in June 1988 for what would be their fourth summit. The Millennium of Christianity in Russia would be celebrated then, he said, and Reagan could visit churches and see for himself.

Overall, their mood was both self-congratulatory and reflective. They had traveled far, Gorbachev remarked, and the journey had often been difficult. But they were reaching a more profound level in their dialogue, a greater trust and understanding. Reagan mused that were they to encounter a threat from another planet, their differences would disappear and they would be united as human beings.

Unlike other summits, the centerpiece of this one, signing the INF Treaty, happened on the first day. That afternoon, in an East Room ceremony carried live on TV, Reagan and Gorbachev signed Russian and English versions of the treaty, which would completely eliminate intermediate-range missiles—859 for the United States and 1,752 for the Soviet Union. Key members of the administration, the Joint Chiefs of Staff, the congressional leadership, and Soviet officials witnessed the signing.

"We can only hope that this history-making agreement will not be an end in itself," Reagan said after they had signed the documents and exchanged pens, "but the beginning of a working relationship that will enable us to tackle the other issues, urgent issues, before us: strategic offensive nuclear weapons, the balance of conventional forces in Europe, the destructive and tragic regional conflicts that beset so many parts of our globe, and respect for the human and natural rights that God has granted to all men."

Gorbachev added a thoughtful statement about what the agreement meant to the world: "May Dec. 8, 1987, become a date that will be inscribed in the history books—a date that will mark the watershed separating the era of a mounting risk of nuclear war from the era of a demilitarization of human life."

With a twinkle in his eye, Reagan added a familiar warning: "We have listened to the wisdom in an old Russian maxim. Though my pronunciation may give you difficulty, the maxim is, *Doveryai no proveryai*—trust but verify."

Gorbachev laughed. "You repeat that at every meeting."

"I like it," Reagan agreed with a broad smile.

The president was restless going into the post-signing meeting. The high point of the day had already passed. He wasn't focused on Gorbachev's explanations of the problems he was having instituting perestroika in the Soviet Union. He broke the seriousness with a joke that was notably tone deaf to the current mood: "An American scholar, on his way to the airport before a flight to the Soviet Union, got into a conversation with his cabdriver, a young man who said that he was still finishing his education. The scholar asked, 'When you finish your schooling, what do you want to do?' The young man answered, 'I haven't decided yet.'" Then, Reagan went on, the scholar flew to Moscow, where he again took a cab from the airport. Speaking Russian, he asked his cabdriver what he wanted to be when he finished his schooling. The cabdriver replied, "They haven't told me yet." The joke landed like a bomb in the room, with

Reagan's team cringing and Gorbachev looking briefly angry. He said he hoped that Reagan would not enlist Jack Matlock to collect anecdotes about the people of Moscow; that would surely harm relations. But they moved on quickly, and later Reagan was apologetic.

The state dinner that evening was a lavish event overseen by Nancy, an astounding feat given the circumstances. Only six weeks earlier, she'd been diagnosed with breast cancer and had undergone a radical mastectomy. Then, days after she returned from the hospital, she learned that her mother had died of a massive stroke.

Kathy Osborne was awed by the first lady's strength. "Probably, they put more into this state dinner than any we'd ever had," she said. "It was so important. It was done very well and very nicely. But here she had to be the perfect First Lady of the United States when she just buried her mother and just went through some very serious surgery. Having gone through a similar situation myself with breast cancer, I was thinking, *This woman has never had a moment to grieve for her mother or for her illness, and here she is being the absolute perfect First Lady for the Russian state dinner.* It was just amazing. But it's just such an example, I think, of what a strong woman she is."

Nancy looked stunning in a long black beaded gown and diamond drop earrings. Raisa also wore black, matching her counterpart in style with a two-piece brocaded gown with pearls. Although it was a black-tie event, Gorbachev and the other Soviets wore business suits—tuxedos just weren't worn in the Soviet Union.

More than a hundred prominent Americans attended the dinner, representing business, politics, the arts, and sports. Joe DiMaggio brought a baseball, hoping to get it signed by both Reagan and Gorbachev. Reagan took it with him to be signed later. They dined on Columbia River salmon with lobster medallions.

In a warm toast, Gorbachev said, "A boundless world stretches far and wide beyond the walls of this house and, may I say, you and I are accountable to it."

Nancy had secured the pianist Van Cliburn to give a recital during dessert. The Gorbachevs were clearly thrilled to see him and exchanged warm hugs with him. They excitedly recalled when Cliburn had come to Moscow in 1958, at the height of the Cold War, to participate in the first International Tchaikovsky Competition. Playing the music of the great Russian masters, Cliburn had won the competition and momentarily opened up a small window of shared values between the nations. Now he sat at the grand piano and began playing "Moscow Nights," an anthem of sorts for Russians. Deeply moved, the Gorbachevs and their entire delegation sang along as Cliburn played. There were many tearful eyes in the room.

The dinner might have been an opportunity for Nancy and Raisa to grow closer. But the uneasy chill persisted. Nancy was offended that Raisa never asked her about the surgery or mentioned her mother's death. At the end of the summit, driving to the airport with Raisa, Barbara Bush brought it up, asking Raisa if she knew about Nancy's surgery. She said yes, but in her country, surgery on the breast would never be mentioned publicly.

Raisa had a habit that irked Nancy of dropping insults into conversation. For example, after she visited the White House for a tour given by the first lady, she told a reporter it was more like a museum, not a place a human being would like to live in. Public fascination with Raisa was high, and Nancy couldn't match that. Americans already knew her.

The Gorbachevs were troubled by a seeming effort to keep

Raisa under wraps. For example, at one point she was scheduled to go on a sightseeing tour of Washington, during which she would stop and interact with groups of Americans. Instead, her car sped by the sites without stopping. Frustrated, she demanded to know why she was being kept inside the car and was told it was for security reasons. But later the press reported it had been her choice. Welcome to the sting of the free press! Raisa also disliked the media characterization of a "cold war" between her and Nancy. Raisa presented herself as being above such petty rivalry.

The next morning, when Gorbachev arrived, Reagan took him into his private study off the Oval Office. He was bouncing Joe DiMaggio's baseball in his hand. "There is something called an American idiom," he told Gorbachev. "We can continue with our rigid ideological positions, or we can play ball"—and he tossed the ball up in the air. "What would you like to do?"

Gorbachev looked Reagan straight in the eye and replied, "Let's play ball."

"If you want inside baseball, *that's* inside baseball," Ken Duberstein observed. (By the way, Reagan got Gorbachev's signature on the ball and added his own, so DiMaggio had his souvenir.)

When they started talking, Reagan immediately launched into a forceful argument about SDI, followed by a rundown by Shultz of the steps they would need to take going forward in reducing strategic offensive arms.

Gorbachev had given up arguing with the president about his favorite program. He finally said that if the United States wanted to go ahead with SDI, it was their business—as long as it was consistent with the arms treaties. That statement, delivered without fanfare, was a huge breakthrough in negotiations.

But Gorbachev had a bone to pick with the American media. In a December 1 interview with Tom Brokaw, he had appeared to say that the Soviets were working on their own SDI program. Now he said that his comments had been distorted. He had not said that—only that the Soviets were working on their own research projects in many areas. He had pointedly said that the Soviets were not developing SDI, and the reporters had gotten it wrong.

They openly discussed what might be achieved in a Moscow summit the following year. Gorbachev, while saying that Reagan was always welcome in his country, added that it would be disappointing if the summit did not produce another agreement, specifically the START treaty. If Reagan didn't think that was possible, he should say so. In Russian, Gorbachev recounted a saying, translated as "If you respect me, don't make a fool of me. Tell me what you want."

Reagan wanted a treaty, too, but getting one would be complicated. As they moved further down the road to disarmament, protections would have to be in place, regional conflicts spurred by Soviet aggression would have to be settled, and progress would have to be made in loosening the USSR's iron hold on East Germany, even if Gorbachev wasn't yet ready to tear down the Berlin Wall.

That evening, the Gorbachevs hosted the Reagans at the Soviet Embassy at a dinner that matched the White House's in grandeur. With vodka and champagne flowing and caviar piled high, the two leaders toasted each other, Gorbachev raising his glass to proclaim, "Until we meet in Moscow!"

The next morning, the final day of the summit, was scheduled to begin at 10:30 A.M., but a call came that Gorbachev was in a meeting at the embassy and would be fifteen minutes late. Fifteen minutes came and went, then thirty, then forty-five. Finally, Fitzwater turned on CNN in the president's secretarial office, thinking it might report Gorbachev's whereabouts. There, filling the screen, was Gorbachev's limo and the sight of the general secretary plunging into the crowds on Connecticut Avenue. Reagan ambled in and stood watching.

He saw Gorbachev engaged in his own PR initiative, and it was going over well with the crowds. Recent polls had shown an 81 percent approval rating for Gorbachev among Americans. Under his leadership, the old Cold War fears had begun to dissipate as people observed that here at last there was a Soviet leader who could get along with the West. They loved his smile, his distinctive birthmark, his fashionable wife, his ease with the public, his westernized mannerisms, the way he called their president by his first name. There was a cachet to being close to a Soviet leader. Americans often took Gorbachev at face value because they liked him, but they couldn't necessarily square their warm feelings for him with the undeniable manifestations of Soviet power around the world: that ugly wall in Berlin, the ongoing war in Afghanistan, the support of Marxist regimes in places such as Nicaragua, Cambodia, and Angola. Not to mention the human rights violations in the Soviet Union itself. But when it came to Gorbachev, they were willing to compartmentalize.

When Gorbachev finally arrived at the White House at noon, Reagan greeted him with a slight smile. "I thought you'd gone home," he said reproachfully.

Gorbachev might not have noticed the edge in Reagan's voice. He was ebullient about the warm response he had received from ordinary Americans. He confessed that he'd been so engaged by the crowd that he'd been reluctant to leave.

That's known by American politicians as "working the crowd," Baker said.

Gorbachev dismissed the idea that it was American style. He'd done it throughout his career. He reminded those present that he had spent most of his career out in the provinces, where it was important to listen to the people, as there was more common sense in the provinces than in the nation's capital—a sentiment Reagan heartily approved of.

At a small luncheon in the Family Dining Room, Reagan and Gorbachev shared reflections on the status of their negotiations. Both were frustrated by the knuckle draggers in their own countries. It was a friendly back-and-forth, replete with pointed anecdotes. Reagan and Gorbachev were certainly on the same page when it came to despising bureaucracy. Reagan recounted an incident from World War II. There was a warehouse full of obsolete records. He'd asked for permission to destroy the documents in order to make room for current documents. The answer came down through the chain of command that he could destroy the documents as long as he first made copies of them.

That reminded Gorbachev of a popular joke about Russian business: Someone bought a case of Russian vodka, and emptied the bottles by pouring out the vodka. He then returned the bottles for money, which he used to buy more vodka.

They continued on in that manner, with much laughter around the table. At that moment, they were just two harried chief executives bemoaning the silliness of bureaucratic tangles that prevented men of vision from doing what they set out to do.

Near the end of the luncheon, a page handed Baker a note from Shultz saying to stretch it out because the diplomats working behind the scenes hadn't been able to agree on a departure statement. Baker whispered to the president, "Maybe you can tell some stories."

Reagan was puzzled, but he launched into more anecdotes as the Russians looked at him curiously. What was happening? They were ready to go.

Another page handed Baker a note: Raisa and Nancy were

in the Red Room alone and did not appear happy. Baker gave it to the president and whispered, "We've got to go." Reagan and Gorbachev soon joined their wives in the library on the ground floor, milling around, waiting. Shultz walked in. "We have not agreed on a departure statement," he said, looking frustrated.

Reagan eyed Gorbachev. "Well, we're going to have to go anyway. My statement will be that we were not able to agree on a departure statement."

Gorbachev recoiled. It meant everything to him that the summit appear to be a success, and if Reagan suggested that the Soviet side had been unwilling to reach a compromise on a statement, he'd look bad. He grimaced. "Oh, all right," he said in English, and they walked out together, smiling as if there had never been an issue.

The final ceremony had been planned with much fanfare; more than five thousand people were crowded onto the South Lawn to observe. Both men gave strong statements, citing the important step that had been taken for peace in the world. But the most striking aspect of their statements was when they spoke from the heart about their personal feelings for each other's people.

"During World War II, when so many young Russians served at the front, the poem 'Wait for Me' became a prayer spoken on the lips of Russian families who dreamed one day of the happiness that their reunion would bring," Reagan said, summoning up a time when the two nations had been aligned in a common goal. "The cause of world peace and world freedom is still waiting, Mr. General Secretary. It has waited long enough. . . . it is good that you came to America, and Nancy and I are pleased to have welcomed you here. Your visit was short, yet I hope you'll take with you a better sense of the spirit and soul of the United States of America. And when you get back to Moscow, please pass on to the Soviet people the best wishes of the American people for a peaceful and prosperous new year."

Gorbachev reached out to Americans with the same tone: "In bidding farewell to America, I am looking forward to a new encounter with it, in the hope that I will then be able to see not only its Capital but also to meet face-to-face with its great people, to chat and to have some lively exchanges with ordinary Americans. I believe that what we have accomplished during the meeting and the discussions will, with time, help considerably to improve the atmosphere in the world at large and in America itself, in terms of its more correct and tolerant perception of my country, the Soviet Union."

The trip made a deep impression on Gorbachev, and it changed his perspective in a significant way. In Washington, he discovered an appreciation for the human factor in negotiations. "Before," he said in remarks to the Politburo on his return to Moscow, "we treated such personal contacts as simply meetings between representatives of opposed and irreconcilable systems. But it turns out that politicians, including leaders of governments if they are really responsible people, represent purely human concerns, interests, and the hopes of ordinary people, [who] are guided by the most natural human motives and feelings."

PART THREE

THREE DAYS IN MOSCOW

CHAPTER 9

THE TRUE MISSION

The point was never just about the arms race for Reagan, or the balance of power, or the adding and subtracting of missiles on either side. From the start, it was about the noble goal of eradicating an existential hazard from the world. The Soviet Union wasn't a threat only because of its weaponry, although weapons made the danger more immediate and tangible. It was a threat because of its ideology, which Reagan believed was a stain on human history.

But Reagan wasn't just a heroic cowboy facing his enemy on a dusty street in a town called Planet Earth, ready to test who was the faster draw; he was a strategist playing a long game, and over the course of his presidency that strategy had evolved on the diplomatic front.

Some of his hard-core supporters surely asked how a man who had once given fiery speeches about the Evil Empire could break bread and sign treaties with the leader of that untrustworthy foe. Had the president softened on the Communist menace? Had the warm handshakes exchanged with Gorbachev weakened the United States' position?

Kenneth Adelman saw it another way. In spite of Reagan's calm style of negotiation, he thought his most effective tool was his unwillingness to compromise on the important things. It was a quality he admired in Abraham Lincoln, and he was happy to make the comparison. "Look at Lincoln," he said. "Lincoln's tenacity in keeping the union together was beyond rational belief. . . . I mean, why should he have this mystical hold? No matter how many lives you're going to save, can't you work out a compromise? There's something about, *No, we're not going to spread slavery anywhere and we're not going to give up any of the union.* It was just a force that everybody had to contend with. It was unstoppable for Lincoln. . . . With Reagan, with Lincoln, and people like that, you don't deal in the real world." By "real," Adelman meant the world of giving in, of being bent by the winds of public opinion or the threat of pain.

There were whispers, plenty of them, that in his final year in office Reagan had lost his edge. Aides spoke of his depression immediately after Iran-Contra, and some of them even worried about the distracted look in his eye, his wandering focus. Later, of course, people would pounce on those remarks as evidence that the initial signs of Alzheimer's disease had already been visible while he was president. But those who knew him well heartily disputed such a characterization. To be sure, the presidency aged all of its occupants, some more than others. But the sheer magnitude of the daily responsibilities would have been impossible had Reagan truly been faltering. As his resolve on the Soviet Union plainly attests, he was as clear as ever in what he set out to do.

Indeed, as he approached his fourth summit with Gorbachev, scheduled for three days in Moscow at the end of May 1988, his sense of mission had never been stronger. If he'd held his rhetorical fire against communism while he and Gorbachev were establishing their relationship and taking cautious steps toward the eradication of nuclear weapons, he now felt liberated to address the issue of human rights head-on.

He sensed that the people of the Soviet Union were ready to do so, even if their leaders were not quite there yet. In a New Year's message to the Soviet people, part of the good-faith exchange he and Gorbachev had continued, Reagan highlighted the achievement of the INF Treaty before turning to the matter of human rights:

> As you know, we Americans are concerned about human rights, including freedoms of speech, press, worship, and travel. We will never forget that a wise man has said that: "Violence does not live alone and is not capable of living alone. It is necessarily interwoven with falsehood." Silence is a form of falsehood. We will always speak out on behalf of human dignity.

When he addressed Congress later in January, he said that the results for peace that they had achieved in seven years had been nothing less than "a complete turnabout, a revolution." He also told them to put on their work shoes, as there was much left to be done. For those who might be tempted to let their guard down in the rosy aftermath of Gorbachev's visit to the United States, he wanted to stress that the battle was only partly won. A treaty signed on nuclear arms was an important step, but the cruel realities of life behind the Iron Curtain had only nominally improved as a result of Gorbachev's reforms.

Part of the caution was an acknowledgment that Gorbachev's position had grown tenuous. By the beginning of 1988, he was racing against time. His political career was in jeopardy as he continued to push for change that was more fundamental than the window dressing even old Party hands approved of. "Talk about reform was one thing," Jack Matlock, now the US ambassador to the Soviet Union, wrote. "Almost everybody did that.

But now it seemed that Gorbachev was encouraging criticism of past practices and even the system itself, and who knew where that might lead?" Matlock sensed a shifting of opinion. Would Gorbachev's ambitions threaten the very existence of the Communist Party? That was the fear among many nervous Party leaders. Gorbachev's own second in command, Yegor Ligachev, was sowing dissent among the hierarchy. The situation had become serious enough that he had received a reprimand from Gorbachev and was rumored to have been relieved of some of his duties in advance of the summit.

Gorbachev was watching his back. At the same time, he dared to hope that the Moscow summit would cement his position, show the Party leaders how he had restored Soviet prestige and caused the Americans to back down in important ways, especially on the START treaty. It was a bold pose, though as Weinberger later noted, "What he didn't understand, what nobody understood, was the fact that Gorbachev was sowing the seeds of his own disaster." He couldn't see the ways that his bold initiatives were wearing away his popularity, that in bringing the Soviet Union into a modern, more open era, he would lose his own place. But that was a worry for another time.

As the summit approached, Gorbachev was most concerned about Reagan's newly abrasive language on human rights. He took note of the speeches Reagan had been giving and thought their tone was offensive. "Could it be that President Reagan's recent remarks represent the groundwork for his visit to the Soviet Union?" he angrily challenged Shultz in April while the secretary of state was in Moscow. "Does he really intend to bring this ideological luggage to Moscow? He must realize that we will answer back. And with what result? We'll have an argument, and we might as well forget everything we have achieved with so much effort. Who needs that?"

No, Shultz assured him, reminding him of all they'd accomplished so far. Reagan was committed to the process. But there was no sugarcoating the hard truths he was determined to speak about.

In a secure internal memo describing his mission for the summit, Reagan wrote:

> My visit to the Soviet Union should not be seen as a dialogue only with the Soviet government, but also as a way of communicating with the Soviet people. I want to emphasize throughout my trip that the democratic values that make our country great are those toward which much of the world—including, we hope, the Soviet Union—is moving. At the same time, I wish to make clear that, while we welcome promises of reform within the USSR, the policies of the United States and the West toward Moscow must be based on Soviet deeds rather than words.

It helped that the Soviet withdrawal from Afghanistan was under way.

Ever since he had taken office, Gorbachev had known that getting out of Afghanistan was absolutely necessary. The question was how. The war was unimaginably costly, not just financially but also in terms of prestige and world opinion. It was a morass, an unwinnable conflict. Finally, in 1988, he set about the painful process of cutting the cord. In advance of the summit, Soviet forces began withdrawing from Afghanistan.

It was a sign of the beginning of the end of Soviet expansionism, which had been the state's model from the outset. Reflecting on this shift, Krauthammer said, "This is an expansionist empire. It's in their blood, it's pre-Communist. And then it all falls apart. It's a terrible paradox for the Russians. They're so big; they have so many frontiers. They have so many potential enemies. But that makes them want to take more territory . . . which makes them bigger. Is it expansionism in their blood? I don't know, but it's defensive. They're always threatened."

Naturally, Reagan was supportive of the Afghanistan withdrawal, although he acknowledged having concerns about what would happen next. (A modern president could surely sympathize with the maddening difficulty of accomplishing anything of real value in Afghanistan.) But Reagan was buoyed by the trend line, which he referred to as a reverse of the "Domino Theory": instead of countries falling to communism, it was *communism* that was in retreat.

Krauthammer could see a vindication of the Reagan Doctrine in the growing resistance to Communist control. "The interesting thing about the Reagan Doctrine is that Reagan never used the term," he said. "Reagan is so smart in a way that he disguised. That was the brilliance of Reagan. He disguised his intelligence, and he was so sure of himself as a person that he didn't need to show off." In that way, Reagan, like Eisenhower, had a winning "hidden hand": the ability, when necessary, to mask his true intentions until the moment was right.

Unfortunately, focusing on high-minded goals wasn't always possible when the nation was awash in frivolous sideshows. The tabloid media environment wasn't as voracious as it is today, but people were still willing to be distracted by juicy gossip when it appeared. In April and May, just as Reagan was preparing for his historic Moscow trip, two biting memoirs by former staff members captured the headlines for days.

Larry Speakes's *Speaking Out: The Reagan Presidency from Inside the White House*, which landed in April, was particularly embarrassing on the eve of the summit. After serving as Reagan's spokesman for just short of six years, he chose that point to reveal that he had invented quotes by the president, most notably a remark he was said to have made to Gorbachev in Geneva: "There is much that divides us, but I believe the world breathes easier because we are talking here together." True or not, it set the media atwitter. Fitzwater and the speechwriters were outraged. It was such an obvious betrayal, with no other purpose than to make the president look inept. After all, hadn't it long been rumored that people were putting words into his mouth? Reagan himself was nonplussed. To his credit, he shrugged it off with a laugh, privately commenting that at least Speakes had gotten it right! In the end, the revelation hurt Speakes more than it hurt Reagan; he was forced to resign from his cushy new job as head of communications for Merrill Lynch.

Then, in May, Don Regan exacted his revenge on Nancy (and by extension Reagan) in *For the Record: From Wall Street to Washington*, which included the bombshell revelation that Nancy relied on a San Francisco astrologer to plot the president's every move. It was extremely mean-spirited and hurtful—George Will called the book "an act of spite." According to Reagan's diary, long hours and days were devoted to discussing Regan's charges. Nancy's explanation was that she had begun talking to the astrologer Joan Quigley as a coping strategy after the assassination attempt and had never taken it too seriously, but that wasn't the way Regan described it. Recalling the agony and humiliation of that period in her memoir, Nancy wrote, "I had become the national laughingstock. I was the butt of countless jokes on television, radio, and in the press. From the moment I got dressed in the morning until the time I got ready for bed, no matter what channel I turned to, there was Don Regan, talking about me and astrology. The man was *everywhere*. It was almost as if he had put a hit out on me."

She apologized profusely to her husband. "I feel terrible about this," she told him. "I've put you in an awful position."

"No, honey, it's all right," Reagan said, ever loving. "I could see what you were going through. It's all right." Reagan was angry at Regan, but there was not much he could do about it. He had more important matters on his mind that May. Fortunately for him, his legacy wouldn't be scorched by the revelation. The same could not be said for Don Regan.

THE SIGNING CEREMONY IN Washington, DC, for the INF Treaty was only the first step in the process of enacting the treaty. It had still required ratification by Congress, and Reagan was pleased when that happened days before his trip to Moscow. But there was more to be done. Everyone wanted to know what great sign of progress would be unveiled in Moscow. Gorbachev desperately wished to show the Politburo a tangible result. Even so, it frustrated both Reagan and Gorbachev that people judged the success of summits by the big reveals. The work of diplomacy was more nuanced, and the negotiations over actual treaties took longer. For example, the elusive deal on START that would reduce US and Soviet strategic arsenals by half was still being debated and would not be accomplished in Moscow. As the date of the summit grew near, Reagan envisioned his mission as a rare opportunity for a personal outreach.

Even with the friendly relationship between Reagan and Gorbachev, there was a sense of mystery about the Soviet leader, as though he stood behind a curtain. In a meeting Reagan had with nongovernmental Soviet experts in early May, James Billington, the Librarian of Congress, urged Reagan to use the summit to learn as much as he could about Gorbachev the man—his personal views and his vision of the future. Billington also advised that while promoting democracy, the president should avoid the "Rodney Dangerfield effect"—an appearance of disrespect—and give the Soviets their due in the struggle for moral recovery.

Reagan agreed with that approach. He had often wondered what had inspired Gorbachev to abandon so many manifestations of Communist doctrine. Reading Gorbachev's new book, *Perestroika*, a treatise on the changes he sought, Reagan saw something he had never expected to see: a leader who wasn't afraid to address the crippling corruption and inefficiency in his government. Perhaps, Reagan thought, Gorbachev had discovered, just as he had, that once you're in office you see things you hadn't before. At the same time, he thought that Gorbachev was deceiving himself in trying to achieve a middle ground, a way to make the socialist state more free, equal, and economically productive. Reagan had never believed that the Soviet Union could be "reformed." However, he was very interested in seeing how far Gorbachev could take his plans.

Also at the meeting was Suzanne Massie, an author and private citizen who had served as an informal advisor to Reagan and a conduit to Gorbachev for years. When she first met the president in 1984, after he had admired her book, *Land of the Firebird: The Beauty of Old Russia*, she was struck by his interest not just in Kremlin politicos but in the Russian people. Now she reminded him that it was important he not in any way look down on the Soviet people but rather show empathy for them. She also mentioned that the people of Leningrad were quite disappointed the president wouldn't be visiting their city. Reagan interrupted her to say that Nancy would be making a day trip to Leningrad during the summit.

Massie urged Reagan to praise the role of Soviet women. He grumbled that whenever he suggested in America that women were a civilizing force, he got castigated by the media. However, he would take her advice; in Moscow, he frequently praised the strength and devotion of Russian women.

Improved bilateral relations, one of the goals of the summit, were also discussed with great enthusiasm. The Russian scholar Maurice Friedberg thought Reagan should suggest opening an American bookstore in Moscow, since Russian literature was so widely available in the United States. The musician and Russia expert Frederick Starr added that cultural and educational exchanges, which were already occurring at Reagan's behest, were beneficial in alleviating some of the anxiety people felt over the changes that were occurring. It was a free-flowing discussion, with many good ideas that strengthened Reagan's commitment to forging a personal bond with the people.

Reagan had a four-part plan for the Moscow summit. As he later explained to reporters:

> As you know, our relationship with the Soviets is like a table. It's built on four legs: arms reduction, resolving of regional conflicts, improvement of human rights within the Soviet Union, and expansion of bilateral exchanges. The Soviets have indicated many times that they'd prefer the discussions be confined to the arms issues alone, but we believe that sustained improvement in relations can't rest stably on one leg. We saw what happened in the detente period of the early seventies. There were arms and trade agreements and what was billed as a general thaw, but because of Soviet behavior in so many areas, these could not be sustained. Weapons are a sign of tensions, not a cause of them. I know all of you have heard me say this time and again, but let me repeat it here: Nations do not distrust each other

because they're armed; they are armed because they distrust each other.

Human rights remained his greatest ambition. In an April 21 speech in Springfield, Massachusetts, he put the Soviets on notice that he had more than arms control on his mind in Moscow. "In the past, the full weight of the Soviet-American relationship all too often seemed to rest on one issue, arms control," he said, calling it "a plank not sturdy enough to bear up the whole platform of Soviet-American relations."

On May 4, just weeks before the summit, he set a more conciliatory tone about human rights in a speech before the National Strategy Forum in Chicago. Instead of lambasting the Soviet Union for its human rights failures, he highlighted the small signs of progress that were being made: "We applaud the changes that have been taking place and encourage the Soviets to go further. We recognize that changes occur slowly, but that's better than no change at all."

He went on to describe the human rights agenda he would be taking to Moscow, which had four parts: freedom of religion, freedom of speech, freedom of movement (including the right to emigrate), and making those rights permanent.

Reagan had begun to see human rights not only as a moral issue but as a pragmatic one for the Soviets. He wanted to frame the idea in such a way that Gorbachev could clearly see its advantages. No longer would human rights be something the West was trying to force down his throat. "I'm going to tackle him on religious freedom—not as a deal with us but as a suggestion to him as an answer to some of his problems," he wrote in his diary.

"What Reagan was doing was putting together a kind of 'four freedoms' presentation, à la FDR," said Fitzwater. FDR's version, in 1941, had named four fundamental freedoms that were the birthright of all people: freedom of speech, freedom of worship, freedom from want, and freedom from fear. Reagan's version, forty-seven years later, included freedom of religion, freedom of speech, freedom of assembly, and freedom of travel. It was, Fitzwater said, an effort to prepare the Soviet people for a better world. "I think he looked at what Gorbachev was doing and said, 'You know, he might not make it, but it looks to me like it's heading there.'"

While stopping in Helsinki on the way to the summit, Reagan made remarks to the League of Finnish-American Societies. He spoke about the Helsinki agreement on human rights, which the Soviet Union had signed along with other nations way back in 1975. In spite of Reagan's objections to some aspects of the agreement, human rights had never been one of them. He now asserted that human rights would be an integral component of the talks in Moscow. "There is no true international security without respect for human rights. . . . The greatest creative and moral force in this new world, the greatest hope for survival and success, for peace and happiness, is human freedom." At the president's side, Shultz was in full agreement and even attended a highly publicized Seder in Helsinki. It set a perfect tone for Moscow.

CHAPTER 10

CRY FREEDOM

The Reagans arrived in Moscow on May 29 to find a polished city scrubbed of its decay. As *Washington Post* journalist Don Oberdorfer described it, "The streets had been cleaned, the trashy residue of the Russian winter had been hauled away, and nearly every place on the official program had been painted and refurbished. The drab, ugly city I had seen in April had become, for a few days at least, a beautiful, gleaming capital."

When Reagan and Gorbachev sat together privately after the arrival ceremony, the tone was open and friendly, their guard down as never before. They were "Ron" and "Mikhail" now, and they marveled at the journey they had taken from Geneva. Both felt that, though it had been difficult, the seeds of their ultimate accomplishments had been planted there. Everything they did now would build on Geneva.

Still, the human rights question was a sticking point. Gorbachev felt that the Soviet Union was moving, albeit slowly, in the right direction. There was more freedom of expression, greater openness in the press, a plan for limited free elections, and experiments in the free market. But certain issues, such as the right of refuseniks to emigrate and the crackdown on dissidents, would take more time. There was only so much he could do. He sincerely hoped that Reagan wouldn't embarrass him on the matter, especially considering that the United States was not without its own issues: civil rights, unemployment, economic inequality, foreign military adventures, consumerism. He also pointed out to Reagan that the United States was engaged in a debate about building a fence between the United States and Mexico, although the analogy didn't fly with Reagan. He informed Gorbachev that a fence might be necessary because so many people wanted to come into the United States, not because they wanted to leave!

The discussion went on, vigorous and sometimes emotional. On that point the two men did not really understand each other. Each felt somewhat aggrieved by the other's position. But Gorbachev was reaching for comity. Perhaps we could cooperate in space, he told the man whose SDI proposal had been a thorn in his side. Reagan agreed and laughed. It seemed as though they were still talking about Heaven—or at least *the heavens*.

The human rights agenda was at the front of Reagan's mind as he sat down with Gorbachev the next day for their first official meeting. It was May 30, Memorial Day in the United States. It was the day Americans honored those who had died on the battlefield. Looking around the table, he realized that the people there were not just honoring those dead but aspiring to a peaceful world. That was a sobering thought.

Gorbachev, too, was thinking about the fight and the peace they sought.

The Russians had a great reverence for their country, with its noble history. They were a proud people who chafed at assaults by the West, including the harsh words Reagan had often directed against them. They wanted peace, but not if it meant abandoning their principles. And so Gorbachev began his remarks with that in mind: "If, as you say in the West, 'politics should reflect the will of the electorate,' then relations between us should grow more cordial. You can see how the Soviet people feel. I understand the American electorate also favors a resolution of differences with the Soviet Union." Stressing that their people and the world at large were looking on with great interest and that any mistake they made would have grave consequences, he warned, "Both of us must play our roles carefully, recognizing the importance of our task and displaying maturity and responsibility in dealing with the problems before us."

In their meetings, Reagan and Gorbachev discussed the matters at hand, the ratification of the INF Treaty, the stalled negotiations on START and the ABM Treaty, and of course, SDI. The tone was different from before, observed Matlock, who said the arguments lacked their usual heat. "The two were like actors wearily reciting a familiar script after it had been decided to postpone indefinitely the play's opening," he noted. That wasn't quite true. In the aftermath of their success with the INF Treaty, there were more cumbersome matters to discuss, including how to constrain strategic arms and reach the 50 percent reduction they had set as a goal in Geneva. That was a far more complex matter, and both sides needed to be sure they got what they expected.

Gorbachev said the dilemma reminded him of a story his granddaughter had recently told him. An old man and woman heard a knock on their door one night. Opening it, they found an egg, which they put under their hen. But when it hatched, a three-headed dragon emerged instead of a chick. Message: Be careful you're not giving birth to a monster.

And of course, there was the lingering question of SDI, which colored everything else. Although Gorbachev had essentially given in on SDI when they had met in Washington, it still bothered him. He pointed out that Reagan might mean well, but he was leaving office in less than eight months. How could he trust that future presidents wouldn't turn SDI into an offensive program? He said wistfully that he wished Reagan's term could be extended, as Roosevelt's had been.

Reagan replied that if the SDI program became workable, it wouldn't be put into effect until all nuclear weapons were eliminated.

Gorbachev countered with the obvious question: If all nuclear weapons were eliminated, why would SDI be necessary?

"It's like a gas mask," Reagan explained. Realistically, even if all nuclear weapons were gone, the technology existed and couldn't be unlearned. There was no guarantee that another bad actor, such as Hitler, would devise weapons one day, and without SDI, the world would be vulnerable.

At that moment, Reagan waved his hand and knocked over a glass of water. He apologized, but Gorbachev found it quite amusing.

"Never mind, Mr. President," he said. "A careless move with a glass of water is no big deal. If it happened with missiles . . ."

They talked for an hour and forty-five minutes and then broke. Earlier, Reagan had expressed his desire to visit a church. Gorbachev had arranged for the president to go to Danilov Monastery, which had been at the heart of the Russian Orthodox Church since its founding in 1282—except for a notable period between 1929 and 1983, when it had been closed and turned into a prison and then later into a factory. It had been the first monastery to be reopened in the modern era, the reason Gorbachev had selected it for a presidential visit. Additionally, it seemed that the monastery was one of Gorbachev's pet showcases, which annoyed Christian dissidents who experienced too many other examples of repression.

In 1929, when the monastery had been taken over by Stalin, there was some fear that its beautiful bells would be destroyed.

Charles Crane, an American businessman, had stepped in and purchased the bells, which were donated to Harvard. There they stayed until being returned to the monastery just that month. It was a historic restoration on the eve of Reagan's visit.

Robed Orthodox monks showed the Reagans around the grounds, including the viewing of stunning icons, artwork Reagan spoke of in his brief address:

> It's been said that an icon is a window between heaven and earth through which the believing eye can peer into the beyond. One cannot look at the magnificent icons created, and recreated here under the direction of Father Zinon, without experiencing the deep faith that lives in the hearts of the people of this land. Like the saints and martyrs depicted in these icons, the faith of your people has been tested and tempered in the crucible of hardship. But in that suffering, it has grown strong, ready now to embrace with new hope the beginnings of a second Christian millennium.

Reagan also pointedly quoted from Aleksandr Solzhenitsyn, the great Russian writer and dissident who had come to symbolize the struggle against oppression: " 'When you travel the byroads of central Russia, you begin to understand the secret of the pacifying Russian countryside. It is in the churches,' Solzhenitsyn wrote. 'They lift their bell towers—graceful, shapely, all different—high over mundane timber and thatch.' "

The day was becoming an ode to freedom, and that afternoon, Reagan continued the theme at a remarkable reception that had been in the works for weeks. As they'd made plans for their visit to Moscow, the Reagans had faced a very serious decision: whether to pay a personal visit to Yuri and Tatyana

Zieman, Jewish refuseniks who had first applied to emigrate from Moscow more than a decade earlier. The plight of the Ziemans had come to Nancy's attention through the wife of a musician named Vladimir Feltsman, who had emigrated the previous year, and their situation had touched her heart. She learned that Yuri had lost his job as a biomedical computer programmer when he had applied to leave and was working as a janitor. He had suffered a brain aneurysm months earlier, and even his doctors had recommended he travel to the West for lifesaving surgery. But the Soviets had turned down his latest appeal shortly before Shultz visited in April. Nancy wanted to do something, and she orchestrated a plan for the Reagans to drop by the Ziemans' apartment to show their support while they were in Moscow. When Gorbachev learned of the plan, he was quite angry. Soon Jack Matlock was summoned for a discussion at Shevardnadze's office. Shevardnadze's deputy, Alexander Bessmertnykh, told the ambassador in no uncertain terms that if the Reagans went ahead with their scheme, it would be an embarrassment to Gorbachev and would place a strain on the summit. It would also be counterproductive for the Ziemans, jeopardizing their chances of leaving soon, if ever.

Bessmertnykh couldn't make any promises, but he implied that if the Reagans agreed not to embarrass Gorbachev in that way, the Ziemans would soon be allowed to leave. (Just in case the Reagans went ahead with the visit anyway, the Soviets painted the Ziemans' apartment and cleaned and patched the street outside their building.)

The Reagans agreed to forgo the drop-by. Instead, they planned an elegant reception in the ballroom of Spaso House, the US ambassador's residence, for nearly a hundred dissidents and refuseniks, including the Ziemans. The Reagans were well aware that it would be an act of courage for those people to attend an event there. Some revealed that they'd received threats from the KGB.

The stories told by the refuseniks were emotional and gripping. The very act of applying to leave had put them and their families in jeopardy. Some had spent time in prison; the careers of many had been terminated; all of them had been subjected to various forms of harassment.

Looking around, Reagan realized that those brave men and women were living embodiments of the quest for freedom that was his main purpose for coming to Moscow. He was inspired by them. "I came here hoping to do what I could to give you strength," he told them. "Yet I already know that it is you who have strengthened me, you who have given me a message to carry back."

In his remarks, he reminded them of the freedoms that were the right of every human, especially those they sought—freedom of religion, freedom of speech, and the freedom to travel. He encouraged them to hold on because change was upon them. He quoted the nineteenth-century Russian poet Alexander Pushkin: "It's time, my friend, it's time. The heart begs for peace; the days fly past, it's time, my friend, it's time." Two months after the summit, the Ziemans were allowed to emigrate to Israel.

Later, a reporter asked press spokesman Gennadi Gerasimov if any harm would come to the refuseniks and dissidents who had met with Reagan. "I don't know," he answered. "I met with President Reagan today, but I don't think I'm going to be harmed in any way by just meeting him."

That evening, the Gorbachevs hosted their guests at a state dinner in the Chamber of Facets, housed in the Palace of Facets, a spectacular fifteenth-century Italian Renaissance–style stone building. The large, dramatic hall, with a central pillar, had once been a ceremonial setting for the czars. In his toast, Reagan turned personal and sentimental:

As wartime allies, we came to know you in a special way. But in a broader sense, the American people, like the rest of the world, admire the saga of the peoples of the Soviet Union. The clearing of the forest, the struggle to build a society, the evolution into a modern state, and the struggle against Hitler's armies. There are other ways, too, that we know you: "Happy or sad, my beloved, you are beautiful," says one of your folk songs, "as beautiful as a Russian song, as beautiful as a Russian soul."

Gorbachev's translator, Igor Korchilov, no doubt echoed many observers when he wrote of Reagan's words and demeanor that night:

As I watched and listened to him, I found it hard to believe that it was happening right here in this "focus of the Evil Empire," which he had castigated so often. That the former sworn enemies were now sharing speeches, but also private jokes and anecdotes, was hard to believe. I could have pinched myself to make sure it was not a dream . . . the ice of the Cold War seemed to be melting before my eyes.

Nancy was seated beside Gorbachev. At one point, he turned to her and said, "You know, your husband and I have a certain . . ."

Seeing that he was struggling for the word, she said, "Let me help you. Chemistry?"

"Yes, chemistry."

"I know you do. I'm very aware of it, and so is my husband."

"It's very rare," said Gorbachev.

REAGAN AND GORBACHEV WERE in Gorbachev's office the second morning of the summit, alone after sitting for a photo op. Before they started their discussion, Reagan pulled out a gift for his friend, a denim jacket. Gorbachev held it up curiously and asked if it was his size. Reagan assured him that he had no way of knowing. "In any case," Gorbachev said, "it was a marvelous souvenir"—one he would keep at home. In return, he gave Reagan a scale model of the Kremlin.

But the best gift was yet to come. Gorbachev said he had something pleasant he wanted to show the president. He grabbed a pile of correspondence from his desk and told him that they were some of the letters and cables people had sent Reagan through the Kremlin, which he wished to pass on. They sat together reading the messages, smiling and laughing:

OUR BABY DAUGHTER, WEIGHING 3100 GRAMS, WAS BORN ON MAY 28TH, THE EVE OF YOUR FIRST VISIT TO OUR COUNTRY. WITH THE BEST OF INTENTIONS, WE WISH TO NAME HER "REAGANA"—YOUR SURNAME WITH THE ADDITION OF THE LETTER "A." WE WANT TO TELL YOU ABOUT THIS AND REQUEST YOUR CONSENT.

WE ARE HAPPY ABOUT YOUR ARRIVAL. WE HAVE JUST HAD A BABY GIRL. WE ASK YOUR PERMISSION TO NAME HER NANCY.

ESTEEMED MR. PRESIDENT: ON THE EVE OF YOUR ARRIVAL IN THE SOVIET UNION OUR SON WAS BORN. AS

A SIGN OF STRENGTHENING FRIENDSHIP BETWEEN THE PEOPLES OF THE USSR AND THE USA WE HAVE DECIDED TO NAME OUR SON RONALD. WE INVITE YOU TO BECOME GODFATHER TO OUR SON.

ON THE DAY OF YOUR ARRIVAL IN OUR COUNTRY—A DAY OF HISTORICAL IMPORTANCE—OUR BABY DAUGHTER WAS BORN. WE HAVE DECIDED TO NAME HER NANCY IN HONOR OF YOUR WIFE. WE WISH YOU PRODUCTIVE WORK AND SUCCESS IN YOUR TALKS FOR THE GOOD OF THE WHOLE WORLD.

Gorbachev went on through the letters, both men beaming at the simple well wishes of the people from far and wide. Reagan was delighted, and Gorbachev promised to send him all the letters. They were still coming in. He hastened to add that they were completely spontaneous and genuine—similar to the types of letters he'd received from Americans after his visit to Washington. Reagan chuckled, imagining all the newly christened baby Mikhails and Raisas in the United States. It was a touching personal moment, highlighting the boundless hopes of ordinary people of both nations. In that way, two leaders with lofty issues on their minds, and burdened by political considerations, were pulled back to Earth by the simple expressions of the citizens who only wanted a peaceful world and better lives.

The letters from the United States were interesting, Gorbachev added. Some questioned whether the interaction between the two nations was worthwhile. He always responded by highlighting the interests at stake for them and for the world, and how the United States and the Soviet Union had a special role to play in that process.

"I have one simple rule," Reagan responded. "You don't get

into trouble by talking to each other, instead of just *about* each other."

Gorbachev then launched into a remarkably candid explanation of what he was trying to accomplish with perestroika. The main thing was democratization, he said. Not just economic, though that was important—especially autonomy in production and among the workers—but also in life. To achieve that, he confided, meant that the Party would need to give up some of the functions it should not have. Interestingly, he stressed that those reforms were not an abdication of socialism; his aim was to bring socialism to its fullest potential. Slapping the coffee table in front of them with the flat of his hand, he added that in socialism they did not want to level things out like a table. The point was, the better producer would be the better earner. The better worker or the better scientist would be paid more. That was a startling statement. Clearly he was still working out how socialism could thrive in what was essentially a market economy.

He was just thinking aloud, he said, but cooperation, expanded trade measures, bilateral exchanges—that was the direction in which they must go.

The key is to eliminate mistrust, Reagan replied simply. Yes, Gorbachev agreed, that was the whole point of what they were doing.

Before the summit, Shultz had urged Reagan to make sure to take a walk in Red Square, which he considered to be one of the greatest sights in the world. Some of the worrywarts at the White House were concerned about the optics—what would the American people make of pictures of Reagan in front of Lenin's tomb? But in Helsinki Shultz brought up the idea again. He told Reagan about the beauty of the square, adding a bit of history: "Red" was the English translation of the Russian word for "beautiful," and the "Beautiful Square" had been named that before communism. (Noting the translation, Korchilov later joked about the American saying "Better dead than Red," noting that " 'Better dead than beautiful' would not have had the same ring.")

Shultz suggested that Reagan say, "Mr. General Secretary, I understand that Red Square is quite a sight to see, and some time during the course of this visit, I'd like to see it." Reagan nodded. He did want to see Red Square. "I'll bet that Gorbachev will say 'great idea,' and he'll wind up being your tour guide," Shultz said. And that's essentially what happened.

They looked perfectly at ease with each other as they strolled out onto the square, stopping to chat with groups of citizens. "There were all these collections of people around the square, maybe eight or ten people in one," Fitzwater said. "And they were all dressed like peasants. The women had on long print floral dresses like the country ladies would wear and babushkas. The men wore suits, but they were workingmen's suits." It was, he thought, a picture of the common people straight out of central casting.

Fitzwater began to notice that some of the questions were odd, coming from ordinary peasants. For example, one elderly woman asked Reagan, "Mr. President, why won't you allow us to see the telemetry from your space shuttle adventures or program?" Another asked about sharing space data, and a third asked a similar technical question.

Then it clicked for Fitzwater. "Look at these people," he said to Baker, who was standing nearby. "The ladies are maids and telephone operators and cleaning ladies from our hotel. And look at the men—they're our drivers from yesterday. Everyone speaks English, which means they're KGB. They dressed them up like peasants."

Baker nodded.

"Howard, should I tell him? Does this matter?" Fitzwater asked.

"Well, I don't know, but . . . yes, you tell him."

Fitzwater went up to Reagan, where he was standing with Gorbachev. "Mr. President, can I have a word for just a second?"

Reagan nodded and backed away two steps.

"These groups are KGB," Fitzwater said quietly. Then he walked away and Reagan returned to his conversations. Reagan's demeanor never changed, and he didn't indicate to Gorbachev that he was onto the ruse. He was just as genial as ever. One could almost hear him thinking, *So what if they're KGB? They're also Russians, just like everyone else.*

There was a side story to Reagan's walk in Red Square that's become the subject of intrigue in recent years. The White House photographer Pete Souza (who would serve under President Barack Obama as well) snapped a picture of Reagan greeting a young boy. Over the boy's left shoulder is a blond man, standing like a tourist with a camera around his neck. Souza later said he was told that the man was Vladimir Putin, and many people thought it looked like him. At the time, Putin, thirty-five, was a KGB functionary serving in East Germany, and the Russian press has scoffed at the idea that he was in Moscow. But Putin's supposed appearance in Reagan's frame became something of a myth, often referenced, and never confirmed, though it is clear that there was a substantial KGB presence in the square that day. Fitzwater weighed in on that during a recent conversation. "I saw the picture," he told this author. "I believe it was him; he denies it. But the picture looks just like him, and now, knowing his personality with thirty years of hindsight, I would bet my life on it that he was there."

As they walked through Red Square, the ABC reporter Sam

Donaldson called out to Reagan, "Do you still think you're in an evil empire?"

Reagan paused. "No," he said firmly, "that was another time, another era." His answer, which seemed casually delivered but might have been planned, had a bracing effect on the Soviet people. "It made them pay attention to the other things he said," Matlock observed, "such as his admiration for Russian women, accustomed to holding a full-time job while maintaining a household in the midst of scarcity, his love for Russian literature and music, his sympathy for the terrible human losses during World War II and to Stalin's terror."

His words in Red Square also scored a victory for Gorbachev. Now he could tell his party leaders, "See, my efforts have changed the American mind." It was as if Reagan had lifted a five-year curse.

Reagan felt exhilarated after his walk in Red Square, but the main event was still to come. That afternoon he had a date with destiny, as he might have described it—a speech at Moscow State University where he would finally present his case to the Soviet people.

CHAPTER 11

THE SPEECH

An enormous bust of Vladimir Lenin, frowning and fierce, poised atop a tall yellow pedestal, loomed over the stage at Moscow State University where Reagan would give his address. To its left was a dramatic mural of the Russian Revolution.

Josh Gilder, the speechwriter assigned to draft Reagan's speech, was aghast when he paid an advance visit to the auditorium and saw the setting.

"I had an instinctive reaction of repulsion," Gilder recalled. The backdrop needed to be changed. Gilder knew that Gorbachev had told people to be helpful, so he said to the official accompanying him, "Okay, the first thing is, the bust of Lenin has to go. Is it movable?"

"Yes," said the official, shaking a bit.

"Wheel it out," Gilder instructed.

The official was nearly in tears. "Second," Gilder said, "cover up the mural."

Agitated, the official hurried off to consult with others.

But as Gilder waited in the hall, his eyes nervously traveling back and forth from the majestic bust to the sweeping mural, he came to a realization: the setting was not demeaning to American values; it was a backdrop that would heighten the power of Reagan's speech. Sitting there, the first line came to him: "Standing here before a mural of your revolution . . ." He quickly told the official that the bust and mural could remain.

And so the dramatic stage was set. But it was still a bit of a shock when the president's aides arrived that day, shortly before the speech. Fitzwater, who was riding in the motorcade behind the president, received a call on his phone. A nervous aide said, "Marlin, when you get here, take a look at this podium where the president's going to be speaking."

"What is it?" Fitzwater asked.

"Lenin . . . a huge statue . . . right above the podium."

"Oh, no," Fitzwater mumbled. Was it a trick? "Here's the problem," he said. "We can't really do anything about this without making a scene." It was too late. Students were already filing into the auditorium.

Like Gilder before him, Fitzwater quickly reached a positive point of view. Later, when someone asked him what he had thought of Reagan standing in front of Lenin for his speech, he had a snappy comeback: "If anybody would ever appreciate Lenin having to spend an hour and a half looking at the backside of Ronald Reagan, it would be the president."

The choice of Moscow State University for Reagan's major speech was loaded with significance. Considered Moscow's finest university, with thirty-five thousand students, it was an imposing structure in Lenin Hills, with a view of the city. Both Gorbachev and his wife were graduates, although neither would be present for the speech. (Nor would Nancy, who was on a day trip to Leningrad.)

The students who crowded into the twelve-hundred-seat auditorium were like students everywhere: informally dressed, their faces a mix of curiosity, excitement, and practiced indifference. They had been raised to distrust and even hate the United States, just as American children had been raised to distrust and hate the Soviet Union. But because they were young and attended a university where ideas were debated, many of them had expanded their thinking. If a poll had been conducted among them, it would probably have shown approval of Gorbachev's reforms. In some circles, perhaps, Reagan was even lionized, just as Gorbachev was by American youth. Those were indeed strange times, the apple cart of conventional thinking upended by their leaders.

Anthony Dolan viewed the Moscow speech as the final flowering of Reagan's philosophy—begun at Westminster with the "ash heap of history," confirmed in Orlando with the "Evil Empire," and furthered in Berlin with "tear down this wall!" In Moscow, Reagan was summoning a vision of the new world that awaited them, already striding forward—as if the Communist state were a mere technicality of history. Some people thought his early speeches were the "old" Reagan and the later speeches were the "new" Reagan, but Dolan saw them as being all of a piece—the continuum of his grander design. Dolan remembered being in the Oval Office the previous December 7, the day before the Gorbachevs had arrived for the Washington summit. Reagan had invited four writers in for a conversation. One of them, Ben Wattenberg, who was mostly associated with Democrats, had asked bluntly, "Have we won the Cold War?"

Hearing that, Dolan had felt overtaken, finding the moment almost extraterrestrial. He stepped outside and viewed the scene from the Rose Garden. "I could see Reagan shifting uneasily in his seat, because he wanted to say yes, but he didn't want to up-end things before the summit," he said. He watched as Reagan gave a standard nonanswer: "We're working on it . . . much is left to be done . . ."

Reagan believed that the Cold War was over, even if he never said it out loud, so the Moscow speech had a markedly different tone than any address he had ever given about communism—

optimistic and futuristic, friendly and even collegial, like old friends making plans.

Dolan thought Gilder was the perfect person to give expression to those thoughts. "Josh had a great understanding of Reagan," he said, recalling the first time he'd taken Gilder into the Oval Office to meet the president. He could feel Gilder "getting" Reagan, listening to him, recognizing his communication genius.

"Most of us understood it wasn't us, it was *him*," Gilder recalled, meaning Reagan. "When I first came on the staff, I asked someone, 'How do I write like Ronald Reagan?' I was told, 'Don't try to. Write the best speech you can and he will make it sound like Ronald Reagan.' He was transformational in this way. Reagan's speeches were remembered because people learned he meant what he said. He had a vision, and every single thing he did as president was part of it. I don't think there's ever been a more consistent politician."

When Gilder returned with a draft, it was beautiful. Reagan loved it. Once again, the nervous Nellies in the State Department and NSC hovered around, worrying about the language. But they soon realized that the speech had no single phrase that might give offense, no line that just *had* to be excised. Its deeper meaning was encased in respectful prose and stirring poetry. It was meant to lift hearts, not rattle cages. And it was pure, unadulterated Reagan. It might have been entitled "Morning in Moscow."

When Reagan strode to the podium, there was polite clapping, but he immediately won over the audience with his opening: "I know you must be very busy this week, studying and taking your final examinations," he said. "So, let me just say, *zhelayu vam uspekha* [I wish you success]."

The speechwriters had lobbied for a different saying—*Ni púkha, ni perá*, literally meaning "Neither fur nor feathers," a traditional good luck wish given to hunters, comparable to the American saying "Break a leg." But Reagan struggled with the exact pronunciation, which was important because it was close to an expression meaning flatulence. So they played it safe with the less colloquial phrasing. It didn't matter. The students applauded enthusiastically.

It was a speech remarkable for its poetry, its subversive seduction, and its subject matter: the technological progress of the current era, the promise available to those modern-day explorers, perhaps sitting in that hall.

Standing here before a mural of your revolution, I want to talk about a very different revolution that is taking place right now, quietly sweeping the globe without bloodshed or conflict. Its effects are peaceful, but they will fundamentally alter our world, shatter old assumptions, and reshape our lives. It's easy to underestimate because it's not accompanied by banners or fanfare. It's been called the technological or information revolution, and as its emblem, one might take the tiny silicon chip, no bigger than a fingerprint. One of these chips has more computing power than a roomful of old-style computers.

But then, ever so subtly, Reagan turned the discourse around, framing the "revolution" as the product of freedom, with the underlying message that it was the reward of an open society. He didn't criticize the Soviet Union; instead, he spoke to the audience of their shared aspirations, based on the assumption that they were collaborators in destiny, seeking common goals. He spoke to them as if they were bound together in a common destiny. He was trying not to persuade them but to inspire them. He didn't shout. He didn't preach. He didn't admonish. He let the warm timbre of his voice wash over the hall. As they listened, the students witnessed the rhetorical gift that Americans had long appreciated: his utter authenticity, the words more convincing because they were spoken from the heart. Time and again he returned to the topic of freedom:

We Americans make no secret of our belief in freedom. . . .

Go to any American town, to take just an example, and you'll see dozens of churches, representing many different beliefs—in many places, synagogues and mosques—and you'll see families of every conceivable nationality worshiping together. Go into any schoolroom, and there you will see children being taught the Declaration of Independence, that they are endowed by their Creator with certain unalienable rights—among them life, liberty, and the pursuit of happiness—that no government can justly deny; the guarantees in their Constitution for freedom of speech, freedom of assembly, and freedom of religion. Go into any courtroom, and there will preside an independent judge, beholden to no government power. There every defendant has the right to a trial by a jury of his peers, usually 12 men and women—common citizens; they are the ones, the only ones, who weigh the evidence and decide on guilt or innocence. In that court, the accused is innocent until proven guilty, and the word of a policeman or any official has no greater legal standing than the word of the accused. Go to any university campus, and there you'll find an open, sometimes heated discussion of the problems in American society and what can be done to correct them. Turn on the television, and you'll see the legislature conducting the business of government right there before the camera, debating and voting on the legislation that will become the law of the land. March in any demonstration, and there are many of them; the people's right of assembly is guaranteed in the Constitution and protected by the police. Go into any union hall, where the members know their right to strike is protected by law. As a matter of fact, one of the many jobs I had before this one was being president of a union, the Screen Actors Guild. I led my union out on strike, and I'm proud to say we won.

But then he added that it wasn't just America or the West that knew about freedom and greatness. In fact, not once in his speech did he criticize the Russian people. Instead, he elevated them with a deep tone of respect, stating that one of the most eloquent passages on human freedom came not from American literature but from the Russian writer Boris Pasternak in the novel *Dr. Zhivago*: "I think that if the beast who sleeps in man could be held down by threats—any kind of threat, whether of jail or of retribution after death—then the highest emblem of humanity would be the lion tamer in the circus with his whip, not the prophet who sacrificed himself. But this is just the point—what has for centuries raised man above the beast is not the cudgel, but an inward music—the irresistible power of unarmed truth."

He was a messenger of hope, seducing them with their own longings, which he knew they had. How could they resist the poignant cry of their countryman? It was not Reagan the outsider they didn't fully trust but Reagan the human being who reminded them of their higher purpose, richly detailed in Russian literature and fully grounded in their hearts. "Is this just a dream?" he asked, his voice growing soft. "Perhaps. But it is a dream that is our responsibility to have come true." The hall was still, the audience rapt. "Your generation is living in one of the most exciting, hopeful times in Soviet history. It is a time when the first breath of freedom stirs the air and the heart beats to the accelerated rhythm of hope, when the accumulated spiritual energies of a long silence yearn to break free." He was reaching out to anyone who felt discouraged, anyone who felt that things could never change. It was the first breath of freedom, and they were there to experience it. He was erasing the conflict that had defined the relationship of their nations and speaking of their shared identity. He was asking them to set aside, if only for a moment, their resistance to democratic principles and think of themselves and the people they could become.

Finally he employed a sentimental tone that brought tears to many eyes. It was Reagan, with his melodic voice, that restored to them the plaintive cry that was in the Russian heart. Reagan had already seen it that week in the excited faces of the crowds in the Arbat, in the fears of the refuseniks, in the serene hope of the monks, in the breathless anticipation in the faces of artists and poets.

I've been told that there's a popular song in your country—perhaps you know it—whose evocative refrain asks the question, "Do the Russians want a war?" In answer it says: "Go ask that silence lingering in the air, above the birch and poplar there; beneath those trees the soldiers lie. Go ask my mother, ask my wife; then you will have to ask no more, 'Do the Russians want a war?'" But what of your one-time allies? What of those who embraced you on the Elbe? What if we were to ask the watery graves of the Pacific or the European battle-fields where America's fallen were buried far from home? What if we were to ask their mothers, sisters, and sons, do Americans want war? Ask us, too, and you'll find the same answer, the same longing in every heart. People do not make wars; governments do. And no mother would ever willingly sacrifice her sons for territorial gain, for economic advantage, for ideology. A people free to choose will always choose peace. . . .

We do not know what the conclusion will be of this journey, but we're hopeful that the promise of reform will be fulfilled. In this Moscow spring, this May 1988, we may be allowed that hope: that freedom, like the fresh green sapling planted over Tolstoy's grave, will blossom forth at last in the rich fertile soil of your people and culture. We may be allowed to hope that the marvelous sound of a new openness will keep rising through, ringing through, leading to a new world of reconciliation, friendship, and peace.

He concluded, smiling at the audience and loving them, those young people so full of possibility. Lenin's gaze did not deter him. He wanted the students to look at *him*, to hear the message he was bringing them. The past was history; the future was theirs to own.

After the speech, he did something very unusual in the Soviet Union: he took questions from the audience. "You could see at first people being a little bit uncomfortable," Duberstein said. "Are we really going to question the president of the United States?" This was Reagan's wheelhouse; he loved to interact with people. He enjoyed the chance to spontaneously chat with the audience, and the questions were certainly not hardballs, although he wouldn't have minded if they were. Sensing that many people in the hall regarded his position as president as somehow imperial, he ended with a down-home story. "Nobody asked me what it was going to feel like to not be president anymore," he said conversationally. "I have some understanding, because after I'd been governor for eight years and then stepped down, I want to tell you what it's like. We'd only been home a few days, and someone invited us out to dinner. Nancy and I both went out, got in the back seat of the car, and waited for somebody to get in front and drive us." The audience laughed; then as one they rose to their feet and gave the president of the United States a standing ovation. Reagan later quipped that while they were cheering, he'd glanced behind him and seen Lenin weeping.

It was an amazing performance. "Here's a guy who throughout his career talked about fighting communism," said Duberstein. "And, you know, really stepping up to the Red threat and even as an actor way back when. And here he is standing in Moscow, in the Soviet Union, delivering this speech about American values. It was kind of a cap to what had been a long road to that moment."

The speech was well received, the *New York Times* declaring "It may have been Ronald Reagan's finest oratorical hour." If there was any sense of disappointment, it was that the media in Moscow didn't give the speech as much attention as expected, a preglasnost throwback. He'd hoped for live television coverage, but that hadn't happened. According to an analysis by the Foreign Broadcast Information Service, all Russian media coverage was selective. Moscow radio covered only a third of the speech, while *Pravda* published a fifth of the speech. The media published synopses rather than exact quotes. While speaking, Reagan had been mindful of addressing all the Soviet people, not just those in the room, but he hadn't quite reached his target audience.

The "odd couple" of press spokesmen, Marlin Fitzwater and Gennadi Gerasimov, jointly met the press later that afternoon. Gerasimov—articulate, sharp, and with a good sense of humor—was up to the fast-paced, tough questioning. In his opening remarks, he was effusive in his description of the events of the day. Serious talks were being held, he emphasized, and sometimes disputes—citing a man in Red Square who had quoted a Russian saying to Reagan and Gorbachev, "The truth is born in disputes." Gorbachev, he said, had added another: "If these disputes are too hot, then the truth evaporates."

Fitzwater, despite his private observation that the "ordinary citizens" in Red Square had been undercover KGB agents, praised the people of Moscow and mentioned how much Reagan had enjoyed meeting them: "The president's reaction was one of great enthusiasm and excitement for the people that he got a chance to talk to and for the description of Red Square and the Kremlin that the General Secretary gave him. He enjoyed that walk [in Red Square] very much—a chance to get out and see the city."

When a reporter suggested that Reagan had looked "tired and listless" that day—an ungenerous assertion, considering his nonstop schedule, culminating with his masterful speech at the university—Gerasimov jumped in to defend him: "After they had a walk on the Red Square, we went up on very high, steep stairs and I will tell you, I felt breathless but the president felt okay."

Fitzwater and Gerasimov sparred with reporters, seeming at ease and almost like a practiced act. When two *Pravda* reporters asked a pair of tough questions of Fitzwater, he joked to Gerasimov, "How come the *Pravda* guy never asks you a question, Gennadi?"

"Well," Gerasimov replied, "we're not supposed to ask questions of each other."

Fitzwater laughed. "I see."

The summit could feel surreal to American staffs and re-porters. They watched the Reagans interact effortlessly with the Russian people, seemingly unconcerned about potential danger. Yet, for the others, being in the heart of Moscow was charged with danger. It was impossible not to summon up im-ages of the Evil Empire they'd been hearing about for years. They knew that most of their rooms were bugged and that the principals, including Reagan, went into "the box" for secure communications. Paranoia was high at the Mezhdunarodnaya Hotel, nicknamed "the Mez," where most staffers and report-ers stayed. Dolan's secretary, whose parents collected salt and pepper shakers from all over the world, was delighted when she received several from the hotel staff as souvenirs. But then she noticed that there was a paper with a printed message rolled up in one of them. She froze. Was it a secret message? A spy communication? She hurried to find Dolan, who told her not to worry. The next day at the embassy, Dolan noticed his secretary talking with a translator. There was a sudden roar of laughter. He went over to look and found out that the secret message was an ad for a Moscow Domino's Pizza. It occurred to him that, at that moment, he might have glimpsed the end of the Cold War.

The evening of Reagan's speech, he and Nancy hosted the Gorbachevs for a small dinner at Spaso House, with a perfor-mance by Dave Brubeck. Nancy glowed, although she'd had a strenuous day, traveling to Leningrad. She'd been accompa-nied by Andrei Gromyko's wife, Lidiya. Raisa had stayed home, as if it were too taxing for her to spend another day with her counterpart. Relations between the two women continued to be chilly. As Helen Thomas put it, "You could have stored meat in the room when those two were together." At one point Raisa had felt compelled to tell reporters, "I don't believe in astrology. I believe in facts and practical things." The press ate it up.

"Mrs. Gorbachev was quite a problem," Ed Rowny remembered, citing a particularly uncomfortable tour she had given Nancy of the Moscow Portrait Gallery.

She kept [Nancy] waiting while she talked to the press about the United States. She complained that the United States was lecturing them on human rights. She added: They've enslaved and kept blacks back for three hundred years. Moreover, they've taken land away from the Indians. Who do they think they are, lecturing us about human rights? I must say, I admired Nancy for keeping her cool and not answering Raisa in kind. She just changed subjects. She comported herself very well.

Relations with Raisa aside, Nancy made the most of the trip. She'd found her Leningrad tour invigorating, and said it was the most beautiful city she had ever visited. She was overwhelmed by the reception she received from the people—many thousands lined the road to welcome her as she drove from the airport. Her only regret was that she hadn't been able to linger longer at the historic sights. Perhaps, she thought, in retirement she and Ron could return for a longer stay and do justice to Leningrad. A visit, once unimaginable, was now just a matter of scheduling.

Reagan was exhilarated by the day. The faces of those students, lifted to hear his words, with all their aspirations and doubts, were just like those of the students in his American audiences. In such moments, frozen in time, he could picture the future he believed would unfold.

CHAPTER 12

MORNING IN MOSCOW

Camera bulbs flashed when reporters were allowed into the room before the final meeting of the summit on Wednesday morning. A reporter shouted a question in Russian to Gorbachev: Had there been any surprises at the summit? Gorbachev was ready for it. That was the point of the summit, he said—to eliminate surprises and build a relationship based on greater predictability.

When the meeting began, Shevardnadze and Shultz each gave a report on where his side stood. In sum, although there would be a ceremony to sign the ratified INF Treaty, only moderate progress had been made on the Strategic Arms Reduction Treaty. Shultz tried to put a positive spin on the negotiations, saying that there were substantial areas of agreement, but there was more work to be done.

Shevardnadze and Shultz spoke of the joint statement from the summit, which their teams had been working on through the night. There were some disagreements, but they had worked out most issues. That's when everything almost fell apart again over a seemingly innocent phrase: "peaceful coexistence."

At their first meeting Gorbachev had handed Reagan a few lines he wanted included in the final joint statement. They read, "Proceeding from their understanding of the realities that have taken shape in the world today, the two leaders believe that no problem in dispute can be resolved, nor should it be resolved, by military means. They regard peaceful coexistence as a universal principle of international relations. Equality of all states, non-interference in internal affairs, and freedom of sociopolitical choice must be recognized as the inalienable and mandatory standards of international relations."

Reagan had glanced at it and seen no problem. He'd turned it over to his staff, and had never given it another moment's thought. But now, when they were finishing up the business of the summit, Gorbachev suddenly asked, "What about the statement I gave you?"

"Well, I know my people negotiated our joint statement all night long. I don't know about this statement. Let me confer with them."

To Reagan's astonishment, Gorbachev erupted in anger. "Why? Why? This is a simple statement. You had no objection to this last Sunday."

"I just want to make sure we all understand the change you want to make," Reagan said.

Gorbachev demanded, "What do you mean? Don't listen to George [Shultz], Ron. George doesn't know anything. He's only the secretary of state. Don't listen to him."

"Well, I want to know what he thinks."

"Don't listen to Frank [Carlucci]. Frank doesn't know. This is about peace and getting along together. What does he know about it? Quit listening to all your aides around you, Mr. President, and think for yourself."

Gorbachev was plainly baffled that the president of the United States would not simply assert his authority but preferred to abide by the recommendations of his advisors. "Should we record," he asked sarcastically, "that the Americans would not agree to the paragraph because of George Shultz or Frank Carlucci? Are they the intransigent parties? Is one of them a revisionist? If not, perhaps we need to look for a scapegoat elsewhere. Perhaps Ambassador Matlock or Assistant Secretary Ridgway?"

Whoa! Fitzwater gaped at the two men. "I thought Reagan might walk out," he said. "Or there might be a fistfight. George Shultz, usually so calm, looked like he was ready to turn the table over. What was going on here?"

Reagan was seated next to Colin Powell. Fitzwater, standing back, saw Powell rip off a corner of his pad and scribble something on it. Then he slid it under the table to Reagan. The president took it, glanced at it, and laid it on the table. Then he told Gorbachev he was going to confer with his people. They gathered at the far side of the room, where Shultz, Carlucci, and the others explained the problem. Gorbachev's addition might have seemed innocuous, but it actually had important implications—as was clear from Gorbachev's fury. "I argued strongly that this represented a return to détente-era declarations that could be variously interpreted, had not stopped the Soviets from invading Afghanistan, and implied, by the phrase 'peaceful coexistence,' a willingness to leave unchallenged areas of Soviet conquest and control," Shultz wrote. In other words, it was a sneaky way of returning to détente. Although it was one of Gorbachev's favorite ideas, Reagan had never supported "peaceful coexistence"—the idea that the United States and the Soviet Union were equal powers with manageable differences. That was a stance he had held throughout his administration, hearkening back to his speech at Westminster. He could never allow "peaceful coexistence" to appear in any statement with his signature.

Returning to Gorbachev, he said, "The answer is no. We're not going to do it."

Gorbachev glowered at him. "Ron, we've got to get rid of these people," he said. "I want to talk to you privately. Let's you and I go down here to the end of the table and have a private talk about this." They walked to the end of the table, away from their advisors. There they stood, toe to toe, and Gorbachev, who was shorter than Reagan, looked up at him and shook his finger in Reagan's face. He was shouting, and his words could be heard: "Think for yourself. Tell me what's wrong with this. What's wrong with this sentence?"

Fitzwater recalled, "President Reagan looked down at him quietly and said, 'We're not accepting it. No. The answer is no.' And Gorbachev's shoulders just collapsed. He dropped his arms, his head went down, and he took a step away. And then he raised back up again, put his arm around Reagan, and said, 'Let's go to the press conference.' " Gorbachev had given in. He knew Reagan well enough to realize that he wouldn't change his mind. The line was struck from the joint statement.

As he walked out of the room, Fitzwater noticed that the piece of paper Powell had handed Reagan was still on the table. He picked it up. It read, "That means you agree to never criticize them again."

Observing the scene, which made the people in the room extremely uncomfortable and even alarmed, Korchilov argued that it was actually a positive moment; Reagan and Gorbachev were treating each other as equals, not with the false deference that masks the truth. "This enabled Gorbachev and Reagan to speak with each other freely and frankly," he concluded, "stepping literally on each other's toes at their last meeting. If they had not become friends in the real sense of the word, they had become partners who held each other in genuine respect."

"Toe to toe": that was the essence of the relationship that had developed between the two men. Such intimacy can expose painful differences, but it has the advantage of being more honest than rhetorical volleys sent from a distance. When Gorbachev cried, "Think for yourself!," he was confronting a friend, not an abstract foe. One cannot imagine Khrushchev shouting that at Eisenhower or Brezhnev at Nixon. Those relationships had existed under layers of subterfuge, making it easier to break off negotiations over the flimsiest excuse. But Reagan and Gorbachev were bonded now; their fights were of the kind that families and friends have.

After the summit, Reagan and Gorbachev gave separate press conferences, and Gorbachev was still smarting. He seemed to be damning the president with faint praise when he said the summit had moved relations "maybe one rung or two up the ladder." He couldn't quite let go of his disappointment that the "peaceful coexistence" language had not made it into the final statement and said, "I believe Mr. Reagan missed an important chance to take a step forward."

By contrast, Reagan stuck to a positive script, praising the tone of the summit and the leadership of Gorbachev. He made a point of crediting Gorbachev for the progress they had made. In Matlock's opinion, those flattering words "probably did more than any other single event to build support in the Soviet Union for Gorbachev's reforms." Gorbachev needed that affirmation from Reagan to prove he was making progress with the United States.

There was no sign of a chill when the Reagans and Gorbachevs met that evening for a performance of the Bolshoi Ballet at the nineteenth-century Bolshoi Theatre. Standing with the Gorbachevs in the royal box while "The Star-Spangled Banner" played, Reagan felt his spirits soar. "To hear that song, which embodies everything our country stands for, so stirringly played by a Soviet orchestra, was an emotional moment that is indescribable," he wrote. "I knew the world was changing."

After the performance, they drove to a private dinner with the Gorbachevs at a guest dacha in a wooded area outside Moscow—a Soviet version of Camp David, some called it. The Shultzes and Shevardnadzes were also invited. Shultz recalled that the mood was warmer and lighter than it had ever been before, with many jokes from both sides—even from Raisa! More seriously, conversation turned to the nuclear disaster at Chernobyl, and Gorbachev expressed how deeply affected he had been by the accident and how it had strengthened his resolve to end the curse of nuclear weapons. He was newly horrified by the thought of the toll a nuclear event of any kind could take.

It was a long dinner—too long, Nancy thought—and it was nearing midnight when they drove back to the city. They were tired, Nancy nearly falling asleep in the car. But as they passed Red Square, Reagan perked up. He wanted to show Nancy Red Square, where he had been with Gorbachev the previous day. She considered pleading tiredness, but later she was glad she hadn't. The square was brightly lit, and they got out of the car and walked toward the building containing Lenin's tomb. Inside, Lenin's body was preserved and displayed in a sarcophagus, open for public viewing during daylight hours. They gazed up at the multicolored swirled domes of St. Basil's Cathedral. Standing in the middle of the square, whose size and majesty symbolized a greatness that was now fading, the Reagans held hands and marveled at the large crowd of spectators waving at them from behind a rope line. How had those people known they'd be there? *They* hadn't even known.

At a friendly departure ceremony at the Kremlin the next morning, Reagan pulled out a copy of the *Time* magazine issue featuring Gorbachev as Man of the Year and asked him to sign it, which he did. "Well, you are now a popular man," Raisa teased her husband. "The president of the United States himself asks you for an autograph." They all laughed, but the moment felt emotional, an ending of sorts. Reagan clasped Gorbachev's hand. "I think you understand we're not just grateful to you and Mrs. Gorbachev, but want you to know we think of you as friends," he said.

Riding to the airport, Reagan peered out the window, enjoying the crowds of people waving at him along the way. He'd noticed it during the entire trip—the happy, welcoming faces in the crowds. He told Duberstein that it was how he knew the trip had been a success—from the faces of the people. He always watched them, trying to make eye contact. "Some presidents, when they get in the limo, think they're in a secure location, they're just going to work," Duberstein said. "Not Reagan. He said, 'These people are giving me the courtesy of coming out to see me. I need to see them, too.'"

As he boarded Air Force One for a side trip to Great Britain to debrief Margaret Thatcher before heading home, Reagan commented on the weather. It was drizzling, and he said to his aides, "We arrived in Moscow in sunshine, and we leave in rain. It means people are crying that we're leaving."

As Air Force One lifted into the sky over Moscow, everyone spontaneously rose to their feet, including the press pool, and sang "God Bless America." Reagan and Nancy led the singing.

"Reagan felt he had hit a grand slam in Moscow," Duberstein said. But there was much more to be done, and his time in office was nearing an end. He had less than eight months to finish his work, and he was humbled by the glacial pace of making history.

Not everyone would characterize the Moscow summit—the centerpiece of this book—as the critical turning point in the end of the Cold War. Some would cite the Geneva summit, when Reagan and Gorbachev had first met face-to-face and where the scaffolding of their future negotiations had been erected. Others would name Reykjavík, in spite of the heated dispute that had ended the summit, because the two sides had reached agreements on important points that they could not take back. Still others would name the Washington summit, not only because that was where an actual treaty had been signed but because it had enhanced the notion of friendship between the two men and their nations.

Moscow, which could not have happened without the other three summits, was transcendent—a coda to Reagan's eight years in office and his life's ambition. In its timing, its tone, and its moral achievement, it did more than any of the others to squarely present the nature of the choice the world was facing. Early in his administration, when Reagan had consigned the Soviet system to "the ash heap of history," many people (especially the Soviets) had misunderstood his words to mean that he was bent on its destruction. Rather, he had been saying that the Soviet system was already collapsing, that history was already marching past it. By the time of the Moscow summit, that fact was evident to everyone, including the Soviets themselves. Yes, they remained a world power. Yes, their arsenal of weapons was still great. But beneath the surface, the economy was in free fall, its citizenry was restless; the architect of perestroika was breaking down the remaining barriers. Reagan's prediction was coming true, as he, if not others, had always known it would.

The collapse of an untenable system did not need a Gorbachev to make it happen, and indeed, when he had first spoken of its inevitable doom, Reagan had not counted on someone like Gorbachev coming into power. He could not have imagined that the Soviets would move closer to his vision of the world so quickly. They had been an intractable force for decades, and then, with Gorbachev, they weren't. That's not to say that the relationship was easy or that Gorbachev had abandoned communism. But he'd left the door open, so that democratization could walk in and take possession.

In the nuclear age, peace is the only viable resolution, and peace is not made in the abstract but between humans. The relationship that developed between the two leaders was transformational. In the often stormy yet enduringly warm collaboration, bitter foes became good-faith negotiators and set the stage for a world that was soon to change. Surely, in 1981, few would have pictured the man whose opposition to communism was like mother's milk walking in Red Square or standing tall on the stage of Russia's premier university to speak passionately about American values. He was there not only because he'd been invited but because Gorbachev had welcomed him in and allowed him to be heard.

Arguably the most important moment of the Moscow visit was Reagan's announcement that the "Evil Empire" was a thing of the past. When the Soviet people witnessed the most ardent public anti-Communist in the world standing in Red Square and embracing a future together with them, it gave them new reason to believe that their leader's reforms were on the right track. Gorbachev himself wrote in his memoirs, "In my view, the 40th president of the United States will go down in history for his rare perception."

When Air Force One at last landed at Andrews Air Force Base in the late afternoon of June 3, Reagan made a statement to the press. "As some of you may have heard, Mr. Gorbachev and I have been trading Russian proverbs this week. But, you know, flying back across the Atlantic today, it was an American saying that kept running through my mind. Believe me, as far as Nancy and I are concerned, there's no place like home."

"You made us proud," Vice President Bush told Reagan

when he welcomed him at Andrews. He assured him that the nation shared his verdict. Americans like to think that their president represents them, not just oratorically but fundamentally—that when other nations see and touch him, they are seeing and touching the essential character of America. Walking through Red Square, standing on a vegetable cart in the Arbat, or casting his long shadow on the statue of Lenin at Moscow State University, Reagan exuded a vigor and a joy that reflected the best side of the United States of America.

HIS TIME IN OFFICE was drawing to a close. On November 8, Vice President George Bush, with his running mate, Dan Quayle, won an overwhelming victory over Democratic candidates Michael Dukakis and Lloyd Bentsen—426 electoral votes and 40 states—to be elected the forty-first president of the United States.

Those who might have considered Bush's victory the beginning of a third Reagan term were soon disabused of the notion. Bush, whose understated personality had given rise to the unfair charge that he was a "wimp," was a very different character from his predecessor. And the decorated World War II aviator was no wimp; that soon became clear. He was about to step into the presidency on his own terms. Gorbachev had reason to be concerned. After all, during the campaign, Bush had said that "the jury is still out" on the Soviet Union. Ironically, early in his vice presidency, when Reagan's rhetoric about the Soviet Union could verge on inflammatory, Bush had privately said he should be less contentious. Now was another time.

Gorbachev had reason to wonder whether negotiations would continue as they had with Reagan. He was frustrated that Bush seemed curt and withdrawn during the transition.

Bush explained the American custom of the president-elect not interfering in foreign policy until he was sworn into office. But as Jon Meacham explained in *Destiny and Power*, "He [Bush] had pledged an essential continuation of Reagan's policies but very much wanted to put his own mark on diplomacy. Thus was born the idea of a wide-ranging Bush review of the Reagan administration's standing positions around the world. There was much to contemplate, especially with the Soviets."

With that in mind, Gorbachev reached out to Reagan in the fall, suggesting one last meeting on December 7 in New York City, during the UN General Assembly. It would be Gorbachev's first visit to New York. Reagan readily agreed. It would not be an official summit, just a friendly get-together and lunch, but Gorbachev had a strategic reason for suggesting it: he wanted to plant a virtual flag on their progress in the hope that the incoming president would stay the course.

According to Colin Powell, the idea was not met with much enthusiasm by Shultz or himself. Everyone assumed Gorbachev's intention was to get close to Bush. He needed to be reminded, Powell said, that in the United States we had only one president at a time. Furthermore, they must emphasize that the meeting would not deal with substance. "No deals. No initiatives. No eleventh-hour surprises pulled on the old leader going out or the new leader coming in," he said of his conversation with Shultz.

"The Vice President did not want this meeting," Powell added. "He did not want to find himself in a room with Gorbachev and get committed, even before he had become President." As Bush's unease grew on the day of the meeting, he told Powell, "I'm not going to get pinned by this guy. I do not want to be hoodwinked by this guy."

"Mr. Vice President," Powell assured him, "we've talked to the Soviets and made it clear to them that this is a courtesy meeting; it is not a summit. We went out of our way to tell everybody it is not a summit, it is a meeting. *Goodbye, Ronnie. Hello, George. How are you doing, Misha?* That's it, and there will be no announcements, pronouncements, or anything like that, so it's okay." Bush, still nervous, said, "All right."

But others saw it as a final opportunity. Ken Duberstein, who had moved into the role of chief of staff after Moscow, when Howard Baker had stepped down to care for his ailing wife, relished the chance for a dramatic final meeting between Reagan and Gorbachev. He was rightly awed by his role in the drama. "Everybody walks into the Oval Office and gets cotton in their mouth," he reflected later, understanding that his place was to be more than a gatekeeper. "Your job is not to tell the president what he wants to know but what he needs to know. You're the one that has to paint the picture of what reality is. You're the person who has to generally say, 'Uh-uh, it doesn't fly.' You're the person who has to say, 'Mr. President, let me take another look at that, let me get better options for you. This decision is not ripe to be made today. Mr. President, let's not go down that path.' . . . You always have to be a reality therapist."

Duberstein was aware that the charge he carried was coming at the end of Reagan's presidency. And he was proud to be the overseer of the final meeting between Reagan and Gorbachev.

They would meet at a site that could not be more weighted in symbolism. Governors Island, only a few hundred yards from Manhattan in New York Harbor, had been a fortress during the Revolutionary War and was now the largest Coast Guard base in the world. Reagan had been there on July 4, 1986, to unveil the newly refurbished Statue of Liberty. From the island, a mile and a half away, Reagan had pushed a button that had released a blue laser beam to Liberty Island, creating a celebratory light show.

Secret documents made public in 2008 describe the content of the meeting and lunch, but the optics were visible for all to see, captured in a stirring photograph of Reagan, Gorbachev, and Bush standing together on a jetty over the water, their coats flapping in the chill wind, and the Statue of Liberty in the background.

Reagan and Gorbachev were glad to see each other. Reagan presented him with a gift: a framed photo of them together in Geneva, where it had all started. The inscription read, "We walked a long way together to clear a path to peace, Geneva 1985—New York 1988."

Gorbachev might have been feeling justifiably proud when he arrived, following a news-making speech at the United Nations in which he declared an end to Soviet aggression in Eastern Europe, with unilateral cuts in Soviet forces totaling 500,000 soldiers and the withdrawal of thousands of tanks.

The speech not only was welcome, it foreshadowed an entirely new world order—a Soviet Union free of aggression. As the *Guardian* wrote approvingly, "The Russian steamroller has loomed over Europe since it first invaded, on the heels of Napoleon's retreat from Moscow in 1812. And as the Soviet leader once again seized the initiative on the world stage yesterday, you could almost feel the earth shifting inside the UN building." In the *New York Times*: "Perhaps not since Woodrow Wilson presented his Fourteen Points in 1918 or since Franklin Roosevelt and Winston Churchill promulgated the Atlantic Charter in 1941 has a world figure demonstrated the vision Mikhail Gorbachev displayed yesterday at the United Nations."

Perhaps more meaningful than the press accolades were the loud cheers and ovations from the floor as Gorbachev delivered the speech, as well as the enthusiastic reactions of some of the old hands in Cold War negotiations. Retired general Andrew Goodpaster, former NATO supreme commander and an indispensable Eisenhower aide, said it was "the most significant step since NATO was founded." Richard Nixon, who was in attendance, pumped Gorbachev's hand afterward and praised him lavishly. Reagan wasn't there for the speech, but he heartily approved when he heard about it.

Bush's advisors were less effusive. Brent Scowcroft, who was on board to become Bush's national security advisor (he'd served the same role under Ford), thought Gorbachev's speech was a manipulative ploy aimed squarely at a change of administrations. "Gorbachev's UN speech had established, with a largely rhetorical flourish, a heady atmosphere of optimism," he said. "He could exploit an early meeting with a new president as evidence to declare the Cold War over without providing substantive actions from a 'new' Soviet Union." But Bush and his people held their fire for the time being.

Lunch at the Coast Guard commandant's residence was friendly, skirting over any policy discussions. Bush was mostly quiet, letting Gorbachev and Reagan reminisce about their meetings since Geneva. "Most of my people thought at the time it would be our only meeting," Reagan said. At one point Gorbachev confessed that he was facing tremendous resistance to his programs from the bureaucracy back home and didn't know if perestroika would succeed. "He turned to Reagan, almost as an older brother, and said, 'What would your advice be?'" recalled Duberstein. "And Reagan said, 'Mr. General Secretary, my friend, the bureaucracy is the same the world over. The only way you can overcome the bureaucracy is to get the people on your side. What that means is less money on missiles and more money for clothing and housing and transportation. It means less money on defense and more money for consumer goods. That's what you have to pursue.'"

Duberstein saw the look in Gorbachev's eyes, and he thought he glimpsed the knowledge that he was done. "If he cut back on the missiles and defense, the military would turn on him. If he cut back on consumer goods and housing, the people would not be on his side. That five-minute exchange really signaled to us that we were winning the Cold War and it was over."

That glimpse of the future notwithstanding, Gorbachev was still playing the angles at lunch. He pointedly addressed Bush, emphasizing his seriousness about his mission and the struggles he was facing in his own country. "In 1985, when I first said there was going to be a revolution, everybody cheered," he said wryly. "They said, yes, we needed a revolution. But by 1987, our revolution was on, and the cheering began to die down. Now in 1988, the revolution still goes on, but the cheering has stopped." He was no doubt referring to his sinking approval ratings at home, so frustrating after all he had tried to accomplish.

Gorbachev tried to gently bait Bush into stating what he thought about the direction Reagan had taken and what the future might hold. Bush gave little indication of where he stood on continuing Reagan's path with the Soviets. He needed time to study the issues, he told Gorbachev, while assuring him he had no intention of stalling. "I'll have the extra incentive of the president in California getting on my case and telling me to get going," he said to laughter.

While their husbands dined on Governors Island, Nancy and Raisa were attending a women's luncheon hosted by the wife of the UN secretary general. Nancy was pleased to see a notable change in Raisa's demeanor. There were none of her customary lectures, and she had an almost emotional reaction to the end of her and Nancy's public relationship. As the two women smiled and held hands, Raisa confided, "I will miss you and your husband. As for the two of us, it was destiny that put us at the place we were, next to our husbands, to help bring about the relationship that our two countries now have."

In a reflective mood, Nancy later surmised that their

awkward relationship had probably been due more to self-consciousness than to antipathy. They had been in such a glaring spotlight, every move and facial expression endlessly debated. How could they not have been nervous and tense? This time, Nancy hadn't minded the adoring crowds swarming around the Gorbachevs when they took to the streets or the massive press reporting on their travels around the city, including a visit to the 107th floor of the World Trade Center. She could see that the Americans' love of the Gorbachevs was a tribute to the relationship her husband had built with them.

On Governors Island, Reagan and Gorbachev walked out to the boats that would shuttle them back to Manhattan. They gripped hands, feeling emotional. "I will be watching you from private life and cheering you on," Reagan promised. And they departed—Reagan to serve out the remaining days of his administration, Gorbachev to face new battles and crises at home (including a deadly earthquake in Armenia, which he had learned about at lunch). "I think the meeting was a tremendous success," Reagan wrote in his diary that day. "A better attitude than at any of our previous meetings. He [Gorbachev] sounded as if he saw us as partners making a better world."

They were men with human flaws, feeling the full burden of their roles, in the moment and in history. They would meet again in different times, but for now they stood poised before the world they cared about, knowing it was no longer solely in their hands. They had pushed their fragile nursling out of the nest, and they could not predict or control the path it would take. But as they clasped hands before the cinematic backdrop of New York's skyline, both recognized that the Cold War was over, even if those around them could not quite see it.

PART FOUR

DREAMS FOR THE FUTURE

CHAPTER 13

THE FALL

"Tomorrow I stop being President," Reagan wrote in his diary right before he went to bed on January 19, 1989. Earlier that evening, his longtime aide Jim Kuhn had rushed upstairs to the residence with a folder of photographs he'd neglected to get signed. Worriedly, he said he knew the Reagans had so much to do but wondered if they could possibly take time to sign them. They both smiled and said of course they would, and Kuhn watched in amazement as they sat on the floor for forty-five minutes and signed every picture.

The preceding weeks had been a flurry of farewell events and packing. Reagan appreciated the accolades flowing in his direction, although he realized they were standard fare for a president on his way out. They'd recede soon enough, he knew, and that was okay. He tried to keep his emotions in check, but they got the better of him—and Nancy, too—on their last visit to Camp David the weekend before. "Of all the things about the presidency, we will miss Camp David the most," he said in a teary farewell to the sailors and marines who had gathered to say good-bye. Nancy, usually so stoic, could not even speak, she was so overcome with emotion.

People kept asking Reagan if he would miss being president. Some, including Gorbachev, expressed regret that he wasn't eligible for a third term. But he was ready to go. "Coming into the White House, you know you have temporary custody of this office and you're going to be leaving," he said. But of course he'd miss it. He'd miss the people, the moments of awe, the chance to shape history. Like every president nearing the end of his time, he'd experience the jarring change occurring in the moment of the transition of power that would send him back to ordinary citizenship. This bittersweet drama, played out at the end of every president's time in office, was part of the essence of American greatness. Everyone expected it and knew it was coming, but it was still a shock to realize that it was the end— the last night you'd lay your head down on that presidential pillow. Nancy captured the experience well: "Nothing can prepare you for living in the White House—and nothing can prepare you for leaving it."

"He was the same man leaving the White House who walked in, other than a knowledge base that was enhanced," Kuhn observed. "I mean, any president, any CEO, any professor or any lobbyist, or any professor-to-be, you want to get smarter every day. With all the information that you have in front of you on a daily basis as President, that knowledge base just grows immensely. But aside from that, he was the same man, personally, who walked in, who left eight years later. Not impacted, not affected by the power, the prestige of that office, because he was just very low key, very unassuming, very self-effacing, a unique man."

In his final weeks, Reagan had time to reflect back on his political life, and he realized that it had all started with FDR. That great man had been the inspiration of his youth, and he hoped that he in turn had given the young people of America even a fraction of the patriotic spirit that his predecessor had. He liked to recall the time he had seen Roosevelt during the

1936 presidential campaign, at a parade in Des Moines when Reagan was twenty-five. "What a wave of affection and pride swept through that crowd as he passed by in an open car . . . a familiar smile on his lips, jaunty and confident, drawing from us reservoirs of confidence and enthusiasm some of us had forgotten we had during those hard years. Maybe that was FDR's greatest gift to us. He really did convince us that the only thing we had to fear was fear itself." The image stayed with him. He always wanted to be the same kind of forceful, inspiring presence.

For his farewell address, Reagan asked Peggy Noonan, who had left the White House after 1986, to return to help him shape the words and ideas that would express his time in the Oval Office. Through December 1988 and into January, she worked with him face-to-face. He wanted to tell two stories, one about a world remade, and the other about a hope—and a warning—for the future. On January 11, 1989, he made his last appearance before the American people, speaking from the Oval Office. He was comfortable at the desk, looking into the camera with that squint, a smile from his eyes, and reaching out through the lens to speak once again in that familiar voice, both resolved and tender.

Of his achievement in brokering a new path of negotiation with the Soviet Union, he said:

> My view is that President Gorbachev is different from previous Soviet leaders. I think he knows some of the things wrong with his society and is trying to fix them. We wish him well. And we'll continue to work to make sure that the Soviet Union that eventually emerges from this process is a less threatening one. What it all boils down to is this: I want the new closeness to con-

tinue. And it will, as long as we make it clear that we will continue to act in a certain way as long as they continue to act in a helpful manner. If and when they don't, at first pull your punches. If they persist, pull the plug. It's still trust but verify. It's still play, but cut the cards. It's still watch closely. And don't be afraid to see what you see.

His warning was different in character from the one Dwight Eisenhower had given twenty-eight years earlier. This was not the threat of bureaucracy or weapons buildup or a military-industrial complex but a threat in the heart of America that required a special vigilance:

There is a great tradition of warnings in Presidential farewells, and I've got one that's been on my mind for some time. But oddly enough it starts with one of the things I'm proudest of in the past 8 years: the resurgence of national pride that I called the new patriotism. This national feeling is good, but it won't count for much, and it won't last unless it's grounded in thoughtfulness and knowledge. . . .

All great change in America begins at the dinner table. So, tomorrow night in the kitchen I hope the talking begins. And children, if your parents haven't been teaching you what it means to be an American, let 'em know and nail 'em on it. That would be a very American thing to do.

And finally, a note of optimism, an ode to the glory of America. Reagan was never embarrassed to let his prose soar; it rarely felt corny coming from him.

The past few days when I've been at that window upstairs, I've thought a bit of the "shining city upon a hill."
The phrase comes from John Winthrop, who wrote it to
describe the America he imagined. What he imagined
was important because he was an early Pilgrim, an early
freedom man. He journeyed here on what today we'd
call a little wooden boat; and like the other Pilgrims, he
was looking for a home that would be free.

I've spoken of the shining city all my political life,
but I don't know if I ever quite communicated what I
saw when I said it. But in my mind it was a tall, proud
city built on rocks stronger than oceans, windswept,
God-blessed, and teeming with people of all kinds living in harmony and peace; a city with free ports that
hummed with commerce and creativity. And if there had
to be city walls, the walls had doors and the doors were
open to anyone with the will and the heart to get here.
That's how I saw it, and see it still.

It's notable that in his final words, Reagan elevated Gorbachev, the man who was now his friend, to a place of respect.
He meant it when he wished him well, thinking of the journey
they had made together and the road Gorbachev still had to
travel. His tone was contemplative in his farewell. He would
not have a direct role in the ending to the story, but he believed
that history would judge the unique collaboration between two
opposing nations kindly.

At a good-bye party thrown by the staff in the East Room,
Duberstein, as emcee, expressed the thoughts of many when
he said, "Mr. President, you fundamentally ended the Cold
War. . . . You started out trying to change America, and you
wound up changing the world. Well done. Well done."

On his final morning, Reagan took the daily walk along the colonnade to the Oval Office and was surprised to find it had been cleared out, except for the desk and rug. Kuhn observed him: "For a moment alone, Reagan stood quietly and gazed around the room, fingers folded lightly in front of him, almost as if in prayer." Then the spell was broken. Duberstein came in, along with Colin Powell. Powell was there to give Reagan his final national security briefing, the shortest and happiest one ever. "The world is quiet today, Mr. President." Reagan thanked him and reached into his pocket, pulling out the nuclear code card. "Here, guys, I don't need this anymore."

"No, Mr. President," Powell said. "Put it back in your pocket. It will automatically be deactivated."

The Bushes and Quayles arrived at the White House for the obligatory coffee, though Nancy could not remember drinking any. The mood, remembered Barbara, was relaxed—"a friendly takeover"—quite different from 1981, when the tension with the Carters had overwhelmed all attempts at polite conversation. Much had been made of the distant relationship between Nancy and Barbara; the Bushes had seldom been invited to the Reagans' private quarters at the White House, and when Nancy gave Barbara a tour during the transition, she was seeing much of it for the first time. The warmth that had grown between Reagan and Bush in their eight years together didn't necessarily trickle down to the first and second ladies. One theory held that Nancy had never forgiven the Bushes for running against her husband in 1980. Although Bush wrote in his diary, "Nancy does not like Barbara," Nancy left Barbara a gift, a beautiful orchid, in her bedroom. A more likely explanation for the sense of distance was that they were different people, in style and sometimes in substance. Indeed, Bush was about to show just how different he was from his California predecessor. Savvy and experienced, a former congressman, ambassador, CIA director, and vice president, he had his own ideas about the future. He and Reagan had forged a close bond over eight years, but now the torch had passed to him and it was on his shoulders to determine his own, and in some sense Reagan's, legacy.

It was cloudy and mild on Inauguration Day. In the car on the way to the Capitol, Reagan cheerily noted the overcast skies. "When I became Governor of California," he told Bush, "just as I placed my hand on the Bible, the sun came through and warmed it." As Bush wrote in his diary, "And sure enough, while we were on the platform, the sun started through." Of course, memories about weather are notoriously shady. There were neither cloudy nor sunny skies at Reagan's gubernatorial inauguration, which happened at night. And the same story is often told of his first inauguration as president. No matter; Bush enjoyed the image of heavenly cooperation.

Barbara held two Bibles—the one George Washington had used for his swearing in and one given to Bush by the congressional prayer group. It was opened to the Beatitudes: "Blessed are the poor in spirit, for theirs is the kingdom of heaven . . . Blessed are the peacemakers, for they shall be called children of God."

After working with Reagan on his farewell, Noonan was asked to help Bush with his inaugural address. "I thought this must be the most special place in history, forty feet down from the retiring president and twenty feet from the incoming president," she told Maureen Dowd of the *New York Times*. "And here I am, sitting on this couch between this president and that one."

In many respects that speech would mark the end of an era. Bush's director of communications, David Demarest, was determined to restore some invisibility to the job, which was the way he thought it should be. He also kept a careful eye on the prose. High-minded oratory was a better fit for Reagan than it was for Bush. It felt authentic because it was, Reagan crafting many of the sentiments himself. He loved to write a poignant phrase, tell a human story. His speeches were full of the resonance of his voice. But what suited Reagan wasn't right for Bush.

Noonan had helped pen Bush's convention acceptance speech the previous August, introducing lines that would both elevate and haunt Bush—calling on America to be "a kinder, gentler nation" and beckoning Americans to create "a thousand points of light" of service. They were lofty sentiments for a prosaic man like Bush.

In general, his speeches as president would be less soaring and more down-to-earth, a style he favored and that was right for him. "I don't like a lot of flowery prose," he told Demarest. "I'm not Ronald Reagan. I'm not an orator; don't try to make me into one."

After the ceremony, the Bushes walked the Reagans to Marine One, where they would begin their journey home. "It was sad telling them good-bye," Barbara wrote, "although he should have felt great, leaving with a very high approval rating and the affection of the nation." Fitzwater recalled that standing on the steps watching the helicopter lift off, he, James Baker, and President Bush all cried. Baker and Fitzwater would be staying on—Baker as secretary of state—and though they were excited about what they were beginning, the full force of what they had lived—*with that man*—fell over them, and they couldn't stop the tears.

In the helicopter heading for Andrews Air Force Base, where the Reagans would board Air Force One (no longer designated as such because Reagan wasn't president) to fly home to California, the pilot performed a ceremonial loop around Washington. Looking down at the White House, Reagan tapped Nancy on the knee. "Look, dear," he said. "There's our little bungalow." And the tears started flowing again. But they looked forward to the descent into normalcy away from that "public housing" in Washington, setting up their regular home, learning where the light switches were—ordinary things.

When Bush entered the Oval Office for the first time as president, he found a note from Reagan in the drawer of his desk. At the top was a cartoon image by Sandra Boynton showing an elephant lying curled up on the ground with a flock of turkeys standing on top of him, pecking away. The inscription read, "Don't let the turkeys get you down." Below, Reagan had written:

Dear George.

You'll have moments when you want to use this particular stationary [*sic*]. Well go to it.

George I treasure the memorys [*sic*] we share with you all the best. You'll be in my prayers. God bless you & Barbara. I'll miss our Thursday lunches.

Ron

Fitzwater, who was in the Oval Office when Bush read the note, said Bush was touched. "What a sweet man," he said fondly.

BUSH TOOK OFFICE IN the company of old faces and new. His foreign policy team was especially strong: James Baker as secretary of state, Brent Scowcroft as national security advisor, and Robert Gates, who would become director of the CIA within a year, as deputy national security advisor. Congressman Dick Cheney stepped down as House minority whip to become secretary of defense after the Senate rejected Bush's first nominee, John Tower, for personal issues and potential conflicts of interest. General Colin Powell stayed on with a new title, chairman of the Joint Chiefs of Staff.

For chief of staff Bush picked John Sununu, a former governor of New Hampshire, a no-nonsense, strong-willed tough guy who was a good balance to Bush's dispassionate nature. Marlin Fitzwater remained on as press secretary.

Those who worked for Bush during his time in Washington, both as vice president and as president, were always struck by his graciousness and innate kindness. One poignant example, related by Gates, involved Scowcroft, whose wife was quite ill:

Brent was so tired . . . he would complete a fifteen-, sixteen-hour day at the White House and then go home and care for his wife. As Brent's wife became sicker during the administration, sometimes the president and I would conspire against Brent and I would find a way during the day to let the president know that Jackie was in the hospital again and so the president would call Brent, maybe at 4:30 or 5:00 in the afternoon, and tell him that he was going over to the residence, that he was done for the day. Then Brent would go to the hospital and I would call the president, and the president would come back to the office and we'd do a couple more hours work.

It was a remarkably kind subterfuge, the type of thing the Bushes were well known for.

"He won't let you be anything but a friend," Powell said of Bush, adding that Barbara was the same way. He remembered meeting her for the first time during Reagan's administration when he sat beside her at an official luncheon. "How do you do, Mrs. Bush? I'm very pleased to be with you," he said. She answered, "Call me Barbara." Powell told her he couldn't do that. "You're the vice president's wife, ma'am. I can't call you Barbara." When she insisted, he said, "My mother would kill me." She responded, "If you don't call me Barbara, *I'll* kill you." And so they became Barbara and Colin, at least in private. It seems like a small thing, but that is the way strong relationships and loyalty are built. Bush, too, chafed at the reverential honorifics and was known to pick up the phone and tell an alarmed aide, "This is George." (Later, when his son became president, he'd begin calls, "It's Forty-one.")

The style points could be deceptive. From the outset, Bush demonstrated that he was his own man, a tough customer, especially with the Soviet Union. Observers were puzzled at his seeming antagonism to continuing a dialogue with Gorbachev in the early months of his administration. Bush was suspicious of Gorbachev and privately thought Reagan had been seduced by the man. Some advisors were whispering in his ear that perestroika was a ruse. Vice President Dan Quayle warned that Gorbachev was nothing more than a "Stalinist in Gucci shoes."

As Bush wrote to his friend Aga Khan shortly after taking office, "I'll be darned if Mr. Gorbachev should dominate world public opinion forever. His system has failed and it's democracy that's on the march." That might have been an opinion shared by many, even Reagan himself with his frequent reminder "Trust but verify."

But Bush's reluctance to make a move didn't play well in public, where it seemed as if he were treading water while Gorbachev boldly publicized one initiative after another. The Bush team thought Gorbachev was showboating in May, when he announced that the Soviet Union would stop supplying arms to Nicaragua. Rather than praising Gorbachev, the administration let it be known that it doubted his sincerity and suspected that his deeds would not match his words. On the defensive in front of the press, Fitzwater made what he called "the worst mistake of my career," accusing Gorbachev of acting like a "drugstore cowboy," not making meaningful proposals. He knew as soon as he spoke that he'd stepped in it. Back in his office, the consequences of his brash words began to sink in as he listened to the press outside calling "Bring out the drugstore cowboy!" He trudged to the Oval Office to meet his fate, and although Bush let the matter drop, the press did not. Fitzwater's name-calling only underscored the administration's inability to present a strong message to the world.

On May 21, 1989, a *New York Times* editorial entitled "Take Me to Your Leader," opened, "Imagine that an alien spaceship approached Earth and sent the message: 'Take me to your leader.' Who would that be? Without doubt, Mikhail Sergeyevich Gorbachev." The editorial added, "It's not likely that most earthlings would instantly think of George Bush."

To be sure, Reagan's relationship with Gorbachev had not been without conflict or controversy. But Bush's recalcitrant attitude, which was echoed by his administration, was incomprehensible. Gorbachev thought the Bush foreign policy team was still immersed in the old Cold War attitudes and couldn't break through them to anticipate, much less orchestrate, a new world. Scowcroft would later admit that this had been somewhat true for him. "The Cold War so profoundly affected all of us," he said. "It infused every part of our lives. It was a pattern of thinking. It was the world that we knew." Bush was also determined to be cautious. He wasn't about to simply rubber-stamp his predecessor's initiatives.

Yet it was obvious that across Eastern Europe the Iron Curtain was dissolving, with Communist regimes in Poland, Hungary, Czechoslovakia, Bulgaria, and Romania on the brink of failure.

If anyone doubted that the world was changing, the wall provided a wake-up call in 1989. Today, we remember the fall of the Berlin Wall as if it had been a spontaneous combustion. But it was an evolving scenario. Gorbachev had received reports of a growing restless energy sweeping the East German population that threatened to erupt.

Visiting East Germany in October, he urged its leaders to be courageous, to embrace perestroika. "Life punishes harshly anyone who is left behind in politics," he warned them. Gorbachev was particularly frustrated with Erich Honecker, the general secretary of the Socialist Unity Party of Germany. Speaking to him, he said, was "like talking to a brick wall." Honecker was immune to the forces of change. He lived in the past and would not even acknowledge the need for new initiatives. He had no interest in easing the tensions.

Weak, physically ill, and on the wrong side of history, Honecker was removed from office in mid-October and replaced by Egon Krenz. Krenz was hardly an improvement on Honecker, and from the standpoint of the leadership, the fall of the wall three weeks later was due to a blunder, not intention.

Attempting to stave off protests, the East German Politburo made some minor changes to travel restrictions in early November. But inexplicably, the official reading the statement to a televised audience on November 9 miscommunicated the extent of the change, leading people to believe that travel was open to every citizen, starting immediately. Almost instantly, thousands of people appeared in the streets, steadily growing in numbers, up to 2 million. The guards were unable to contain them, and there was just enough confusion about the official announcement that they weren't sure they should try.

With pickaxes and hammers, and eventually cranes and bulldozers, the people of Berlin tore down the wall in an epic act of resistance. Crowds gathered in the night like a spontaneous eruption, young people pulling themselves up onto the flat top of the wall and raising their arms in victory. It was giddy and joyous and full of wonderment. Decades later, people who were young on that day still speak with awe of getting a call from a family member or friend: "Go to the wall, go to the wall"—and without question they had raced to see what was happening and then joined the throngs. In an instant, the terrible, oppressive barrier to freedom came apart in a breathtaking rebellion.

Hearing the news, Scowcroft rushed to the Oval Office, where he was joined by Fitzwater. No one was sure what was happening, but they turned on CNN in the study off the president's office and watched.

"Do you want to make a statement?" Fitzwater asked.

"Why?" The president looked at him curiously.

"Why?" Fitzwater was surprised at the response. "This is an incredibly historic day," he said. "People will want to know what it means."

Bush was quiet for a moment. He knew that what people wanted was boastful American chest thumping—*We won, you lost*—and he just wasn't going to feed into it. "Listen, Marlin," he finally said, "I'm not going to dance on the Berlin Wall. The last thing I want to do is brag about winning the cold war, or bringing the wall down."

Even so, Fitzwater convinced him that he had to make a statement. The public would expect it. Reluctantly, Bush agreed to speak to a press pool in the Oval Office. Later, Fitzwater might have regretted his insistence, because Bush's performance before the press was lackluster.

"You don't seem elated," CBS correspondent Lesley Stahl said with surprise after he'd finished.

"I am not an emotional kind of guy," he replied with a shrug.

"Well, how elated are you?"

"I'm very pleased."

White House aides watched the performance with dismay. What was wrong with the president? Boy, some of them mumbled, Reagan would have knocked this moment out of the park. Fitzwater understood what Bush was trying to do—or, rather, what he was trying *not* to do—but it was agonizing.

Many Americans who tuned in to the news saw Reagan on the screen, speaking to Sam Donaldson from his office in Los Angeles. His face was serene, and his voice was quiet and confident. When Donaldson asked him if he had thought it would come so soon, the former president smiled. "Well, I didn't know when it would come, but I'll tell you, as an eternal optimist I believed with all my heart that it was in the future."

When Donaldson, citing the "ash heap of history" speech, asked him if he felt vindicated, Reagan did not take the opportunity to boast about a win. "The people have seen that communism had its chance and it doesn't work," he said.

BAKER WOULD WHOLEHEARTEDLY DEFEND what he deemed Bush's "prudence and perspicacity," saying "He got a lot of grief from the media for not being more emotionally exuberant about the fact that the wall had come down. And he said, Wait a minute. We're going to have to continue to deal with these people, and I'm not going to stick it in their eye. He was so wise on that, really. Everybody thought he was wrong, but he was right."

Reagan had to be thinking about his own role in the drama, although he was no longer center stage. It was undeniable that Gorbachev had allowed it to happen; it had been his forceful challenge to East Berlin, his decision not to prevent it. "Mr. Gorbachev, tear down this wall!" Reagan had cried, and in effect that was what happened. The feared crackdown from Moscow didn't come. Indeed, Gorbachev had been telegraphing a hands-off policy toward Eastern Europe and, by extension, Germany. When the wall fell that night, Gorbachev wasn't even awakened by his advisors. Once the East German leadership saw that Soviet tanks would not be rolling in the streets, it had no choice but to stand down. The next day, the Politburo did not even hold an emergency meeting.

Chernyaev wrote in his diary, "The Berlin Wall has collapsed. This entire era in the history of the socialist system is over." But the reality was more nuanced. Yes, the wall had fallen, but East Germany was still under Communist control; that had not changed. And although many people were calling for German reunification, that wasn't such a simple matter. Despite the agonies of the divided Germany, many Europeans, from both the east and the west, were uneasy about a united Germany, since their last experience of it had involved two wars of aggression. Now they wondered what was to prevent a reunited Germany from abusing its strength. In their superb book on the end of the Cold War, *At the Highest Levels: The Inside Story of the End of the Cold War*, historian Michael Beschloss

and foreign policy analyst Strobe Talbot painted a picture of
the dread that was lurking in European halls of power: "Twice
in the twentieth century, German militarism and expansionism had plunged the world into war. Russians, Poles, and other
neighbors of Germany were not eager to test the proposition that
1914 and 1939 were aberrations; nor were the British, French,
and other peoples who had suffered directly at German hands."
For his part, Gorbachev thought it was important for Germany
to remain part of the Warsaw Pact, an ally of the Soviet Union.
His view was not just doctrinal but an economic necessity as
the union shrank. The antipathy to a unified Germany was also
personal for him, as it was for many East Bloc nations. They,
too, had suffered from the aggression of Germany. Visiting a
Soviet POW cemetery in Germany earlier in the year, where
hundreds of thousands of people had perished during World
War II, Raisa had made an uncharacteristically emotional statement: "Decades have passed, but even today, there is no Soviet
family that does not mourn relatives who met a tragic, untimely
death in those terrible years." So the question of German reunification was far from being settled, even as bulldozers cleared
away the detritus of the fallen wall.

Meanwhile, Bush was taking heat in the media and from
Democrats about being too timid in foreign relations. Everyone wanted to know why he and Gorbachev had not yet had
a summit. People just didn't understand. Gates said, "I think
both Brent and I believed, and I think maybe the president believed, that the Reagan administration had gotten out ahead of
itself in the last six or eight months of 1988 in dealing with the
Soviet Union, that their aspirations had outrun reality and had
outrun the capacity of the government to absorb and deal with
what they were trying to do. In particular, Bush wanted to see
if Gorbachev's actions would match his words before the UN."

Unbeknown to all but a handful of people, Bush had reached out to Gorbachev at the end of the summer of 1989, proposing an informal summit that December, at a removed location out of the spotlight. The two men had decided to keep the meeting a secret, Bush joking that they both knew how to keep secrets. Bush had told only Baker, Scowcroft, and Fitzwater that there would be a summit, although the word prematurely leaked out that the leaders would meet on the Mediterranean island of Malta in December. Notably, it was mere weeks after the fall of the Berlin Wall.

As a former navy man, Bush enjoyed the setting of the talks, to be held on two ships, one American, one Soviet, side by side in the harbor. Each leader would stay on his own ship, and meetings would alternate between the two. For him, the American ship, the USS *Belknap*, had a sentimental appeal. But according to Fitzwater, Gorbachev wasn't fond of warships, with their tight quarters and Spartan accommodations. In addition to the *Slava*, which was barely used, he brought the *Maxim Gorky*, a Soviet cruise ship. "The *Gorky* was a long way from battleship gray," Fitzwater recalled. "It had red carpets throughout, floor-to-ceiling mirrors in most rooms and hallways, and gold chandeliers in the dining and meeting areas."

On his way to Malta, Gorbachev met with Pope John Paul II, the first visit of a Soviet head of state to the Vatican. Gorbachev wanted to signal his openness toward more religious freedom in the Soviet Union and his interest in establishing ties with the Vatican. The pope, whose birth name was Karol Wojtyła, had been raised in Poland, and thus had a natural affinity for the Poles' struggles under communism. Having suffered under Nazi oppression as a young man and then under Soviet domination after the war, which had made the practice of his faith a dangerous act, he knew firsthand the peril many people in his homeland and elsewhere were facing in their quest for religious freedom. He used the pulpit of his papacy to support Solidarity in Poland and advocate for human rights around the world. He and Reagan had established common cause on that issue.

Reagan had been an admirer of the pope before he took office, but what had really cemented their relationship was their "dubious distinction" (Reagan's words) of suffering assassination attempts only six weeks apart in 1981. When they met for the first time the following June, they spoke about their common experience, marveling at their miraculous survival. They agreed that they'd both been spared in order to do God's will in the world, their mission the fall of communism and the demise of the Soviet Union. In a public statement after their meeting, the pope underscored the unique American role in the quest for peace: "With faith in God and belief in universal human solidarity may America step forward in this crucial moment in history to consolidate her rightful place at the service of world peace. . . . My final prayer is this: that God will bless America so that she may increasingly become and truly be and long remain one nation under God, indivisible, with liberty and justice for all."

Those two men of faith, a Catholic and a Protestant, were deeply joined in their higher purpose. In the coming years they spoke often about the persecution and even martyrdom of people of all faiths under Soviet rule. After his presidency, Reagan once welcomed Polish visitors to his office in California. Pointing to a picture of the pope on the wall, he said, "He is my best friend."

Gorbachev had always been testy on the subject of religious freedom, which Reagan consistently pressed. He felt that people did not appreciate how far the Soviet Union had come on the matter.

There were small signs that the atheistic shield was cracking. In September, Baker and Shevardnadze, meeting in Wyoming for negotiations, exchanged gifts. Baker gave Shevardnadze a pair of cowboy boots. Shevardnadze presented Baker with an enamel picture of Jesus preaching. "You see," Shevardnadze said, "even we communists are changing our worldview."

When Gorbachev arrived at the Vatican, the pope invited him to meet privately for a brief time. He spoke to Gorbachev in Russian, telling him he'd been practicing the language so they could talk directly. He made it clear to Gorbachev that his was a larger mission, a nonpolitical quest, telling him that although he criticized communism, he also criticized the vices of capitalism. And he pressed him, saying that religious freedom was at the heart of it all. But he said, "It would be wrong for someone to claim that changes in Europe and the world should follow the Western model. This goes against my deep convictions. Europe, as a participant in world history, should breathe with two lungs."

Gorbachev replied, "This is a very appropriate image." But he bristled a bit when the pope lectured him on religious freedom. "At one point President Reagan tried to teach me how to conduct matters in our country," he said. "I told him that we would not be able to have a conversation like that. A conversation can only happen on the basis of realism and mutual respect. I told him: you are not a teacher and I am not a student. You are not a prosecutor and I am not a defendant. So, if we want to talk about politics, about how to change the world for the better, then we have to do it as equals. He understood this and we were able to do what we did."

The conversation was polite and deferential, the pope saying little as Gorbachev defended his reforms, mentioning his efforts in Poland and inviting the pope to visit the USSR. Gorbachev left pleased with the meeting and the idea of opening official relations with the Vatican in the near future.

As the parties arrived in Malta, a storm was forecast, but they were able to meet on the first morning. "We are not here to upstage Gorbachev," Bush had reminded his team when they landed in Malta. "Our problems are too serious for PR. We want to know how much change he can accommodate."

Sitting down with Gorbachev on the *Gorky*, Bush said candidly, "There are people in the United States who accuse me of being too cautious. It is true, I am a cautious man, but I am not a coward, and my administration will seek to avoid doing anything that would damage your position in the world."

Almost apologetic for his long months of silence—dubbed "the Bush pause"—he then picked up on the conversation from Governors Island, as if it had happened a week before, not a year before. "I agree completely with what you said in New York," he told Gorbachev, stating that the world would be a better place if perestroika were a success. The Cold War had given way to an era of cooperation, but what that entailed was still sketchy.

When the discussion turned to Germany, Bush wanted Gorbachev to know that he was willing to proceed cautiously. "If our Democrats criticize my timidity, let them do it," he said. "I do not intend to jump up on the wall because too much is at stake on this issue."

Gorbachev laughed. "Well, jumping on the wall is not a good activity for a president."

But as he had told the pope, he was growing frustrated by the regular references to "Western values." Why are openness and democracy Western values? he asked with some bitterness. Had Germany been displaying "Western values" between 1937 and 1945? He sought his due for his hard labor pressing for reform. He felt they had moved beyond the point where he was on the "other" side.

"Why don't we use the term 'democratic values,'" Baker suggested, and Gorbachev was pleased with that.

Later that day, the gale descended on Malta with greater force than expected—a twenty-year storm, they called it. Sixty-mile-an-hour winds sent huge waves crashing against the *Belknap*, hammering it as the seasick Americans tried to hold on. The situation was less dire for the Soviets aboard the *Gorky*, which was moored at the dock. A formal dinner hosted by Gorbachev was planned on the *Gorky*, and Bush instructed the captain to find a way to get there. Again and again, the navy crew tried to steady the ship against a small dock that was placed alongside so the president and his team could depart. But the waves buffeted the dock as if it were a piece of cardboard, pulling it away. As his green-gilled staff looked on, Bush kept insisting that they were going to the dinner. At one point, Fitzwater recalled, "The president walked out to the edge of the ship, grabbed the cable handrail in that particular area, and exclaimed with great enthusiasm, 'Let's go!'" Everyone—except the president—was relieved when the captain said no.

With calmer waters the next day, they resumed meetings, discussing a second summit in Washington the following June, when they would hopefully reach agreement on a START treaty. The high point of the summit was the joint press conference, where Bush and Gorbachev beamed and kidded as if they were old buddies. They announced that they had entered an era of "enduring cooperation" leading to "lasting peace." Barbara and Raisa were equally warm. As the teams mingled with reporters, chatting and shaking hands, many observers concluded that it was the moment the Cold War ended. Of course that designation had already been announced on Governors Island. But no matter; Reagan would have been heartened to see the scene, a fulfillment of all he'd done.

The June 1990 summit was very productive, with a robust trade agreement and commitments to reduce long-range nuclear missiles. The trade deal was immensely important to Gorbachev; he nearly begged the president to agree to it. He desperately needed a win back home, and Bush understood that. Shortly before the summit, Jack Matlock had sent a cable detailing Gorbachev's problems at home, calling him "an embattled leader":

> THE SUCCESS OF GORBACHEV'S EFFORTS TO MODERNIZE SOVIET SOCIETY AND AT THE SAME TIME KEEP THE FEDERATION TOGETHER APPEARS INCREASINGLY PROBLEMATIC. DEMOCRATIZATION AND MARKET REFORMS ARE HERE EXAGGERATING REGIONAL, ETHNIC, AND CLASS TENSIONS AND THUS COMPLICATING THE FORGING OF THE NATIONAL CONSENSUS NEEDED FOR FURTHER REFORMS.

According to Matlock, Gorbachev was getting it from both sides—not only from the hard-liners resistant to change but from the "social forces his reforms have unleashed."

The most difficult conversation of the summit involved Germany. With Germans clamoring for reunification and the freedom to join NATO, Gorbachev was on his heels. He pleaded with Bush to see it from the Soviet standpoint, to proceed more slowly and cautiously—to remember the past.

Bush was sympathetic, but he urged Gorbachev to look beyond that narrow view. "Your concern, your mistrust toward the united Germany are too deep, they ignore the fifty-year-old democratic experience of Germany," he said bluntly. He added kindly, "At the same time, one can understand your fears. We also fought Hitler, but our losses do not stand any comparison with the 27 million Soviet lives sacrificed in the armed struggle with Nazi Germany." That memory, however, could not rule policy, he said. He told Gorbachev, "As it seems to me, our approach to Germany is more realistic, and has better timing. Because the processes of German unification are unfolding faster than any of us could have imagined, and there is no force that can put a brake on them. That is why the mistrust oriented toward the past is an especially bad adviser here."

Aggrieved, Gorbachev bit back: "You are extremely concerned about the health of united Germany, from which you calculate the health of NATO. You are so concerned about it that you forget about the health and interests of the Soviet Union. And this, in its turn, does not help either stability or predictability at all."

"NATO is the anchor of stability," Bush insisted.

"But two anchors are better," Gorbachev argued. "As a seaman, you should be able to understand it."

"And where will we find the second anchor?"

"In the East," Gorbachev declared but then seemed to lose his train of thought. "What it would be concretely—let our ministers think about it."

"Yes, let them think about it," Bush agreed. "But we have to take into account the exceptional pace of German unification."

Gorbachev was arguing that NATO and the Warsaw Pact could coexist as joint stabilizing forces. Bush knew that was a fantasy. Gorbachev seemed adamant, but then, in the course of the conversation, he came to a stunning conclusion that must have surprised his foreign policy team, proposing that they leave it up to Germany to decide. He suggested this language: "The United States and the Soviet Union agree that united Germany, upon reaching the final settlement, taking into account the results of World War Two, would decide on its own which alliance she would be a member of."

Bush, nodding in agreement, suggested a slight—though deeply meaningful—change. "I would propose a somewhat different formulation," he said. "The United States is unequivocally in favor of united Germany's membership in NATO, however, if it makes a different choice, we would not contest it, we will respect it."

"I agree. I accept your formulation," Gorbachev said.

Looking on, Baker was immediately aware that that was an impossible construct. "Whatever you say, but the simultaneous obligations of one and the same country toward the WTO [Warsaw Treaty Organization] and NATO smack of schizophrenia."

Gorbachev brushed his concern aside. "It is only for a financier, who puts cents together into dollars. Politics, however, is sometimes a search for possible in the sphere of unfamiliar."

"But obligations to the [Warsaw Pact] and NATO are adversarial obligations," Baker insisted, getting what amounted to a shrug. It was a tremendous sticking point. But in the eyes of the Americans, Gorbachev had already conceded, perhaps without fully realizing it. Given the choice, they knew which way Germany would go. And indeed, in October there was German reunification under NATO.

The takeaway from the summit, Chernyaev wrote in his diary, was that "the USSR and the United States are no longer enemies." Baker agreed. "The discussion that took place at the summit meeting in early June of 1990 was a turning point in world history," he said. "For months, the president's speechwriters had included a phrase in speeches saying 'The Cold War is over.' And routinely I crossed it out and crossed it out and crossed it out. After this meeting, I came to the conclusion that this time I could leave it in the president's speeches. Why? Because the fundamental building of the Cold War focused on Germany, on the division of Germany, and the subsequent division of Europe. And nothing could be more symbolic of the end of that period of history than the unification of Germany inside NATO."

That was all well and good, but back home in Russia, many people viewed the summit as nothing more than a PR campaign by Gorbachev. Meanwhile, Boris Yeltsin, who had revived his power as the newly elected head of the Russian Parliament, was intent on making himself and his more radical reforms the main story.

After the meetings, Bush invited Gorbachev to join him at Camp David, his first visit. Riding the president's golf cart along the trails, they came to one of Bush's prized locations, the horseshoe pit. Bush asked Gorbachev if he'd ever played horseshoes. Gorbachev said no. Hopping out of the golf cart, Bush asked him if he'd like to try. Gorbachev agreed and got a ringer on his first throw. That delighted Bush, who had the horseshoe mounted on a plaque, which he presented to Gorbachev at dinner that night.

In September, the Reagans paid a visit to the Gorbachevs in Moscow. Reagan and Gorbachev beamed and wrapped their arms around each other, hugging with genuine warmth, and even Nancy and Raisa seemed glad to be together again. Remembering their last visit in May 1988, Reagan marveled, "There have been so many changes in those two years and four months that I am beginning to understand how Rip Van Winkle must have felt."

It might have been an effort to put a happy face on what was clearly a time of great crisis for Gorbachev. The next year unfolded with one disruption after another in the increasingly disunited Soviet Union. Ironically, Gorbachev's perestroika paved the way for the growing strength of Yeltsin.

Even with all the stresses of forging a new government and the blowback from hard-liners and reformers alike, Gorbachev never betrayed any discouragement. He was a problem solver, focused on solutions. His masterstroke was the creation of a Union Treaty, which would ease the way for independence for Soviet states and create a road map for going forward. But it was a heavy lift, and it didn't help that Yeltsin was an increasingly outspoken critic. Gorbachev thought Yeltsin was excessively self-interested; he wanted to rule his own roost of Russia as if it were the whole story. Condoleezza Rice, a Soviet scholar and future secretary of state under George W. Bush, put it this way: "Yeltsin created parallel structures in the Russian republic that effectively ripped the heart out of the Soviet Union. After all, what was the Soviet Union without Russia at its core?"

GORBACHEV WAS EXHAUSTED. HE planned a getaway on August 4, 1991, to his estate in Foros, Crimea, overlooking the Black Sea, with Raisa, their daughter, Irina, and her husband and two young children. They relaxed and read, swam and took long walks. Gorbachev found it hard to rest. Uncertainty about the signing of the Union Treaty and his growing unpopularity at home plagued him. There had even been whispers of an impending coup, which he did not believe.

Late on Sunday afternoon, August 18, after they had been vacationing for two weeks, Gorbachev was in his office reading a newspaper when there was a tap on his door. It was his chief bodyguard, Vladimir Medvedev, telling him that a group had arrived unannounced to speak to him. They were his own people—his chief of staff, two Central Committee secretaries, the head of the KGB directorate in charge of his security, and a high-ranking general—but Gorbachev was immediately suspicious. He picked up a phone to call out, but the line was dead. He tried other phones. All the lines were dead.

"Don't leave me," Gorbachev said to Medvedev, then went into his bedroom to speak to Raisa.

"Something bad has happened," he told her. He didn't know why the men were there or why the phone lines had been cut, but he warned, "It may end badly for all of us, the whole family. We've got to be ready for anything."

Raisa, whose steely nature had suffered much criticism on the public stage, proved her mettle by rising from her seat and bravely vowing "Whatever you decide, I'll be with you, no matter what."

By the time Gorbachev returned to his office, the group of visitors had already made themselves at home there. They told him that a committee had been set up to take over the country because it was in a state of emergency. They pressured him to sign a declaration of emergency. He refused, and they demanded his resignation.

Gorbachev was enraged. "I had promoted all these people and now they were betraying me!" he wrote indignantly about his state of mind at that moment. He tried to persuade them that they must discuss the matter in a levelheaded way and within the framework of the constitution. They were not moved. At one point his personal secretary—who worked for him!—told Gorbachev he didn't understand the nature of the trouble the country was in. "Shut up, you asshole!" Gorbachev shouted. "Who are you to lecture me on what's going on?"

Gorbachev saw what was happening. It was a coup by the weak-spined hard-liners. He would not give in to them. Unable to secure Gorbachev's compliance, the group rose to leave. As they walked out, Gorbachev's patience was spent. He swore at them "Russian-style." They returned to Moscow, leaving Gorbachev and his family under house arrest without access to outside communication. (His bodyguard, who had promised to stay by his side, abandoned him.) A public announcement followed from Moscow that Gorbachev was ill and the Committee on Emergency Rule was taking over.

Chernyaev, who was staying in another building on the premises, finally learned what was happening and made his way to Gorbachev's dacha, where he found him lying on a bed making notes. He was calm and clearheaded but grim. Chernyaev wasn't so composed. He began swearing, and Gorbachev said, "Yes, this may not end well, but I have faith in Yeltsin. He won't give in to them. He won't compromise. But that means blood."

The conspirators had told Gorbachev that Yeltsin would be arrested. In fact, Yeltsin was still nominally free at that point, holed up in the parliamentary "White House," receiving calls from around the world, and even ordering food from Moscow's Pizza Hut.

Suddenly he looked out and saw army tanks rolling up outside. Infuriated, he leapt up and strode out of the building. Approaching a tank, he climbed on top of it in a bold challenge. "Soldiers, officers, generals," he cried in his finest moment, "the clouds of terror and dictatorship are gathering over the whole country. They must not be allowed to bring eternal night."

Inspired by Yeltsin, thousands of Russians poured into the streets around the "White House" in the next couple of days, demonstrating that they were unwilling to go back to the old ways. The Gorbachevs knew nothing of that. Throughout the siege, Mikhail and Raisa thought they and their family might be murdered, or injured in some way, as Tsar Nicholas II and his family had been during the revolution that had given birth to the Soviet Union. They worried about food and vowed to eat only what they had with them, lest food from the outside be poisoned. Their deepest fears were over the fate of their daughter and her family, especially the small children, who were tucked away out of sight. Heartsick, Raisa suffered what appeared to be a ministroke and lay in bed with Gorbachev hovering beside her, wondering if it was the end of everything.

In Washington, Bush monitored the situation as best he could. The response was muted. The United States could not afford to jump into the fray, and it would be inappropriate to do so. But he spoke to Yeltsin and eagerly waited for word from Gorbachev.

With defiance from the population and a lack of support from the military, the coup folded by August 21. A delegation of the plotters rushed to the Crimea, hoping to provide a credible explanation to Gorbachev and save their skins. He placed them under arrest and refused to see them until communications were restored and a proper delegation arrived. He spoke to Yeltsin on the phone and then to Bush.

"My God, I'm glad to hear you," Bush said.

Gorbachev was relieved, too, and his aides and guards were giddy with victory. But he knew his power was unraveling.

Stepping off the plane, finally home, he lingered in front of the camera, saying he wanted "to breathe the air of freedom in Moscow."

In the aftermath of the coup, Gorbachev lost much of his influence. It was the beginning of the end. Many, including Yeltsin, turned on him, blaming him for being asleep at the wheel, for allowing so many old hard-liners to retain influence—in effect, for having made the coup possible. Meanwhile, Yeltsin, restless for power and reflecting the wave of change that was occurring, sparred with Gorbachev, even though they agreed on fundamentals. But quickly now, a massive change was taking place, leaping beyond Gorbachev's slow and steady march for change.

From the time he had entered office in 1985, Gorbachev had set out to transform the Soviet Union. He had always used the language of reform, not destruction. But he was not attuned to the reality that once the supporting beams of the Soviet Union were knocked down, there would be nothing to prevent the house from collapsing. "This was one of his blind spots," Robert Gates said. "He didn't understand the role of fear and mythology in maintaining control."

The final blow to Gorbachev's stature came when Yeltsin met with leaders of Ukraine and the Republic of Belarus in early December, behind his back, announcing the formation of the Commonwealth of Independent States. The Soviet Union was dead. Gorbachev would step down. Yeltsin would assume power as president of the new Russian state. The end would come on Christmas Day.

Ted Koppel of ABC had a camera crew waiting to film Gorbachev as he arrived at his office on the final day. "I'm feeling absolutely calm, absolutely free," Gorbachev told him. He noted that what they were observing was a peaceful transition of power in a place where it had never occurred before. "Even in this I have turned out to be a pioneer."

He spent several hours in his office, taking calls and signing correspondence. His most emotional call was with Bush, who was celebrating Christmas with his family at Camp David. Bush said he hoped they would meet again, perhaps at Camp David, where the horseshoe pit was still in good condition.

At last Gorbachev left his office to make his farewell address, which was poignant for a hope expressed but yet to be fulfilled. "We're now living in a new world," he declared. "An end has been put to the cold war and to the arms race, as well as to the mad militarization of the country, which has crippled our economy, public attitudes, and morals. The threat of nuclear war has been removed."

He was honest about his failings, acknowledging "Of course, there were mistakes made that could have been avoided, and many of the things that we did could have been done better. But I am positive that sooner or later, someday, our common efforts will bear fruit and our nations will live in a prosperous, democratic society."

He stood tall, maintaining a confident pose, but there were tears in his weary eyes.

Across the world in California, Reagan, Gorbachev's partner in change, had recently dedicated his presidential library in Simi Valley, joined by every living president—Bush, Ford, Carter, and Nixon—and their wives, along with Lady Bird Johnson, Caroline Kennedy, and John Kennedy, Jr. The library that day looked like a shining city on a hill, the sun beaming over the land below.

"Eighty years is a long time to live, and yet within the course of only a few short years I have seen the world turned upside down and conventional wisdom utterly disproved," Reagan told the gathering. "Visitors to this mountaintop will see a great jagged chunk of the Berlin wall, hated symbol of, yes, an evil empire, that spied on and lied to its citizens, denying them their freedom, their bread, even their faith. Well, today that wall exists only in museums, souvenir collections and the memories of a people no longer oppressed. It is also a reminder that a strong America is always desirable—and necessary in our world."

Heads craned to look at the obelisklike piece of the wall, over nine feet tall and splattered with brilliantly colored graffiti. Stripped of its ominous history, the relic of a time now gone, it was beautiful and even joyful. Afterward, many people couldn't resist touching its ragged surface, just to make sure it was real.

CHAPTER 14

WITHOUT FIRING A SHOT

One day, while Gorbachev was still in power, Dick Cheney received a visitor to his office, a young Russian activist and reformer, who had been involved in the prodemocracy movement. They talked for an hour about the state of things in Russia, and when the young man rose to leave, Cheney asked him where he was going next.

"I'm going to California," he replied. "I'm going to see President Reagan, the father of perestroika."

Cheney sat him back down on the couch. "Now, explain this to me," he said. "I thought Gorbachev was the father of perestroika."

"No," the man insisted, "Ronald Reagan is the father of perestroika."

Cheney was struck by his point. "It was his assessment," he said, "that it was in fact the Reagan policy of firmness, the U.S. military buildup, the threat of SDI, that all of those things had precipitated the circumstances, caused the conclusion on the part of Gorbachev and those around him that they could not compete with the United States on those terms and they had to fundamentally change their system."

All over the world, and especially in those places most impacted by the Soviet scourge, people were waking up to their new reality and feeling grateful to Reagan. Ordinary people, released from a form of bondage in former Communist bloc countries, were moved to make personal pilgrimages to California and pay homage to him. In late 1993, an elderly Romanian woman walked into Reagan's office, asking to see him. Without hesitation, Reagan's assistant Peggy Grande ushered her in. "When she entered his office and saw President Reagan," Grande wrote, "she instantly dropped to her knees and bowed at his feet. She started sobbing loudly and uncontrollably, kissing the president's feet—literally kissing them—with tears falling on his shoes."

Such incidents happened again and again. So if you want to know if Reagan won the Cold War, ask the young man. Ask the old woman. Ask the people of Berlin. Ten months after the fall of the wall, on a visit to Germany, the Reagans found themselves greeted in the streets by thousands of cheering Berliners. When they walked with German chancellor Helmut Kohl through the area where the wall had once stood and used a hammer and chisel to carve out a chunk, the crowd roared, "Danke, Herr Reagan!" To this day, Berliners have a reverence for Reagan that has never dimmed.

On another postpresidency visit to Gdańsk, at the site where Lech Wałęsa heroically started a union revolution that eventually brought down communism in Poland, thirty thousand people stood in the pouring rain to see Reagan. They waited while he met with Wałęsa, and when he walked outside, they burst into song. He tried to speak, but they kept singing. Puzzled, Reagan asked Wałęsa what they were singing. He replied, "May you live 100 years."

"Ronald Reagan won the Cold War without firing a shot," Margaret Thatcher declared in 1991. People have argued about that ever since, particularly asking the question, Is it Reagan or Gorbachev who should get the credit? It is easy to imagine both men laughing at the question and recognizing it as a simplification, if not a fantasy. Theirs was a rare and surprising partnership. Just think what might have been had Chernenko lived another three or four years as the Soviet leader, dooming Gorbachev's perestroika; or if Reagan had died in the assassination attempt; or if Mondale had defeated Reagan in 1984. Any one of those circumstances could have changed the course of Cold War history, in the wrong direction. It is more accurate to say that their partnership, bolstered by the cries for freedom from across Eastern Europe and around the world, won the Cold War. People can argue that the Soviet system was failing anyway, but thanks to the enduring faith of Reagan, and the determination of Gorbachev, it was a peaceful transition.

Yet only one of those men truly believed in freedom from the bottom of his heart. Reagan's calculation that Gorbachev was a different kind of Soviet leader allowed him to make some bold moves, but always in the context of achieving a noble goal. He never compromised on democracy, always operated by the light of that guiding star. He succeeded with a combination of grit, temperament, flexibility, and shrewdness. He came into office railing against the Soviet Union, the Evil Empire. For his entire first term, he refused to meet with Soviet leaders. But then, with Gorbachev, his instincts finely tuned for an opening, he had the courage to change the conversation. As James Baker summed up his philosophy of governance: "Pragmatism without principles is cynicism. But principles without pragmatism are often powerless."

It's hard to overestimate the significance of the change. The conflict between the United States and the Soviet Union seemed embedded in decades of thought and rhetoric. It wasn't easy to shake loose, to present another vision. Scowcroft reflected the common view when he said, "Generally speaking, the U.S.-Soviet confrontation—or the East/West confrontation, whatever—was a fixture of the scene as much as the fact that there was a France, Germany, United States, Soviet Union, and that it was to be managed and manipulated, not to be changed."

Reagan believed that the Soviet system was doomed, but the question of how that would come about and what would be left in its wake filled his thoughts. War was out of the question. Peaceful coexistence was out of the question. He had the tenacity to sit through countless hours of conversation and bursts of brutal conflict with Gorbachev to work out a third option. His genuine interest, in turn, allowed a friendship to develop that speeded up the progress of perestroika. The abiding friendship between Reagan and Gorbachev is one of the big stories of the Cold War's end. Reagan might have repeated "Trust but verify" too often for Gorbachev's liking, but in the end the emphasis was on trust.

In that way, Reagan demonstrated that one can be strong without being confrontational. One can be a catalyst for change without being mired in the mud. "He learned that you can find ways, even when you're adversaries, to work things out if you just get to the table and do it," Peter Hannaford said. "I believe that always stayed with him. The way it played out means I think he should get a very large degree of the credit for it. His predecessors worked for it, and they all contributed to some degree. Most of the big events happened in George Bush's term, but they were things that were all set in motion before him, as I think he would be the first to agree. So, I think that's the most important thing Reagan did."

Reagan gets little credit for being a grand strategist, but ultimately, the clever way he used SDI might have been the most significant weapon in his arsenal. "Star Wars" never came to pass; it was widely mocked at home and abroad and was barely mentioned after Reagan left office. But later, analysts in both Russia and the United States agreed that more than any other strategy, Reagan's insistence on a strategic defense initiative put the Soviets on the run. Aware of their economic problems and their weakening hand in the world, they knew they could not compete. SDI was like a ghost, invoking terror, even though it was only an idea, a wisp of smoke.

Through it all, Reagan's belief in a better tomorrow seduced the Soviet people, making them more responsive to Gorbachev's reforms. His speech at Moscow State University was a decisive moment in that quest. It was an invitation that young people in particular were ready to accept. He might have used the speech to oratorically dismantle the socialist belief system and issue a call to action, as he did in the speech at the Brandenburg Gate. Instead, he captivated the audience with stories of their potential, just over the horizon. He employed their own cultural images and poetry to show them what they could now become.

"He painted in primary colors, but when he governed he also used pastels," Duberstein said. "He wanted to bring people together, and he listened to allies as well as adversaries: 'Focus on what you can accomplish, and push the ball down the field. You can't just do Hail Mary passes, you need three yards and a cloud of dust'—I think that was Vince Lombardi. He was somebody who looked for solutions, not just for problems."

Reagan was humble about his achievements. Dismissing the label "the Great Communicator," he said, "I never thought it was my style or the words I used that made a difference: it was the content. I wasn't a great communicator, but I communicated great things."

ONLY THE LUCKY AMONG us see their childhood dreams come true. Reagan was one of them. But luck is not a free pass from suffering or indignity. Life is never fair, though we want it to be. And so Alzheimer's disease, which had killed his beloved mother, came for Reagan, too, placing him in the shadows for a decade before his death in 2004.

One of his last public appearances was a large eighty-third birthday party in Washington, DC, in February 1994—what he quaintly called "the forty-fourth anniversary of my thirty-ninth birthday." It also served as a fund-raiser for the Republican National Committee. The hall was packed—2,200 of his old friends and aides and supporters, spanning the decades, including former prime minister Margaret Thatcher, for whom he reserved his fondest words of affection.

He still looked like himself, straight-backed, dark-haired, and ruddy-cheeked, joking about his age: "As most of you know, I'm not one for looking back. I figure there will be plenty of time for that when I get old."

His remarks that night were bait for the Republican audience: jokes about President Bill Clinton and the Democrats, recollections of his achievements. His voice cracked a little at the end as he expressed his deepest gratitude to those gathered: "Thank you for being there, and for being *here*. And thank you for making this evening a memory I will cherish forever. Until we meet again, God bless you, my friends."

But for the most part, they would not meet again. Before the year was out, the terms of Reagan's final time on earth had been set. At the Reagan Museum, a video plays, on a continuous loop, a reading of Reagan's letter to the American people on November 5, announcing that he had Alzheimer's. "I now begin the journey that will lead me into the sunset of my life," he wrote. "I know that for America there will always be a bright

dawn ahead." His letter to the American people and the world
was a final act of courage and humility—the public reckoning
of a truth teller refusing to be shamed by life's cruel fate. Visitors entering that room stand stock-still, watching the video,
surprised to find tears in their eyes after all this time. Teachers
whisper to their classes about the meaning of Alzheimer's as
the children solemnly watch and listen. But then, shaking themselves loose of the sadness, visitors enter the final room, where
Reagan's warm smile and sparkling voice, restored again on a
giant screen, beckon them to believe. And when they walk out
into the sun, they are smiling, just as he would have wanted.

"The last enemy that will be abolished is death," the scrip-
tures say. And those who treasure Reagan's legacy can easily
apply that belief to him. He had always been larger than life,
and now he was larger than death, a man whose impact on the
world would outlast him, no matter how unsettled the future
became.

He died on June 5, 2004, and his two great political friends
traveled to Washington for his state funeral. Margaret Thatcher
revealed that when Reagan had been planning his funeral while
still in office (something presidents are required to do), he had
asked her to speak at his service. However, she was herself ill by
that point, so she had taped her eulogy before Reagan's death,
and it would be played at the service, which she attended.

Mourning his friend, Gorbachev was emotional, saying that
Reagan was a man who had been fated to be by his side in the
most important endeavor of the last years of the twentieth century. Gorbachev's sorrow was tempered by the knowledge of
what they had done together. In a *New York Times* op-ed entitled "A President Who Listened," Gorbachev wrote poignantly
of the main lesson of their work together:

I think that the main lesson of those years is the need for dialogue, which must not be broken off whatever the challenges and complications we have to face. Meeting with Ronald Reagan in subsequent years I saw that this was how he understood our legacy to the new generation of political leaders.

The personal rapport that emerged between us over the years helped me to appreciate Ronald Reagan's human qualities. A true leader, a man of his word and an optimist, he traveled the journey of his life with dignity and faced courageously the cruel disease that darkened his final years. He has earned a place in history and in people's hearts.

Visitors to the Reagan Library can pause in contemplation at the outdoor granite memorial site where Reagan and Nancy are buried. The epitaph is pure Reagan:

I know in my heart that man is good, that what is right will always eventually triumph and there is purpose and worth to each and every life.

Upward of 2 million people every year read those words and stroll the lush grounds, amid the blooming flowers, peering over the cliff at the valley below. On a clear day, they can see the ocean and the world beyond.

THE LAST WORD

2018

February 20, 2018
James S. Brady Press Briefing Room (named for President
Reagan's first press secretary wounded in the assassination
attempt on Reagan)

Reporters were ready to pounce when White House Press Secretary Sarah Sanders walked confidently to the briefing room podium. After a short statement about the mass shooting at Marjory Stoneman Douglas High School in Parkland, Florida, which had stunned the nation six days earlier, Sanders opened it up for questions. It was the first time reporters would have a shot at asking them since Special Counsel Robert Mueller and his team indicted a host of Russians a few days earlier for various illegal activities tied to the 2016 election.

MSNBC's Hallie Jackson was prepped and ready when Sanders gave her the nod.

"Does the President now acknowledge what the Special Counsel indictments made clear, which is that Russians not only tried to meddle, but interfere and influence the 2016 election?" Jackson asked.

Without missing a beat, the White House Press Secretary answered and then pushed back on the underlying premise.

"Absolutely. And the president has acknowledged that multiple times before. He acknowledged it during the transition, he acknowledged it during a press conference in Poland, and he acknowledged it for a third time at a press event in Poland. He has stated several times," she said, adding quickly, "it's very clear that Russia meddled in the election. It's also very clear that it didn't have an impact on the election. And it's also very clear that the Trump campaign didn't collude with the Russians in any way for this process to take place."

But it was the next rhetorical defense that Sanders had obviously spent some time preparing beforehand. She said, "What I can tell you is that the president has been extremely tough on Russia. He helped push through $700 billion to rebuild our military. I can assure you Russia is not excited about that. He has helped export energy to Eastern Europe. I can assure you, Russia is not excited about that. He has put and upheld sanctions that the Obama administration put in place. He has upheld those. He has closed three diplomatic properties that were Russia's, here in the United States. He has taken a number of actions against Russia and put pressure on them. He has helped arm the Ukrainians." In a strong defense, Sanders argued that President Trump had actually been more decisive than previous administrations.

As of this writing, Special Counsel Mueller has not concluded his investigation into alleged Russian collusion with the 2016 Trump campaign. The President has repeatedly called the collusion allegation a "hoax" and the nonstop focus and media coverage of the issue "fake news." At this moment, we don't know what we don't know, but the Trump administration has been working hard to show how tough it has been on Russia even as all of this has been going on—with some success. Going forward, he faces the challenge of figuring out, as presidents

before him have tried to do, how to maximize a relationship
with a nation that remains a frequent foe and an untrustworthy
partner.

The Cold War officially ended more than a quarter century
ago, with the collapse of the Soviet Union. Many people thought
that Russia and the former Soviet-aligned nations would not
only become immediately democratized, but would also be
seamlessly integrated into the larger family of nations under
NATO. But bedrock Soviet principles were not just ideologically driven; they were culturally driven. And it wasn't so easy
to abandon history and culture for uncertain alliances. The ensuing decades saw a hardening of mutual distrust between the
United States and Russia.

There was a common belief that once the Cold War was
won, the prospect of an arms race would evaporate and the
world would be safe for democracy. Reagan had always known
better. His wisdom was reflected in his insistence on pressing
for SDI. When Gorbachev scoffed, Reagan reminded him that
they could not know what might happen with other bad actors
in the world. Reagan looked at the future and knew true peace
was not as simple as defeating just one foe.

In Reagan's time, the nuclear threat was a faceoff between
two powers. Today, nine nations have nuclear programs—the
United States, Russia, the United Kingdom, France, China, India, Pakistan, Israel, and North Korea. Iran threatens, and it
is naïve to think a nuclear Iran is impossible. For the first time
since the Cuban Missile Crisis, people have experienced a real
fear of nuclear disaster, this time from North Korea. As the
sirens blared and the messages shot out in Hawaii on January
13, 2018—"BALLISTIC MISSILE THREAT INBOUND TO
HAWAII, SEEK IMMEDIATE SHELTER. THIS IS NOT A
DRILL"—families huddled in bathtubs and hotel ballrooms,

saying goodbye to their loved ones, thinking they were all just moments away from nuclear incineration. Hawaii's false alarm was just the latest moment to bring the North Korean nuclear threat home. It is a threat that is real and urgent.

Reagan's SDI was essentially the grandfather to the modern-day Missile Defense System, which the US military is working hard to perfect in order to provide a shield against North Korean nuclear aggression. The system took a lot longer than Gorbachev thought the 1980s SDI would take to build and test, but missile defense is now a crucial part of the US defense of the homeland.

When Vladimir Putin was first in office as president of Russia between 2000 and 2008, many in the George W. Bush administration, including Vice President Dick Cheney, were suspicious of him, fearing that "once a KGB officer, always a KGB officer." Even so, Bush attempted a "reset" in relations, famously saying, "I looked the man in the eye. I was able to get a sense of his soul." He imagined that he and Putin could reach a common framework. It never came to be.

In the Obama administration, people were still talking about a reset. Secretary of State Hillary Clinton went so far as to deliver a plastic "RESET" button to the Russian Foreign Minister (with the wrong Russian word for "reset" printed on top). That didn't work so well either. By the time Putin returned to the presidency in 2012, after four years out of office, relations had begun to deteriorate once more. President Obama was ineffective in reaching out to Putin, and was toothless in his criticism of Russian aggression in the Ukraine.

In Russia, Mikhail Gorbachev, now in his mid-eighties, has been an outspoken critic of the flaws in the Russian system, and of Putin himself. Asked by the BBC in late 2016 whether Putin ever asked his advice, he replied, "He knows everything already."

Gorbachev is deeply concerned about the current threat of nuclear war. When Trump took office in 2017, Gorbachev publicly urged him and Putin to work together to halt what he called "the new arms race." And Trump seemed intent on engineering another "reset" with Putin, especially a joint effort to fight terrorism. But Trump's interest in working with Putin has been complicated by the ongoing Mueller investigation and the necessity of confronting Russian aggression. The question is: Will an emboldened Russia feel less inclined to pursue a destructive agenda after the latest US moves?

The answer is unclear. On March 1, 2018, Putin, running for reelection, gave a provocative state-of-the-nation speech, highlighting the development of new strategic nuclear weapons. Although the weapons are not yet operational, Putin was bullish in his challenge, stating, "I want to tell all those who have fueled the arms race over the last fifteen years, sought to win unilateral advantages over Russia, introduced unlawful sanctions aimed to contain our country's development: all what you wanted to impede with your policies have already happened. . . . You have failed to contain Russia."

There is debate whether the threat is real, or whether Putin was engaged in some old-fashioned electioneering to appease his base. But it can't be denied that the modern security reality is layered in complexity. The menace doesn't come only from nuclear weapons. Global terrorism isn't reliant on sophisticated weaponry. And today we live in an era where a cyber-threat can jeopardize democracy, accessing invisible pathways that we have yet to uncover. We know that a newly aggressive Russia does not threaten us just from the skies but also from within.

It is also true that the Russians or the Soviets have been attempting to undermine American democracy and commit espionage against the US government for more than eight decades. That's what a young Ronald Reagan was worried about in those early anti-Communist Hollywood days.

It is a daunting challenge for any president to juggle all of the hot spots and hazards while still portraying strength on the world stage. Some have questioned the administration's overall foreign policy strategy and have surmised that any given decision also seems to go through the most important filter of what it means for President Trump personally. Still, there are real signs the president has it in him to rise to the occasion of our era and deliver a forceful message if he chooses to do so. While Presidents Trump and Reagan are very different personalities and very different people, on important occasions Trump has given speeches that sounded—dare I say—Reaganesque.

Less than six months into his presidency, Trump gave a speech in Warsaw, Poland's Krasinski Square, a speech that one could hear Reagan delivering—similar in its tone and content. He spoke reverently of Polish courage during the Warsaw uprising in World War II, was blunt about the challenges the global community faced today, and presented an uplifting view of the future for free nations.

He challenged Russia to cease its destabilizing activities in Ukraine and its support for hostile regimes in Syria and Iran. And in words Reagan might have used, he criticized "the steady creep of government bureaucracy" that robs nations of wealth and hampers their ability to innovate. But mostly he talked about shared values:

> Americans, Poles, and the nations of Europe value individual freedom and sovereignty. We must work together to confront forces, whether they come from inside or out, from the South or the East, that threaten over time to undermine these values and to erase the bonds of cul-

ture, faith, and tradition that make us who we are. If left unchecked, these forces will undermine our courage, sap our spirit, and weaken our will to defend ourselves and our societies.

But just as our adversaries and enemies of the past learned here in Poland, we know that these forces, too, are doomed to fail if we want them to fail. And we do, indeed, want them to fail. They are doomed not only because our alliance is strong, our countries are resilient, and our power is unmatched. . . . Our adversaries . . . are doomed because we will never forget who we are. And if we don't forget who [we] are, we just can't be beaten. Americans will never forget. The nations of Europe will never forget. We are the fastest and the greatest community. The world has never known anything like our community of nations.

President Trump gave another soaring speech in Riyadh, Saudi Arabia, speaking to leaders from the Arab world about fighting radical jihadists and terrorism—blunt rhetoric in the heart of Islam that one could also hear Reagan delivering.

In addition to the similar rhetoric in big speeches, Trump and Reagan also have this in common: both men were and are underestimated. Reagan, the Hollywood actor, who was "just delivering lines," and Trump, the billionaire businessman/reality TV star, who most days has said or tweeted at least one thing that has shocked or appalled establishment Washington—to the delight of his supporters.

I cover this administration daily, and yes, it has been like drinking from a fire hose. If President Reagan were alive today, after reading oral histories and talking to aides and friends, I'm pretty sure he'd advise President Trump not to let the attacks or negative stories or jokes bother him. There are a host of differences between the two men, but this might be the biggest. Reagan would not let the brutal criticism of the day, the pointed opinion pages, what he saw as the TV networks' one-sided coverage, the late-night comics' jokes, the aggressive speeches from the House and Senate floor affect him. Reagan's press secretary, Marlin Fitzwater, put it this way when we spoke: "Reagan took all that and just shoved it aside. I always remember people would ask me, 'How does he put up with Sam Donaldson yelling at him and being crude sometimes?' It never bothered Reagan a bit. Sam would yell at him, and the president would say to me, 'What's he saying, Marlin?' And I'd say, 'Well, I'm not sure I heard it all, Mr. President, but he thinks our policy is wrong here.' And the President would invite me into the Oval Office and he'd say, 'Now here's what you tell him . . .' and he would go through this long dissertation on what I should tell Sam Donaldson about this problem. I mean Reagan just always believed if he got 'em, he could convince 'em. And he never resented the press in any way."

You may remember, in 1987, Marist Student Council President Bret Baier had a real problem with the yelling Sam Donaldson in that Rose Garden event, but Fitzwater says President Reagan did not.

Whether Trump will take what I think Reagan's advice would have been—to get out of his own way—is yet to be seen. President Trump is a counterpuncher, a trait honed in the rough and tumble real estate world of New York City. A different style—perhaps closer to another Reagan quote, "When you can't make them see the light, make them feel the heat."

We have no way to know what the future holds for this administration or this president. Two things are clear: (1) Like Reagan, President Trump changed the paradigm. While the jury is still out on the end result of that tectonic shift, the entire game changed in the way Washington worked—or what was important—once President Trump took office. And (2) No matter what happens going forward, in the words of President Reagan, this country, this Republic "is not a fragile flower." It's tremendously resilient, not because of its government, but because of its people.

Over the past four years, researching and then writing about the optimism and pragmatism of President and General Dwight D. Eisenhower, and then the optimism and fortitude of President Ronald Reagan that led to the end of the Cold War, I came to appreciate that both leaders had the ability to get big things across the finish line. We know Trump has this capability. He managed to push Congress to get a massive tax bill through, and he signed it into law; he managed to nominate and help shepherd conservative judge Neil Gorsuch to fill a vacant seat on the US Supreme Court. Many of his initiatives are welcomed by conservatives. He has also shown boldness on the world stage; he ordered the US military to step up the attacks on ISIS, and the group was largely obliterated in Iraq and Syria in the first nine months of his presidency.

But he also faces a world in disarray, demanding skilled leadership. "The twenty-first century will either be a century of disastrous intensification of a deadly crisis, or the century in which mankind becomes morally more pure and spiritually healthier," Mikhail Gorbachev wrote in *The New Russia*. "I am convinced that we are called upon to do our part to ensure the triumph of humanity and justice." This is the challenge that faces Trump and other modern leaders. Perhaps beyond the grave, Ronald Reagan would echo Gorbachev's sentiment, and his view would be optimistic. He knew that no matter how the political pendulum swings, the resilience of this country shines through.

In President Reagan's last message to the American people,

announcing he was suffering from Alzheimer's disease, he reserved his final words for an enduring faith in America. "When the Lord calls me home, whenever that day may be," he wrote, "I will leave with the greatest love for this country of ours and eternal optimism for its future."

Amen.

ACKNOWLEDGMENTS

Like *Three Days in January*, *Three Days in Moscow* would not have happened without the amazing hard work and dedication of my coauthor, Catherine Whitney. Catherine's ability to adapt my ideas and voice in the same back-and-forth process that made *Three Days in January* work so well makes *Three Days in Moscow* really shine. She did a tremendous job culling important details from thousands of pages of library documents, biographies, oral histories, and my interviews.

The team would not have been complete without our intrepid researcher, Sydney Soderberg, digging up gems at the Reagan, Bush, and Eisenhower libraries.

Professionals at presidential libraries are the gatekeepers of the history and wisdom of our highest office. The Ronald Reagan Presidential Library opened its doors to me and allowed me inside their remarkable store of knowledge and insight. In particular, I would like to thank Joanne Drake, chief administrative officer, who was enthusiastic about my book and made sure I had everything I needed; archivist Ray Wilson, who was so generous with his time and input; audio visual archivist Michael Pinckney, who helped select wonderful photos for the book; and chief marketing officer Melissa Giller, for taking me through every aspect of the library and bringing Reagan's presidency to life for me. I am also grateful to John Heubusch, executive director of the Reagan Foundation for his constant support.

Thanks, too, to archivists Doug Campbell and Buffie Hollis at the George H. W. Bush Presidential Library, who helped give substance to President Bush's role in the end of the Cold War. I also returned to the Eisenhower Library for research into the relationship between our thirty-fourth and fortieth presidents, and am grateful as always to the wonderful professionals there, especially acting director Tim Rives and archivist Mary Burtzloff. Meredith Sleichter, the executive director of the Eisenhower Foundation, was also helpful.

Many people added their voices to this project, and were generous in sharing their experiences and perceptions. I am especially grateful to those who served under Reagan or reported on his presidency and gave me the benefit of their wisdom: Charles Black, Anthony Dolan, Kenneth Duberstein, Marlin Fitzwater, Josh Gilder, Charles Krauthammer, Gilbert Robinson, George Shultz, and Chris Wallace. Many others offered priceless insights for the book and the Fox documentary. I am also extremely grateful to the Miller Center/UVA for their devotion to recording the oral histories of many staffers, who paint a vivid picture of what it was like to serve under Reagan. The Miller Center does a tremendous service to our nation's historical memory.

Special thanks to the team at William Morrow, led by our editor, Peter Hubbard. Peter's confidence that we could deliver again gave us comfort that we actually could. Peter and his team—Liate Stehlik, Lauren Janiec, Lynn Grady, Nick Amphlett, and Tavia Kowalchuk—came up with a rock-solid plan to give *Three Days* the boost it needed to launch.

As always, thanks to my manager, Larry Kramer, and book agent, Claudia Cross with Folio Literary Group, for their encouragement and excellent handling of day-to-day logistics, which made it easier for me to juggle work, family, and another book and book tour.

Thank you to my employer, Fox News, for allowing me the leeway to spend time on this and for doing a one-hour documentary scheduled to run at book launch.

And a very special thank-you to my family—my wife, Amy, and my two sons, Paul and Daniel. Time away and late nights made the prospect of another book "daunting," but they could not have been more supportive of me.

Through it all, I have been grateful to President Ronald Reagan, who is an uplifting presence to this day—always reminding us of the greatness of our nation and what we can still become. Reagan's courage, resolve, and tireless pursuit of peace are an enduring gift to the world. His wisdom resonates still. I feel enormously privileged to tell his story.

RONALD REAGAN'S SPEECH AT MOSCOW STATE UNIVERSITY

May 31, 1988

Thank you, Rector Logunov, and I want to thank all of you very much for a very warm welcome. It's a great pleasure to be here at Moscow State University, and I want to thank you all for turning out. I know you must be very busy this week, studying and taking your final examinations. So, let me just say zhelayu vam uspekha [I wish you success]. Nancy couldn't make it today because she's visiting Leningrad, which she tells me is a very beautiful city, but she, too, says hello and wishes you all good luck.

Let me say it's also a great pleasure to once again have this opportunity to speak directly to the people of the Soviet Union. Before I left Washington, I received many heartfelt letters and telegrams asking me to carry here a simple message, perhaps, but also some of the most important business of this summit: It is a message of peace and good will and hope for a growing friendship and closeness between our two peoples.

As you know, I've come to Moscow to meet with one of your most distinguished graduates. In this, our fourth summit, General Secretary Gorbachev and I have spent many hours together, and I feel that we're getting to know each other well. Our discussions, of course, have been focused primarily on many of the important issues of the day, issues I want to touch on with you in a few moments. But first I want to take a little time to talk to you much as I would to any group of university students in the United States. I want to talk not just of the realities of today but of the possibilities of tomorrow.

Standing here before a mural of your revolution, I want to talk about a very different revolution that is taking place right now, quietly sweeping the globe without bloodshed or conflict. Its effects are peaceful, but they will fundamentally alter our world, shatter old assumptions, and reshape our lives. It's easy to underestimate because it's not accompanied by banners or fanfare. It's been called the technological or information revolution, and as its emblem, one might take the tiny silicon chip, no bigger than a fingerprint. One of these chips has more computing power than a roomful of old-style computers.

As part of an exchange program, we now have an exhibition touring your country that shows how information technology is transforming our lives—replacing manual labor with robots, forecasting weather for farmers, or mapping the genetic code of DNA for medical researchers. These microcomputers today aid the design of everything from houses to cars to spacecraft; they even design better and faster computers. They can translate English into Russian or enable the blind to read or help Michael Jackson produce on one synthesizer the sounds of a whole orchestra. Linked by a network of satellites and fiber-optic cables, one individual with a desktop computer and a telephone commands resources unavailable to the largest governments just a few years ago.

Like a chrysalis, we're emerging from the economy of the Industrial Revolution—an economy confined to and limited by the Earth's physical resources—into, as one economist titled his book, "The Economy in Mind," in which there are no bounds on human imagination and the freedom to create is the most precious natural resource. Think of that little computer chip. Its value isn't in the sand from which it is made but in the microscopic architecture designed into it by ingenious human minds. Or take the example of the satellite relaying this broadcast around the world, which replaces thousands of tons of copper mined from the Earth and molded into wire. In the new economy, human invention increasingly makes physical resources obsolete. We're breaking through the material conditions of existence to a world where man creates his own destiny. Even as we explore the most advanced reaches of science, we're returning to the age-old wisdom of our culture, a wisdom contained in the book of Genesis in the Bible: In the beginning was the spirit, and it was from this spirit that the material abundance of creation issued forth.

But progress is not foreordained. The key is freedom—freedom of thought, freedom of information, freedom of communication. The renowned scientist, scholar, and founding father of this university, Mikhail Lomonosov, knew that. "It is common knowledge," he said, "that the achievements of science are considerable and rapid, particularly once the yoke of slavery is cast off and replaced by the freedom of philosophy." You know, one of the first contacts between your country and mine took place between Russian and American explorers. The Americans were members of Cook's last voyage on an expedition searching for an Arctic passage; on the island of Unalaska, they came upon the Russians, who took them in, and together with the native inhabitants, held a prayer service on the ice.

The explorers of the modern era are the entrepreneurs, men with vision, with the courage to take risks and faith enough to brave the unknown. These entrepreneurs and their small enterprises are responsible for almost all the economic growth in the United States. They are the prime movers of the technological revolution. In fact, one of the largest personal computer firms in the United States was started by two college students, no older than you, in the garage behind their home. Some people, even in my own country, look at the riot of experiment that is the free market and see only waste. What of all the entrepreneurs that fail? Well, many do, particularly the successful ones; often several times. And if you ask them the secret of their success, they'll tell you it's all that they learned in their struggles along the way; yes, it's what they learned from failing. Like an athlete in competition or a scholar in pursuit of the truth, experience is the greatest teacher.

And that's why it's so hard for government planners, no matter how sophisticated, to ever substitute for millions of individuals working night and day to make their dreams come true. The fact is, bureaucracies are a problem around the world. There's an old story about a town—it could be anywhere—with a bureaucrat who is known to be a good-for-nothing, but he somehow had always hung on to power. So one day, in a town meeting, an old woman got up and said to him: "There is a folk legend here where I come from that when a baby is born, an angel comes down from heaven and kisses it on one part of its body. If the angel kisses him on his hand, he becomes a handyman. If he kisses him on his forehead, he becomes bright and clever. And I've been trying to figure out where the angel kissed

you so that you should sit there for so long and do nothing."
[Laughter]

We are seeing the power of economic freedom spreading
around the world. Places such as the Republic of Korea, Sin-
gapore, Taiwan have vaulted into the technological era, barely
pausing in the industrial age along the way. Low-tax agricultural policies in the subcontinent mean that in some years India
is now a net exporter of food. Perhaps most exciting are the
winds of change that are blowing over the People's Republic
of China, where one-quarter of the world's population is now
getting its first taste of economic freedom. At the same time,
the growth of democracy has become one of the most powerful political movements of our age. In Latin America in the
1970's, only a third of the population lived under democratic
government; today over 90 percent does. In the Philippines, in
the Republic of Korea, free, contested, democratic elections are
the order of the day. Throughout the world, free markets are the
model for growth. Democracy is the standard by which governments are measured.

We Americans make no secret of our belief in freedom. In
fact, it's something of a national pastime. Every 4 years the American people choose a new President, and 1988 is one of those
years. At one point there were 13 major candidates running in
the two major parties, not to mention all the others, including
the Socialist and Libertarian candidates—all trying to get my
job. About 1,000 local television stations, 8,500 radio stations,
and 1,700 daily newspapers—each one an independent, private
enterprise, fiercely independent of the Government—report on
the candidates, grill them in interviews, and bring them together for debates. In the end, the people vote; they decide who
will be the next President. But freedom doesn't begin or end
with elections.

Go to any American town, to take just an example, and you'll see dozens of churches, representing many different beliefs—in many places, synagogues and mosques—and you'll see families of every conceivable nationality worshiping together. Go into any schoolroom, and there you will see children being taught the Declaration of Independence, that they are endowed by their Creator with certain unalienable rights—among them life, liberty, and the pursuit of happiness—that no government can justly deny; the guarantees in their Constitution for freedom of speech, freedom of assembly, and freedom of religion. Go into any courtroom, and there will preside an independent judge, beholden to no government power. There every defendant has the right to a trial by a jury of his peers, usually 12 men and women—common citizens; they are the ones, the only ones, who weigh the evidence and decide on guilt or innocence. In that court, the accused is innocent until proven guilty, and the word of a policeman or any official has no greater legal standing than the word of the accused. Go to any university campus, and there you'll find an open, sometimes heated discussion of the problems in American society and what can be done to correct them. Turn on the television, and you'll see the legislature conducting the business of government right there before the camera, debating and voting on the legislation that will become the law of the land. March in any demonstration, and there are many of them; the people's right of assembly is guaranteed in the Constitution and protected by the police. Go into any union hall, where the members know their right to strike is protected by law. As a matter of fact, one of the many jobs I had before this one was being president of a union, the Screen Actors Guild. I led my union out on strike, and I'm proud to say we won.

But freedom is more even than this. Freedom is the right

to question and change the established way of doing things. It is the continuing revolution of the marketplace. It is the understanding that allows us to recognize shortcomings and seek solutions. It is the right to put forth an idea, scoffed at by the experts, and watch it catch fire among the people. It is the right to dream—to follow your dream or stick to your conscience, even if you're the only one in a sea of doubters. Freedom is the recognition that no single person, no single authority or government has a monopoly on the truth, but that every individual life is infinitely precious, that every one of us put on this world has been put there for a reason and has something to offer.

America is a nation made up of hundreds of nationalities. Our ties to you are more than ones of good feeling; they're ties of kinship. In America, you'll find Russians, Armenians, Ukrainians, peoples from Eastern Europe and Central Asia. They come from every part of this vast continent, from every continent, to live in harmony, seeking a place where each cultural heritage is respected, each is valued for its diverse strengths and beauties and the richness it brings to our lives. Recently, a few individuals and families have been allowed to visit relatives in the West. We can only hope that it won't be long before all are allowed to do so and Ukrainian-Americans, Baltic-Americans, Armenian-Americans can freely visit their homelands, just as this Irish-American visits his.

Freedom, it has been said, makes people selfish and materialistic, but Americans are one of the most religious peoples on Earth. Because they know that liberty, just as life itself, is not earned but a gift from God, they seek to share that gift with the world. "Reason and experience," said George Washington in his Farewell Address, "both forbid us to expect that national morality can prevail in exclusion of religious principle. And it is substantially true, that virtue or morality is a necessary spring of popular government." Democracy is less a system of government than it is a system to keep government limited, unintrusive; a system of constraints on power to keep politics and government secondary to the important things in life, the true sources of value found only in family and faith.

But I hope you know I go on about these things not simply to extol the virtues of my own country but to speak to the true greatness of the heart and soul of your land. Who, after all, needs to tell the land of Dostoyevski about the quest for truth, the home of Kandinski and Scriabin about imagination, the rich and noble culture of the Uzbek man of letters Alisher Navoi about beauty and heart? The great culture of your diverse land speaks with a glowing passion to all humanity. Let me cite one of the most eloquent contemporary passages on human freedom. It comes, not from the literature of America, but from this country, from one of the greatest writers of the 20th century, Boris Pasternak, in the novel "Dr. Zhivago." He writes: "I think that if the beast who sleeps in man could be held down by threats—any kind of threat, whether of jail or of retribution after death—then the highest emblem of humanity would be the lion tamer in the circus with his whip, not the prophet who sacrificed himself. But this is just the point—what has for centuries raised man above the beast is not the cudgel, but an inward music—the irresistible power of unarmed truth."

The irresistible power of unarmed truth. Today the world looks expectantly to signs of change, steps toward greater freedom in the Soviet Union. We watch and we hope as we see positive changes taking place. There are some, I know, in your society who fear that change will bring only disruption and discontinuity, who fear to embrace the hope of the future— sometimes it takes faith. It's like that scene in the cowboy movie "Butch Cassidy and the Sundance Kid," which some here in

Moscow recently had a chance to see. The posse is closing in on the two outlaws, Butch and Sundance, who find themselves trapped on the edge of a cliff, with a sheer drop of hundreds of feet to the raging rapids below. Butch turns to Sundance and says their only hope is to jump into the river below, but Sundance refuses. He says he'd rather fight it out with the posse, even though they're hopelessly outnumbered. Butch says that's suicide and urges him to jump, but Sundance still refuses and finally admits, "I can't swim." Butch breaks up laughing and says, "You crazy fool, the fall will probably kill you." And, by the way, both Butch and Sundance made it, in case you didn't see the movie. I think what I've just been talking about is perestroika and what its goals are.

But change would not mean rejection of the past. Like a tree growing strong through the seasons, rooted in the Earth and drawing life from the Sun, so, too, positive change must be rooted in traditional values—in the land, in culture, in family and community—and it must take its life from the eternal things, from the source of all life, which is faith. Such change will lead to new understandings, new opportunities, to a broader future in which the tradition is not supplanted but finds its full flowering. That is the future beckoning to your generation.

At the same time, we should remember that reform that is not institutionalized will always be insecure. Such freedom will always be looking over its shoulder. A bird on a tether, no matter how long the rope, can always be pulled back. And that is why, in my conversation with General Secretary Gorbachev, I have spoken of how important it is to institutionalize change—to put guarantees on reform. And we've been talking together about one sad reminder of a divided world: the Berlin Wall. It's time to remove the barriers that keep people apart.

I'm proposing an increased exchange program of high school

students between our countries. General Secretary Gorbachev mentioned on Sunday a wonderful phrase you have in Russian for this: "Better to see something once than to hear about it a hundred times." Mr. Gorbachev and I first began working on this in 1985. In our discussion today, we agreed on working up to several thousand exchanges a year from each country in the near future. But not everyone can travel across the continents and oceans. Words travel lighter, and that's why we'd like to make available to this country more of our 11,000 magazines and periodicals and our television and radio shows that can be beamed off a satellite in seconds. Nothing would please us more than for the Soviet people to get to know us better and to understand our way of life.

Just a few years ago, few would have imagined the progress our two nations have made together. The INF treaty, which General Secretary Gorbachev and I signed last December in Washington and whose instruments of ratification we will exchange tomorrow—the first true nuclear arms reduction treaty in history, calling for the elimination of an entire class of U.S. and Soviet nuclear missiles. And just 16 days ago, we saw the beginning of your withdrawal from Afghanistan, which gives us hope that soon the fighting may end and the healing may begin and that that suffering country may find self-determination, unity, and peace at long last.

It's my fervent hope that our constructive cooperation on these issues will be carried on to address the continuing destruction and conflicts in many regions of the globe and that the serious discussions that led to the Geneva accords on Afghanistan will help lead to solutions in southern Africa, Ethiopia, Cambodia, the Persian Gulf, and Central America. I have often said: Nations do not distrust each other because they are armed; they are armed because they distrust each other. If this globe is to live in peace and prosper, if it is to embrace all the possibilities of the technological revolution, then nations must renounce, once and for all, the right to an expansionist foreign policy. Peace between nations must be an enduring goal, not a tactical stage in a continuing conflict.

I've been told that there's a popular song in your country—perhaps you know it—whose evocative refrain asks the question, "Do the Russians want a war?" In answer it says: "Go ask that silence lingering in the air, above the birch and poplar there; beneath those trees the soldiers lie. Go ask my mother, ask my wife; then you will have to ask no more, 'Do the Russians want a war?'" But what of your one-time allies? What of those who embraced you on the Elbe? What if we were to ask the watery graves of the Pacific or the European battlefields where America's fallen were buried far from home? What if we were to ask their mothers, sisters, and sons, do Americans want war? Ask us, too, and you'll find the same answer, the same longing in every heart. People do not make wars; governments do. And no mother would ever willingly sacrifice her sons for territorial gain, for economic advantage, for ideology. A people free to choose will always choose peace.

Americans seek always to make friends of old antagonists. After a colonial revolution with Britain, we have cemented for all ages the ties of kinship between our nations. After a terrible Civil War between North and South, we healed our wounds and found true unity as a nation. We fought two world wars in my lifetime against Germany and one with Japan, but now the Federal Republic of Germany and Japan are two of our closest allies and friends.

Some people point to the trade disputes between us as a sign of strain, but they're the frictions of all families, and the family of free nations is a big and vital and sometimes boisterous one. I can tell you that nothing would please my heart more than in my lifetime to see American and Soviet diplomats grappling with the problem of trade disputes between America and a growing, exuberant, exporting Soviet Union that had opened up to economic freedom and growth.

And as important as these official people-to-people exchanges are, nothing would please me more than for them to become unnecessary, to see travel between East and West become so routine that university students in the Soviet Union could take a month off in the summer and, just like students in the West do now, put packs on their backs and travel from country to country in Europe with barely a passport check in between. Nothing would please me more than to see the day that a concert promoter in, say, England could call up a Soviet rock group, without going through any government agency, and have them playing in Liverpool the next night. Is this just a dream? Perhaps, but it is a dream that is our responsibility to have come true.

Your generation is living in one of the most exciting, hopeful times in Soviet history. It is a time when the first breath of freedom stirs the air and the heart beats to the accelerated rhythm of hope, when the accumulated spiritual energies of a long silence yearn to break free. I am reminded of the famous passage near the end of Gogol's "Dead Souls." Comparing his nation to a speeding troika, Gogol asks what will be its destination. But he writes, "There was no answer save the bell pouring forth marvelous sound."

We do not know what the conclusion will be of this journey, but we're hopeful that the promise of reform will be fulfilled. In this Moscow spring, this May 1988, we may be allowed that hope: that freedom, like the fresh green sapling planted over Tolstoy's grave, will blossom forth at last in the rich fertile soil of your people and culture. We may be allowed to hope that the marvelous sound of a new openness will keep rising through, ringing through, leading to a new world of reconciliation, friendship, and peace.

Thank you all very much, and *da blagoslovit vas gospod*— God bless you.

NOTES

INTRODUCTION

xi *"I want to talk"*: Ronald Reagan, "Remarks and a Question-and-Answer Session with the Students and Faculty at Moscow State University," May 31, 1988, Ronald Reagan Presidential Library, Simi Valley, CA; https://www.reaganlibrary.gov/sites/default/files/archives/speeches/1988/053188b.htm.

xi *"Freedom is the"*: Ibid.

xv *"Governor and then"*: Author interview with Marlin Fitzwater, July 19, 2017.

xvi *"Freedom is never more"*: Reagan used these lines in a number of speeches, including his gubernatorial inauguration address on January 5, 1967; reaganlibrary.org.

PROLOGUE: THE WALK

1 *"If someone had told me"*: Nancy Reagan, *My Turn: The Memoirs of Nancy Reagan* (New York: Random House, 2011).

3 *"People in the Soviet"*: Marina Darmaros, "Boris Yeltsin: Ups and Downs in the Eyes of the World," *Russia Beyond*, February 2, 2011.

3 *"His growing loneliness"*: Andrei Grachev, *Gorbachev's Gamble: Soviet Foreign Policy and the End of the Cold War* (New York: Wiley, 2008).

4 *"Mr. President"*: Memorandum of Conversation, The President's First One-on-One Meeting with General Secretary Gorbachev, May 29, 1988, National Security Archive.

4 *"In the past"*: Ibid.

4 *Nancy disliked Raisa's*: Nancy Reagan, *My Turn*.

5 *A cartoon by*: Len "Boro" Borozinski cartoon, *Phoenix Gazette*, June 3, 1988.

5 *As they strolled*: George de Lama, "Nancy, Raisa: Roses, 'Nyets,'" Chicago Tribune Service, May 30, 1988.

5 *The private meeting*: Memorandum of Conversation, The President's First One-on-One Meeting with General Secretary Gorbachev, May 29, 1988, National Security Archive.

6 *"We thought she was"*: Author interview with Marlin Fitzwater, July 19, 2017.

7 *"This was the last"*: Ibid.

8 *"This is either"*: Ibid.

9 *"She's with us!"*: Nancy Reagan, *My Turn*; also author interview with Marlin Fitzwater, July 19, 2017.

9 *"we just lost"*: Author interview with Marlin Fitzwater, July 19, 2017.

9 *"It was clearly"*: Author interview with Chris Wallace, July 18, 2017.

10 *"We represent two"*: Memorandum of Conversation, Geneva Summit, November 19, 1985, National Security Archive.

10 *"Sometimes the best act"*: Author interview with Kenneth Duberstein, October 26, 2017.

CHAPTER 1: DREAM MAKER

15 *Ronald Reagan often told*: Ronald Reagan, *An American Life: The Autobiography* (New York: Simon and Schuster, 1990).

15 *"I've always said"*: Lyn Nofziger, oral history with Stephen Knott et al., March 6, 2003, Ronald Reagan Oral History Project, UVA Miller Center/Ronald Reagan Presidential Library.

16 *"He lets me come"*: Nancy Reagan, *My Turn: The Memoirs of Nancy Reagan* (New York: Random House, 2011).

16 *"sunny aloofness"*: Robert Draper, "Obama's BFF," *New York Times*, July 26, 2009. [Notably, Draper made this reference in a piece about President Obama.]

16 *"I've never had trouble"*: Ronald Reagan, *An American Life*.

16 *"warmly ruthless"*: Martin Anderson, oral history with Jim Young, December 11 and 12, 2001, Ronald Reagan Oral History Project, UVA Miller Center/Ronald Reagan Presidential Library.

16 *"In his lifetime"*: "Eulogy for Ronald Reagan," June 11, 2004, Margaret Thatcher Foundation; https://www.margaretthatcher.org/document/110360.

17 *"I thought I married"*: Nancy Reagan, *My Turn*.

18 *"He loved shoes"*: Ronald Reagan with Richard G. Huber, *Where's the Rest of Me?* (New York: Duell, Sloan and Pearce, 1965). [Note: Reagan wrote two memoirs, this first published just before he began his political career.]

18 *"I wanted to let"*: Ronald Reagan, *An American Life*.

19 *"If you're the child"*: Lou Cannon, interview on "The Reagan Years: The Making of a President," *CNN Perspective*, February 11, 2001.

19 *"I learned from"*: Ronald Reagan, *An American Life*.

20 *"Times were tough"*: Ronald Reagan, "Remarks During a Homecoming and Birthday Celebration in Dixon, Illinois," February 6, 1984, The American Presidency Project; http://www.presidency.ucsb.edu/ws/?pid=39366.

20 *"My existence turned"*: Ronald Reagan, *An American Life*.

20 *"house of magic"*: Ronald Reagan, *Reagan: A Life in Letters*,

ed. Kiron K. Skinner, Annelise Anderson, and Martin Anderson (New York: Free Press, 2003).

21 *"I'm damned if anyone"*: Ronald Reagan, *Where's the Rest of Me?*

22 *"When the credits roll"*: Bonnie Angelo, *First Mothers: The Women Who Shaped the Presidents* (New York: William Morrow, 2000).

22 *"She had a natural"*: Ronald Reagan, *An American Life.*

22 *"To higher, nobler things"*: *Reagan's Country*, Reagan Foundation Member Newsletter, 2012.

23 *"I wonder what"*: *Reagan's Country*, Reagan Foundation Member Newsletter, 2012; http://home.reaganfoundation.org/site/DocServer /ReaganMomentsEssayJuly2012.pdf?docID=886.

23 *"Just between us"*: Ronald Reagan, *A Life in Letters.*

24 *"I discovered that night"*: Ronald Reagan, *An American Life.*

24 *"We attended a college"*: Ronald Reagan, "Your America to Be Free," 1957 Commencement Address at Eureka College in Illinois, reagan 2020.us.

26 *With Reagan sitting there*: Ronald Reagan, *An American Life.*

26 *From then on*: Ibid.

27 *"Rock, sometimes when"*: Film *Knute Rockne, All American*, 1940, Warner Bros. Preserved in the National Film Registry.

28 *Worried that the press*: Author interview with Marlin Fitzwater, July 19, 2017.

28 *More than any other project*: Ronald Reagan, *Where's the Rest of Me?*

29 *"a great president"*: Adam Miller, "Wyman Hails Her 'Great' Ex," *New York Post*, June 12, 2004.

29 *"In every story"*: Michael Reagan, *On the Outside Looking In* (New York: Zebra, 1988).

29 *"Are you and your son"*: Sam Donaldson, *Hold On, Mr. President* (New York: Random House, 1987).

30 *"At the early onset"*: Michael Reagan, *Lessons My Father Taught Me: The Strength, Integrity, and Faith of Ronald Reagan* (New York: Humanix Books, 2016).

32 *"I didn't realize it"*: Ronald Reagan, *An American Life.*

CHAPTER 2: A POLITICAL EVOLUTION

33 *The hearing room*: "Ronald Reagan and Albert Maltz, Testimony Before HUAC 1947," U.S. Congress, House, Committee on Un-American Activities Hearing, October 23, 1947.

34 *"Perhaps part of it"*: Ronald Reagan, *Where's the Rest of Me?*; see also Stephen Vaughn, *Ronald Reagan in Hollywood: Movies and Politics* (Cambridge, UK: Cambridge University Press, 1994); Jennifer Latson, "Walt Disney, Ronald Reagan and the Fear of Hollywood Communism," *Time*, October 20, 2014.

34 *"'Suddenly,' he wrote"*: Ronald Reagan, *Where's the Rest of Me?*

35 *"Well, sir"*: Ronald Reagan, Testimony before the U.S. Congress, House Committee on Un-American Activities, Hearing, October 23, 1947; https://ia802607.us.archive.org/23/items/hearingsregar din1947aunit/hearingsregardin1947aunit.pdf.

37 *when he returned*: Reagan, *Where's the Rest of Me?*

38 *Ironically, it was*: Nancy Reagan, *My Turn*; see also Ronald Reagan, *Where's the Rest of Me?*

39 *"If ever God"*: Ronald Reagan, *An American Life*.

40 *"Those GE tours"*: Ibid.

40 *"Whether we admit it"*: Matthew Dallek, *The Right Moment: Ronald Reagan's First Victory and the Decisive Turning Point in American Politics* (Oxford University Press, 2004).

40 *Frequently, on the road*: Nancy Reagan, *I Love You, Ronnie: The Letters of Ronald Reagan to Nancy Reagan* (New York: Random House, 2000).

41 *"Every family has problems"*: Nancy Reagan, *My Turn*.

41 *"I'm counting on you"*: Nancy Reagan, *I Love You, Ronnie*.

41 *"He was easy to love"*: Ron Reagan, *My Father at 100: A Memoir* (New York: Penguin Group, 2011).

42 *"an odd sibling rivalry"*: Patti Davis, *Dateline NBC*, November 14, 2004.

42 *"I think you could"*: Ron Reagan, *Today*, March 7, 2004.

43 *"This is the issue"*: Ronald Reagan, "A Time For Choosing," http://www.americanrhetoric.com/speeches/ronaldreaganatimeforchoosing.htm.

43 *"one bright spot"*: Matthew Dallek, *The Right Moment*.

43 *"I didn't know"*: Ronald Reagan, *An American Life*.

43 *"I have a feeling"*: Merriman Smith, oral history with John Luter, January 3, 1968, Columbia University Oral History Project, Dwight D. Eisenhower Library, Abilene, Kansas.

44 *"Extremism in the"*: Barry Goldwater, "Address Accepting the Presidential Nomination at the Republican National Convention in San Francisco," July 16, 1964, The American Presidency Project; http://www.presidency.ucsb.edu/ws/index.php?pid=25973.

44 *"a race that"*: Larry J. Sabato, "How Goldwater Changed Campaigns Forever," *Politico Magazine*, October 27, 2014.

45 *"He believed basically"*: Stuart Spencer, oral history with Jim Young et al., November 15 and 16, 2001, Ronald Reagan Oral History Project, UVA Miller Center/Ronald Reagan Presidential Library.

45 *Reagan laughed*: Ronald Reagan, *An American Life*.

46 *"When Jack Warner"*: This was a story Reagan repeated on many occasions in various settings. (It always got a laugh, even long after he was in the White House.) It's recorded in the *Public Papers of the Presidents: Ronald Reagan 1988–1989*.

47 *"There was something about him"*: Lyn Nofziger, oral history with Stephen Knott et al., March 6, 2003, Ronald Reagan Oral History Project, UVA Miller Center/Ronald Reagan Presidential Library.

47 *"the best communicator"*: Stuart Spencer, oral history with Jim Young et al., November 15 and 16, 2001, Ronald Reagan Oral History Project, UVA Miller Center/Ronald Reagan Presidential Library.

47 *"But there is a problem"*: Ronald Reagan, *Reagan: A Life in Letters*, ed. Kiron K. Skinner, Annelise Anderson, and Martin Anderson (New York: Free Press, 2003).

47 *"There are lots of people"*: Stuart Spencer, oral history with Jim Young et al., November 15 and 16, 2001, Ronald Reagan Oral History Project, UVA Miller Center/Ronald Reagan Presidential Library.

48 *"Dear Mr. President"*: Ronald Reagan's handwritten letter to President Eisenhower, June 10, 1966, Dwight D. Eisenhower Library.

48 *"Ronald Reagan for"*: Matthew Dallek, *The Right Moment*.

49 *"because when Reagan"*: William French Smith, "Evolution of the Kitchen Cabinet 1965–1973," Ronald Reagan Gubernatorial Era Series, 1989.

49 *"Never eat with them"*: Michael Deaver, oral history with Jim Young et al., September 12, 2002, Ronald Reagan Oral History Project, UVA Miller Center/Ronald Reagan Presidential Library.

49 *"Keeping up with"*: Nancy Reagan, *My Turn*.

49 *"Reagan was a"*: Matthew Dallek, *The Right Moment*.

50 *"Crisscrossing California"*: "Ronald for Real," *Time*, October 7, 1966.

51 *"government by cabinet"*: Edwin Meese III, *With Reagan: The Inside Story* (Washington D.C.: Regnery Gateway, 1992).

52 *"He had to face up"*: Stuart Spencer, oral history with Jim Young et al., November 15 and 16, 2001, Ronald Reagan Oral History Project, UVA Miller Center/Ronald Reagan Presidential Library.

CHAPTER 3: THE GREATEST STAGE

53 *"You won't have Nixon"*: Richard Nixon, press conference, November 7, 1962, video; https://www.youtube.com/watch?v=_RMSb-tS_OM.

53 *"For these critical years"*: Richard M. Nixon, Letter to the Citizens of New Hampshire, January 31, 1968, Richard Nixon Presidential Library and Museum.

55 *"When I came back"*: Chris Bachelder, "Crashing the Party: The Ill-Fated 1968 Presidential Campaign of Governor George Romney," *Michigan Historical Review* (Fall 2007).

55 *"There was a split"*: Lyn Nofziger, oral history with Stephen Knott et al., March 6, 2003, Ronald Reagan Oral History Project, UVA Miller Center/Ronald Reagan Presidential Library.

56 *"motive was just as pure"*: Paul Laxalt, oral history with Jim Young et al., October 9, 2001, Ronald Reagan Oral History Project, UVA Miller Center/Ronald Reagan Presidential Library.

57 *"He'd always remind us"*: Ibid.

57 *"His biggest trouble"*: Eisenhower letter to Walter Thayer, October 24, 1966, post-presidential archives, Dwight D. Eisenhower Library.

57 *A story Eisenhower related*: Dwight D. Eisenhower, *The Eisenhower Diaries*, ed. Robert H. Ferrell (New York: W. W. Norton & Co., 1976).

58 *"For years in"*: Norman Mailer, *Miami and the Siege of Chicago: An Informed History of the Republican and Democratic Conventions of 1968* (New York: World Publishing Co., 1968).

59 *"idiosyncratic conservatism"*: Steven Hayward, "Ronald Reagan: Conservative Statesman," Heritage Foundation, June 4, 2013; http://thf_media.s3.amazonaws.com/2013/pdf/mapt09.pdf.

59 *"I'll never forget it"*: Paul Laxalt, oral history with Jim Young et al., October 9, 2001, Ronald Reagan Oral History Project, UVA Miller Center/Ronald Reagan Presidential Library.

59 *"You know, if I"*: Peter Hannaford, oral history with Stephen Knott et al., January 10, 2003, Ronald Reagan Oral History Project, UVA Miller Center/Ronald Reagan Presidential Library.

60 *"An interesting thing"*: Ibid.

61 *Deaver got a phone call*: Michael Deaver, oral history with Jim Young et al., September 12, 2002, Ronald Reagan Oral History Project, UVA Miller Center/Ronald Reagan Presidential Library.

61 *"To err is human"*: Ronald Reagan, *Ronald Reagan in His Own Words*, ed. Tyler Richmond (Seedbox Press, 2011).

61 Newsweek *called him:* "Ready on the Right—Ronald Reagan," *Newsweek*, March 24, 1975.

61 *"It's time for us all"*: Ibid.

63 *"You shouldn't be making"*: Paul Laxalt, oral history with Jim Young et al., October 9, 2001, Ronald Reagan Oral History Project, UVA Miller Center/Ronald Reagan Presidential Library.

63 *"I just don't think"*: Michael Deaver, oral history with Jim Young et al., September 12, 2002, Ronald Reagan Oral History Project, UVA Miller Center/Ronald Reagan Presidential Library.

63 *"He doesn't look"*: Nancy Reagan, *My Turn*.

64 *"In my opinion"*: Ronald Reagan, "Announcement for Presidential Candidacy and Press Conference," November 20, 1975, Ronald Reagan Presidential Library and Museum.

64 *"Okay, so here we are"*: Martin Anderson, oral history with Jim Young, December 11 and 12, 2001, Ronald Reagan Oral History Project, UVA Miller Center/Ronald Reagan Presidential Library.

65 *"Okay, you borrow"*: Ibid.

65 *"If you were to stand"*: Adam Wren, " 'It Was Riotous': An Oral History of the GOP's Last Open Convention: Twenty Republican Party Figures Remember 1976," *Politico*, April 5, 2016. [Specifically, recollection of Reagan supporter Ernest Angelo.]

67 *"You know what I regret"*: Nancy Reagan, *My Turn*.

67 *The following morning*: Michael Deaver, oral history with Jim Young et al., September 12, 2002, Ronald Reagan Oral History Project, UVA Miller Center/Ronald Reagan Presidential Library.

68 *"Am I being asked"*: Ibid.

69 *"They suggested I write"*: Ronald Reagan, "Remarks at the Republican National Convention," August 19, 1976, Ronald Reagan Presidential Library and Museum.

69 *"We nominated the wrong guy"*: Adam Wren, " 'It Was Riotous': An Oral History of the GOP's Last Open Convention," *Politico*, April 5, 2016.

70 *"I'll lay me down"*: Lee Edwards, "When Reagan Almost Won: The 1976 GOP Convention," *Daily Signal*, April 15, 2016.

71 *Ten days after*: Richard Allen, oral history with Stephen Knott, May 28, 2002, Ronald Reagan Oral History Project, UVA Miller Center/Ronald Reagan Presidential Library.

72 *According to Hannaford*: Peter Hannaford, oral history with Stephen Knott et al., January 10, 2003, Ronald Reagan Oral History Project UVA Miller Center/Ronald Reagan Presidential Library.

74 *"he became Teddy Roosevelt"*: Andrew E. Busch, *Reagan's Victory: The Presidential Election of 1980 and the Rise of the Right* (Lawrence: University Press of Kansas, 2005).

74 *so-called malaise speech*: Jimmy Carter, "Address to the Nation on Energy and National Goals: 'The Malaise Speech,'" July 15, 1979, The American Presidency Project; http://www.presidency.ucsb.edu/ws/?pid=32596.

75 *Some analysts believe*: Chris Whipple, "Ted Kennedy: The Day the Presidency Was Lost," ABC News, August 31, 2009.

76 *"To me our country"*: "Ronald Reagan Announcement for Presidential Candidacy," November 13, 1979, Ronald Reagan Presidential Library and Museum.

77 *"It was conventional wisdom"*: Author interview with Charles Black, August 23, 2017.

78 *"We made a decision"*: Ibid.

79 *Reagan biographer Craig Shirley*: Craig Shirley, *Reagan Rising: The Decisive Years, 1976–1980* (New York: Broadside Books, 2017).

79 *But his masterstroke*: Ibid.

79 *"Charlie, where's John?"*: Author interview with Charles Black, August 23, 2017.

80 *"One of the most amazing things"*: Michael Deaver, oral history with Jim Young et al., September 12, 2002, Ronald Reagan Oral History Project, UVA Miller Center/Ronald Reagan Presidential Library.

80 *"Reagan almost choked"*: Ibid.

81 *"Out of a clear blue"*: Jon Meacham, *Destiny and Power: The American Odyssey of George Herbert Walker Bush* (New York: Random House, 2015).

81 *"life seems to be governed"*: Jimmy Carter, *White House Diary* (New York: Farrar, Straus and Giroux, 2010).

82 *"There was a distinct sense"*: Busch, *Reagan's Victory*.

82 *"The only strategic mistake"*: Patrick Caddell, oral history with Jim Young, November 29, 1982, Ronald Reagan Oral History Project, UVA Miller Center/Jimmy Carter Presidential Library, Atlanta, GA.

83 *"I had a discussion"*: "The Carter-Reagan Presidential Debate," October 28, 1980, Commission on Presidential Debates; http://www.debates.org/index.php?page=october-28-1980-debate-transcript.

83 *"It might be well"*: Ibid.

84 *"And there we stood"*: Nancy Reagan, *My Turn*.

84 *"I was bitter"*: Rosalynn Carter, *First Lady from Plains* (New York: Houghton Mifflin, 1984).

84 *"the chill in her manner"*: Nancy Reagan, *My Turn*.

85 *Carter lectured Reagan*: Carl Brauer, *Presidential Transitions: Eisenhower Through Reagan* (New York: Oxford University Press, 1986).

85 *"Reagan recalled verbatim"*: Douglas Brinkley, *The Unfinished Presi-*

dency: Jimmy Carter's Journey Beyond the White House (New York: Viking, 1998).

86 *"Allowing Ronald Reagan"*: Brinkley, *The Unfinished Presidency.*

CHAPTER 4: A REVOLUTION OF IDEAS

87 *"Have you got"*: Michael K. Deaver, *A Different Drummer: My Thirty Years with Ronald Reagan* (New York: HarperCollins, 2001).

88 *"Do I have to?"*: Ibid.

89 *In preparing the speech*: Ken Khachigian, "Reagan's Timeless Inaugural Message," RealClear Politics, January 21, 2016; https://www .realclearpolitics.com/articles/2016/01/21/reagans_timeless_inaugu ral_message_129383.html.

90 *"In this present crisis"*: Ronald Reagan, "Inaugural Address," January 20, 1981, The American Presidency Project; http://www.presi dency.ucsb.edu/ws/?pid=43130.

93 *"I've had my differences"*: Nancy Reagan, *My Turn.*

94 *"The true-hearted conservatives"*: Carl Brauer, *Presidential Transitions.*

95 *"The chief of staff"*: James A. Baker, III, with Steve Fiffer, *"Work Hard, Study ... and Keep Out of Politics!"* (Evanston, IL: Northwestern University Press, 2008).

96 *Deaver had surprised Reagan*: Deaver, *A Different Drummer.*

96 *"The Meese-Baker-Deaver combination"*: Hedrick Smith, "The Presidential Troika," *New York Times*, April 19, 1981.

97 *"We spent a lot"*: Lyn Nofziger, oral history with Stephen Knott et al., March 6, 2003, Ronald Reagan Oral History Project, UVA Miller Center/Ronald Reagan Presidential Library.

97 *"He notified me"*: Caspar Weinberger, oral history with Stephen Knott, November 19, 2002, Ronald Reagan Oral History Project, UVA Miller Center/Ronald Reagan Presidential Library.

98 *It appears that Reagan*: Archives, Ronald Reagan Presidential Library.

98 *"from the beginning"*: Caspar Weinberger, oral history with Stephen Knott, November 19, 2002, Ronald Reagan Oral History Project, UVA Miller Center/Ronald Reagan Presidential Library.

99 *"Look, the NSC"*: Richard Allen, oral history with Stephen Knott, May 28, 2002, Ronald Reagan Oral History Project, UVA Miller Center/Ronald Reagan Presidential Library.

99 *Allen introduced Reagan*: Ibid.

100 *"We're going to make history"*: Handwritten notes from cabinet meeting, February 13, 1981, 1:45 pm, Ronald Reagan Presidential Library.

101 *Early on he tangled*: Caspar Weinberger, oral history with Stephen Knott, November 19, 2002, Ronald Reagan Oral History Project, UVA Miller Center/Ronald Reagan Presidential Library.

101 *"Is this what we want"*: Ibid.

101 *Stockman's star might have risen*: William Greider, "The Education of David Stockman," *The Atlantic*, December 1981.

102 *"See, the thing about Reagan"*: Martin Anderson, oral history with

Jim Young, December 11 and 12, 2001, Ronald Reagan Oral History Project, UVA Miller Center/Ronald Reagan Presidential Library.

103 *the frequent laughter*: Kathleen Osborne, oral history with Jim Young and Stephen Knott, April 26, 2003, Ronald Reagan Oral History Project, UVA Miller Center/Ronald Reagan Presidential Library.

103 *"so many of his decisions"*: Howard Baker, oral history with Stephen Knott, August 24, 2004, Ronald Reagan Oral History Project, UVA Miller Center/Ronald Reagan Presidential Library.

103 *David Gergen*: David Gergen, *Eyewitness to Power: The Essence of Leadership; Nixon to Clinton* (New York: Simon & Schuster, 2000).

103 *"Why do you like Reagan?"*: Edward Rowny, oral history with Stephen Knott, March 17, 2016, Ronald Reagan Oral History Project, UVA Miller Center/Ronald Reagan Presidential Library.

103 *Deaver recalled that*: *The American Experience*, PBS, February 23, 1998.

104 *"In my experience"*: Author interview with Charles Black, November 13, 2017.

104 *On one occasion*: Howard Baker, oral history with Stephen Knott, August 24, 2004, Ronald Reagan Oral History Project, UVA Miller Center/Ronald Reagan Presidential Library.

104 *"That was right"*: Martin Anderson, oral history with Jim Young, December 11 and 12, 2001, Ronald Reagan Oral History Project, UVA Miller Center/Ronald Reagan Presidential Library.

105 *"Herbert Hoover with a smile"*: Hugh Sidey, "The Art of Political Insult," *Time*, June 20, 1983.

105 *"I was kind of"*: Max Friedersdorf, oral history with Stephen Knott et al., October 24 and 25, 2002, Ronald Reagan Oral History Project, UVA Miller Center/Ronald Reagan Presidential Library.

106 *"I thought we had"*: Ronald Reagan, *An American Life*.

106 *He was a uniter*: Author interview with Kenneth Duberstein, August 22, 2017.

107 *"Reagan found the formula"*: Ibid.

107 *"bird in a gilded cage"*: Ronald Reagan, *The Reagan Diaries*, ed. Douglas Brinkley (New York: HarperCollins, 2007).

108 *In the confusing early moments*: Michael Deaver, oral history with Jim Young et al., September 12, 2002, Ronald Reagan Oral History Project, UVA Miller Center/Ronald Reagan Presidential Library.

109 *"Reagan had a habit"*: Ibid.

109 *"Honey, I forgot"*: Nancy Reagan, *My Turn*.

109 *"Constitutionally, gentlemen"*: Caspar Weinberger, oral history with Stephen Knott, November 19, 2002, Ronald Reagan Oral History Project, UVA Miller Center/Ronald Reagan Presidential Library.

110 *"George Bush struck"*: William Safire, "Essay: One Fell Short," *New York Times*, April 2, 1981.

110 *As the historian Jon Meacham*: Jon Meacham, *Destiny and Power: The American Odyssey of George Herbert Walker Bush* (New York: Random House, 2015).

110 *"The crisis had passed"*: Ibid.

111 *Strom Thurmond managed*: Max Friedersdorf, oral history with Ste-

phen Knott et al., October 24 and 25, 2002, Ronald Reagan Oral History Project, UVA Miller Center/Ronald Reagan Presidential Library.

111 *"It's amazing how sound"*: Ronald Reagan, *The Reagan Diaries*.

112 *Shultz was in London*: George P. Shultz, oral history with Stephen Knott and Jim Young, December 18, 2002, Ronald Reagan Oral History Project, UVA Miller Center/Ronald Reagan Presidential Library.

CHAPTER 5: THE TRUMPET CALL

115 *"just purring along"*: Martin Anderson, oral history with Jim Young, December 11 and 12, 2001, Ronald Reagan Oral History Project, UVA Miller Center/Ronald Reagan Presidential Library.

115 *A month earlier*: Michael Deaver, oral history with Jim Young et al., September 12, 2002, Ronald Reagan Oral History Project, UVA Miller Center/Ronald Reagan Presidential Library.

117 *"I write for the ear"*: Ronald Reagan, *An American Life*.

117 *"Sometimes, speech writers"*: Ibid.

118 *"The Soviet Union would remain"*: Ronald Reagan, *The Humor of Ronald Reagan: Quips, Jokes and Anecdotes from the Great Communicator*, ed. Malcolm Kushner (Menasha, WI: Museum of Humor Press, 2011).

118 *"By the way"*: Ibid.

118 *"We have every right"*: Ronald Reagan, "First Inaugural Address," January 20, 1981, Ronald Reagan Presidential Library and Museum.

119 *"If you don't have any strength"*: Author interview with George P. Shultz, December 2, 2017.

120 *But walking back*: Richard Allen, oral history with Stephen Knott, May 28, 2002, Ronald Reagan Oral History Project, UVA Miller Center/Ronald Reagan Presidential Library.

121 *"It called to mind"*: George Will, letter to Ronald Reagan, May 18, 1982, Ronald Reagan Presidential Library.

121 *"We had a truck"*: Author interview with Anthony Dolan, May 2, 2017.

121 *"They always thought"*: Ibid.

123 *"We're approaching the end"*: Robert C. Rowland and John M. Jones, *Reagan at Westminster: Foreshadowing the End of the Cold War* (College Station, TX: Texas A&M University Press, 2010).

124 *was "remarkable"*: Margaret Thatcher, *The Downing Street Years* (New York: HarperCollins, 1993).

124 *"Of course"*: Ronald Reagan, *An American Life*.

125 *In one late-night*: Michael Deaver, oral history with Jim Young et al., September 12, 2002, Ronald Reagan Oral History Project, UVA Miller Center/Ronald Reagan Presidential Library; also, text of call in declassified NSC papers, Ronald Reagan Presidential Library.

125 *The general media reaction*: Rowland and Jones, *Reagan at Westminster*.

126 *"One of my jobs there"*: Author interview with George P. Shultz, December 2, 2017

126 *"They are in very bad"*: Ronald Reagan, *The Reagan Diaries*, ed. Douglas Brinkley (New York: HarperCollins, 2007).

127 *"If we truly believe"*: Ronald Reagan, *Reagan, In His Own Hand: The Writings of Ronald Reagan that Reveal His Revolutionary Vision for America*, ed. Kiron K. Skinner, Annelise Anderson, and Martin Anderson (New York: Simon and Schuster, 2001).

127 *"Reagan's view was"*: Kenneth Adelman, oral history with Stephen Knott, September 30, 2003, Ronald Reagan Oral History Project, UVA Miller Center/Ronald Reagan Presidential Library.

127 *"psychological optimism"*: Charles Krauthammer, "Ash Heap of History: Reagan's Westminster Address 20 Years Later," Remarks made at a panel discussion held at the Heritage Foundation, June 3, 2002.

128 *"Bill, I never met"*: William P. Clark, oral history with Stephen Knott, August 17, 2003, Ronald Reagan Oral History Project, UVA Miller Center/Ronald Reagan Presidential Library.

129 *"Do you think"*: Reagan, *An American Life.*

129 *"I strongly feel"*: Letter from Nixon to Ronald Reagan, Ronald Reagan Presidential Library.

130 *"There was no question"*: Ronald Reagan, Press Conference, November 11, 1982, The American Presidency Project.

130 *"The d—n media"*: Ronald Reagan, *The Reagan Diaries.*

130 *Robert P. Dugan, Jr.*: Letter to Ronald Reagan, December 3, 1982, Ronald Reagan Presidential Library.

131 *In preparing for the event*: Aram Bakshian, oral history with Stephen Knott, January 14, 2002, Ronald Reagan Oral History Project, UVA Miller Center/Ronald Reagan Presidential Library.

131 *"Long after I left"*: Ibid.

131 *Among the lines excised*: Author interview with Anthony Dolan, May 2, 2017.

132 *"The greatest evil"*: C. S. Lewis, *The Screwtape Letters* (London: Geoffrey Bles, 1942).

132 *When Bakshian saw the draft*: Aram Bakshian, oral history with Stephen Knott, January 14, 2002, Ronald Reagan Oral History Project, UVA Miller Center/Ronald Reagan Presidential Library.

132 *"terms so strong"*: David Gergen, *Eyewitness to Power: The Essence of Leadership; Nixon to Clinton* (New York: Simon & Schuster, 2000).

132 *"Just send him the draft"*: Author interview with Anthony Dolan, May 2, 2017.

133 *"I kept wondering"*: Gergen, *Eyewitness to Power.*

133 *"Once he [the president] saw"*: Aram Bakshian, oral history with Stephen Knott, January 14, 2002, Ronald Reagan Oral History Project, UVA Miller Center/Ronald Reagan Presidential Library.

133 *"I hate to admit it"*: Gergen, *Eyewitness to Power.*

134 *"The other day"*: Ronald Reagan, "Remarks at the Annual Convention of the National Association of Evangelicals in Orlando, Florida," March 8, 1983, Ronald Reagan Presidential Library.

135 *What Bakshian called*: Aram Bakshian, oral history with Stephen Knott, January 14, 2002, Ronald Reagan Oral History Project, UVA Miller Center/Ronald Reagan Presidential Library.

135 *Nancy Reagan, who frequently*: Nancy Reagan, *My Turn.*

135 *In the* New York Times: Anthony Lewis, "Abroad at Home; Onward, Christian Soldiers," *New York Times*, March 10, 1983.

136 *"'You've destroyed twenty years'"*: Caspar Weinberger, oral history with Stephen Knott, November 19, 2002, Ronald Reagan Oral History Project, UVA Miller Center/Ronald Reagan Presidential Library.

136 *"a passive containment"*: Ibid.

136 *"marks a revival"*: Arthur Schlesinger, Jr., "Pretension in the Presidential Pulpit," *Wall Street Journal*, March 17, 1983.

137 *"Dear Mr. Willoughby"*: Ronald Reagan, letter to William Willoughby, Ronald Reagan Presidential Library.

137 *Reagan introduced*: Ronald Reagan, "Address to the Nation on Defense and National Security," March 23, 1983, Ronald Reagan Presidential Library and Museum.

138 *"He didn't share that"*: Kenneth Adelman, oral history with Stephen Knott, September 30, 2003, Ronald Reagan Oral History Project, UVA Miller Center/Ronald Reagan Presidential Library.

138 *As he told Edward Rowny*: Edward Rowny, oral history with Stephen Knott, March 17, 2016, Ronald Reagan Oral History Project, UVA Miller Center/Ronald Reagan Presidential Library.

139 *"We get your dust"*: James Haggerty, oral history with Ed Edwin, March 2, 1967, Columbia University Oral History Project, Dwight D. Eisenhower Presidential Library.

140 *"it left me greatly depressed"*: Ronald Reagan, *The Reagan Diaries*.

140 *"I feel the Soviets"*: Ibid.

CHAPTER 6: RON AND MIKHAIL

141 *"There is a bear"*: Ronald Reagan TV ad: "The Bear," video; https://www.youtube.com/watch?v=NpwdcmjBgNA.

141 *"Throughout this whole period"*: Stuart Spencer, oral history with Jim Young et al., November 15 and 16, 2001, Ronald Reagan Oral History Project, UVA Miller Center/Ronald Reagan Presidential Library.

141 *"In the beginning"*: George J. Church, "Men of the Year: Ronald Reagan and Yuri Andropov," *Time*, January 2, 1984.

142 *"I believe that 1984"*: Ronald Reagan, "Address to the Nation and Other Countries on United States-Soviet Relations," January 16, 1984, Ronald Reagan Presidential Library.

144 *Even though Mondale*: Peter J. Wallison, *Ronald Reagan: The Power of Conviction and the Success of His Presidency* (New York: Basic Books, 2004); see also Walter Mondale, *The Good Fight: A Life in Liberal Politics* (New York: Scribner, 2010).

144 *"You already are"*: 1984 1st Presidential Debate: Reagan vs. Mondale, C-Span Historical Archives.

145 *"If TV can tell"*: Walter Mondale, interview with Jim Lehrer, *The MacNeil/Lehrer NewsHour*, May 25, 1990.

145 *"I'd have been having"*: Peter Robinson, *How Ronald Reagan Changed My Life* (New York: Harper, 2003).

146 *"He was a Californian"*: Caspar Weinberger, oral history with Stephen

Knott, November 19, 2002, Ronald Reagan Oral History Project, UVA Miller Center/Ronald Reagan Presidential Library.

146 *"I'd lay my phone"*: Kathleen Osborne, oral history with Jim Young and Stephen Knott, April 26, 2003, Ronald Reagan Oral History Project, UVA Miller Center/Ronald Reagan Presidential Library.

146 *"Whisper peace"*: Nancy Reagan, *My Turn*.

147 *"There were no visible signs"*: Lou Cannon, "Reagan, Gromyko Meet in 'Exchange of Views,'" *Washington Post*, September 29, 1984.

147 *"You ain't seen nothing yet"*: Anthony Lewis, "Abroad at Home; 'You Ain't Seen Nothing Yet,'" *New York Times*, November 8, 1984.

147 *Over lunch, Thatcher related*: "Thatcher-Reagan Meeting at Camp David," record of conversation, December 28, 1984, Ronald Reagan Presidential Library.

149 *The public inaugural was scheduled*: Francis X. Clines, "Reagan Sworn in for 2nd Term; Inaugural Parade Dropped as Bitter Cold Hits Capital," *New York Times*, January 21, 1985.

149 *"Today, we utter"*: Ronald Reagan, "Inaugural Address," January 21, 1985, The American Presidency Project; http://www.presidency.ucsb.edu/ws/index.php?pid=38688.

149 *But he had a warning*: Address Before a Joint Session of the Congress on the State of the Union, February 6, 1985. Ronald Reagan Presidential Library and Museum.

151 *"Regan spends an hour"*: Max Friedersdorf, oral history with Stephen Knott et al., October 24 and 25, 2002, Ronald Reagan Oral History Project, UVA Miller Center/Ronald Reagan Presidential Library.

151 *"They keep dying"*: Jason Saltoun-Ebin, *Dear Mr. President . . . : Reagan/Gorbachev and the Correspondence That Ended the Cold War* (CreateSpace, 2011).

152 *"Do not rush"*: Paul Kengor, *The Crusader: Ronald Reagan and the Fall of Communism* (New York: Harper, 2006).

152 *"We were poor"*: Mikhail Gorbachev, *Memoirs* (New York: Doubleday, 1996).

153 *"She bewitched me"*: Ibid.

153 *"We have a division"*: Maureen Dowd, "The Iceland Summit: Charm and Cough Drops; Raisa Gorbachev's Reyjkavik Visit: A Public Relations Coup for Moscow," *New York Times*, October 12, 1986.

153 *"A dead-end political situation"*: Mikhail Gorbachev, *The New Russia* (Cambridge, UK: Polity Books, 2016).

154 *"The people were happy"*: Gorbachev, *Memoirs*.

154 *"One of the most crucial"*: Andrei Grachev, *Gorbachev's Gamble: Soviet Foreign Policy and the End of the Cold War* (New York: Wiley, 2008).

155 *A secret poll*: Charles W. Dunn, ed., *The Enduring Reagan* (Lexington: University Press of Kentucky, 2009).

155 *"Those old verities"*: Ronald Reagan, "Address Before a Joint Session of the Irish National Parliament," June 4, 1984, The American Presidency Project.

156 *"However strange it may seem"*: Grachev, *Gorbachev's Gamble*.

157 *"You can be assured"*: Saltoun-Ebin, *Dear Mr. President*.

157 *"It is not an easy task"*: Ibid.

158 *"His strongest suit"*: George P. Shultz, oral history with Stephen Knott, Jim Young, et al., December 18, 2002, Ronald Reagan Oral History Project, UVA Miller Center/Ronald Reagan Presidential Library.

159 *"I was strongly opposed"*: Caspar Weinberger, oral history with Stephen Knott, November 19, 2002, Ronald Reagan Oral History Project, UVA Miller Center/Ronald Reagan Presidential Library.

160 *There was only one condition*: Donald T. Regan, *For the Record: From Wall Street to Washington* (New York: Random House, 1990).

161 *"They're not going"*: Loretta Tofani, "Regan 'Misspoke' in Remarks on Women," *Washington Post*, November 25, 1985.

162 *His staff felt less assured*: Kenneth Adelman, oral history with Stephen Knott, September 30, 2003, Ronald Reagan Oral History Project, UVA Miller Center/Ronald Reagan Presidential Library.

162 *"The juices were flowing"*: Ronald Reagan, *The Reagan Diaries*, ed. Douglas Brinkley (New York: HarperCollins, 2007).

162 *Reagan was tired*: Kenneth Adelman, oral history with Stephen Knott, September 30, 2003, Ronald Reagan Oral History Project, UVA Miller Center/Ronald Reagan Presidential Library.

163 *It was bitterly cold*: James Kuhn, oral history with Stephen Knott, March 7, 2003, Ronald Reagan Oral History Project, UVA Miller Center/Ronald Reagan Presidential Library.

163 *"He comes down the stairs"*: Kenneth Adelman, oral history with Stephen Knott, September 30, 2003, Ronald Reagan Oral History Project, UVA Miller Center/Ronald Reagan Presidential Library.

163 *The optics of it*: "Reagan," *American Experience*, PBS, February 23, 1998.

164 *"He used to drive"*: Frank Carlucci, oral history with Phillip Zukow, Stephen Knott, and Don Oberdorfer, August 28, 2001, Ronald Reagan Oral History Project, UVA Miller Center/Ronald Reagan Presidential Library.

164 *Outside, Don Regan*: James Kuhn, oral history with Stephen Knott, March 7, 2003, Ronald Reagan Oral History Project, UVA Miller Center/Ronald Reagan Presidential Library.

164 *"Are you out"*: George P. Shultz, *Turmoil and Triumph: My Years as Secretary of State* (New York: Scribner, 1993).

165 *Through interpreters*: Memorandum of Conversation, Reagan-Gorbachev Meetings in Geneva, First Plenary Meeting, November 19, 1985, The White House/Ronald Reagan Presidential Library.

165 *"Dad, you're late"*: Kenneth Adelman, oral history with Stephen Knott, September 30, 2003, Ronald Reagan Oral History Project, UVA Miller Center/Ronald Reagan Presidential Library.

165 *"When he came out"*: Kenneth Adelman, oral history with Stephen Knott, September 30, 2003, Ronald Reagan Oral History Project, UVA Miller Center/Ronald Reagan Presidential Library.

166 *"Well, he's a new kind"*: Ibid.

166 *In reply, Gorbachev opened*: Memorandum of Conversation, Reagan-

Gorbachev Meetings in Geneva, Second Plenary Meeting, November 19, 1985, The White House/Ronald Reagan Presidential Library.

166 *Adelman felt that*: Kenneth Adelman, oral history with Stephen Knott, September 30, 2003, Ronald Reagan Oral History Project, UVA Miller Center/Ronald Reagan Presidential Library.

166 *There was a boathouse*: Ibid.

166 *Reagan made a personal appeal*: Memorandum of Conversation, Reagan-Gorbachev Meetings in Geneva, Second Private Meeting, November 19, 1985, The White House/Ronald Reagan Presidential Library.

167 *As they walked back*: Ibid.

167 *Shultz observed that*: Shultz, *Turmoil and Triumph*.

167 *their wives were having*: Memorandum of Conversation, Mrs. Reagan's Tea for Mrs. Gorbachev, November 19, 1985, The White House/Ronald Reagan Presidential Library.

167 *"That Raisa Gorbachev is"*: Michael R. Beschloss, *Presidential Courage: Brave Leaders and How They Changed America 1789–1989* (New York: Simon and Schuster, 2008).

168 *"Mr. President, I have to"*: Shultz, *Turmoil and Triumph*.

168 *"Suddenly everyone was talking"*: Ibid.

168 *On Wednesday*: Memorandum of Conversation, Reagan-Gorbachev Meetings in Geneva, Third Private Meeting, November 20, 1985, The White House/Ronald Reagan Presidential Library.

168 *"We'll share SDI with you"*: Memorandum of Conversation, Reagan-Gorbachev Meetings in Geneva, Third Plenary Meeting, November 20, 1985, The White House/Ronald Reagan Presidential Library.

168–169 *"Gorbachev thought it was whacko"*: Kenneth Adelman, oral history with Stephen Knott, September 30, 2003, Ronald Reagan Oral History Project, UVA Miller Center/Ronald Reagan Presidential Library.

169 *"He was intense"*: Shultz, *Turmoil and Triumph*.

169 *"I just thought"*: Ibid.

169 *"maybe there was a little"*: Ronald Reagan, *An American Life*.

170 *"As I flew back"*: Ronald Reagan, "Address Before a Joint Session of the Congress following the Soviet–United States Summit Meeting in Geneva," Nov. 21, 1985, Ronald Reagan Presidential Library.

CHAPTER 7: ICELAND FREEZE

172 *Letters flew back and forth*: Jason Saltoun-Ebin, *Dear Mr. President . . . : Reagan/Gorbachev and the Correspondence That Ended the Cold War* (CreateSpace, 2011); also archives of the Ronald Reagan Presidential Library.

172 *"I consider your"*: Ibid.

172 *"Both of us have"*: Ibid.

172 *"I attach special significance"*: Ibid.

173 *"I see a good augury"*: "New Year's Messages of President Reagan and Soviet General Secretary Gorbachev," January 1, 1986, The American Presidency Project; http://www.presidency.ucsb.edu/ws/?pid=36367.

174 *"Just over a month ago"*: Ibid.

174 *In January, Gorbachev grabbed*: Serge Schmemann, "Gorbachev Offers to Scrap A-Arms Within 15 Years," *New York Times*, January 16, 1986.

175 *"pie in the sky"*: "Thatcher Calls Nuclear Free World 'Pie in the Sky,'" UPI, March 28, 1986.

175 *"I think President Reagan"*: James Baker, "Reagan," *The American Experience*, PBS, February 23, 1998.

176 *"There is no way"*: Ronald Reagan, *The Reagan Diaries*, ed. Douglas Brinkley (New York: HarperCollins, 2007).

176 *"And I want to say"*: Ronald Reagan, "Address to the Nation on the Explosion of the Space Shuttle Challenger," January 28, 1986, Ronald Reagan Presidential Library and Museum.

177 *It had long been*: Peter Hannaford and Charles D. Hobbs, *Remembering Reagan* (New York: Regnery Publishing, 1995).

178 *"Well, we know that"*: Ronald Reagan, "The President's News Conference," April 9, 1986, The American Presidency Project; http://www.presidency.ucsb.edu/ws/index.php?pid=37105.

178 *"What are we to make"*: Saltoun-Ebin, *Dear Mr. President.*

178 *"aggressive criminal action"*: Jonathan A. Becker, *Soviet and Russian Press Coverage of the United States: Press, Politics and Identity in Transition* (London: Palgrave Macmillan, 1999).

178 *"This is also the night"*: Ronald Reagan, "Remarks at the Annual White House Correspondents Dinner," April 17, 1986, The American Presidency Project; http://www.presidency.ucsb.edu/ws/index.php?pid=37150.

179 *"The offer was rejected"*: Jack F. Matlock, Jr., *Reagan and Gorbachev: How the Cold War Ended* (New York: Random House, 2004).

179 *"They launched an unrestrained"*: Mikhail Gorbachev, *Memoirs* (New York: Doubleday, 1996).

179 *"his personal Cuban missile crisis"*: Grachev, *Gorbachev's Gamble.*

179 *"Look at the Chernobyl catastrophe"*: James Graham Wilson, *The Triumph of Improvisation: Gorbachev's Adaptability, Reagan's Engagement, and the End of the Cold War* (Ithaca, NY: Cornell University Press, 2014).

180 *"mad as h—l"*: Ronald Reagan, *The Reagan Diaries.*

181 *The Soviet leader wrote*: Mikhail Gorbachev, letter to Ronald Reagan, September 14, 1986, National Security Archive, George Washington University, Washington, DC.

181 *"I could see"*: Grachev, *Gorbachev's Gamble.*

181 *"I opted for Iceland"*: Ronald Reagan, *The Reagan Diaries.*

182 *"They will get Daniloff"*: Gorbachev, discussion with assistants on preparations for Reykjavík, September 29, 1986, National Security Archive, George Washington University, Washington, DC.

182 *Chernyaev shared Gorbachev's fondest hopes*: Anatoly C. Chernyaev, *My Six Years with Gorbachev* (University Park: Pennsylvania State University Press, 2000).

182 *"In order to move Reagan"*: Ibid.

183 *"As far as the SDI"*: Ibid.

183 *"The American people"*: George P. Shultz, Memorandum to the Pres-

ident, October 2, 1986, National Security Archive, George Washington University, Washington, DC.

184 *In an intriguing addendum*: Richard Solomon, memo to Ronald Reagan, National Security Archive, George Washington University, Washington, DC.

185 *"something out of an"*: Kenneth Adelman, oral history with Stephen Knott, September 30, 2003, Ronald Reagan Oral History Project, UVA Miller Center/Ronald Reagan Presidential Library.

185 *"If observers sometimes regard"*: Shultz, *Turmoil and Triumph*.

186 *"There is a Russian saying"*: Memorandum of Conversation, Reagan-Gorbachev, First Meeting, October 11, 1986, National Security Archive, George Washington University, Washington, DC.

186 *"He could well afford"*: Shultz, *Turmoil and Triumph*.

187 *"I've given you"*: Memorandum of Conversation, Reagan-Gorbachev, Second Meeting, October 11, 1986, National Security Archive, George Washington University, Washington, D.C.

187 *"If we both eliminate"*: Shultz, *Turmoil and Triumph*.

188 *"This all depends"*: Memorandum of Conversation, Reagan-Gorbachev, Final Meeting, October 12, 1986, National Security Archive, George Washington University, Washington, DC.; see also Shultz, *Turmoil and Triumph*.

188 *He scribbled a note*: Shultz, *Turmoil and Triumph*.

189 *"I'd just never seen"*: James Kuhn, oral history with Stephen Knott, March 7, 2003, Ronald Reagan Oral History Project, UVA Miller Center/Ronald Reagan Presidential Library.

189 *"the two leaders"*: Grachev, *Gorbachev's Gamble*.

189 *"I still feel"*: Shultz, *Turmoil and Triumph*.

190 *"Mr. President," he said*: James Kuhn, oral history with Stephen Knott, March 7, 2003, Ronald Reagan Oral History Project, UVA Miller Center/Ronald Reagan Presidential Library.

191 *"He [Gorbachev] tried to act"*: Ronald Reagan, *The Reagan Diaries*.

191 *"My first, overwhelming intention"*: Gorbachev, *Memoirs*; also Gorbachev's reflections on Reykjavík on the flight to Moscow, October 12, 1986, National Security Archive, George Washington University, Washington, DC.

192 *"In a way"*: Shultz, *Turmoil and Triumph*.

CHAPTER 8: "TEAR DOWN THIS WALL!"

193 *Howard Baker was*: Howard Baker, oral history with Stephen Knott, August 24, 2004, Ronald Reagan Oral History Project, UVA Miller Center/Ronald Reagan Presidential Library.

194 *"Some of us"*: Tom Wicker, "The Shovel Brigade," *New York Times*, November 23, 1986.

194 *"He chewed me out"*: Max Friedersdorf, oral history with Stephen Knott et al., October 24 and 25, 2002, Ronald Reagan Oral History Project, UVA Miller Center/Ronald Reagan Presidential Library.

195 *"What are you telling"*: Nancy Reagan, *My Turn*.

195 *Reagan was resistant*: Ibid.

195 *"Mr. President, this"*: Frank Carlucci, oral history with Phillip Zukow, Stephen Knott, and Don Oberdorfer, August 28, 2001, Ronald Reagan Oral History Project, UVA Miller Center/Ronald Reagan Presidential Library.

196 *"Help," he pleaded*: Author interview with Ken Duberstein, October 26, 2017.

197 *Reporters such as Chris Wallace*: Author interview with Chris Wallace, July 18, 2017.

197 *"I liked everybody"*: Author interview with Marlin Fitzwater, July 19, 2017.

198 *"Regan just could not"*: Ibid.

198 *"A few months ago"*: Ronald Reagan, "Address to the Nation on the Iran Arms and Contra Aid Controversy," March 4, 1987, Ronald Reagan Presidential Library and Museum.

199 *"As difficult as it is"*: Cheryl Hudson and Gareth Davies, eds., *Ronald Reagan and the 1980s: Perceptions, Policies, Legacies* (New York: Palgrave Macmillan, 2008).

200 *"it has been a long time"*: Jason Saltoun-Ebin, *Dear Mr. President . . . : Reagan/Gorbachev and the Correspondence That Ended the Cold War* (CreateSpace, 2011).

201 *"Isn't it strange"*: Romesh Rafnesar, *Tear Down This Wall: A City, a President, and the Speech that Ended the Cold War* (New York: Simon and Schuster, 2009).

202 *"we will never"*: "Kohl Assails Berlin Wall; East Germans March in Tribute to It," *Los Angeles Times*, August 14, 1986.

202 *In April, Dolan*: Author interview with Anthony Dolan, October 23, 2017.

202 *"From the air"*: Peter Robinson, *How Ronald Reagan Changed My Life* (New York: Harper, 2003).

203 *"The two of you thought"*: Ibid.

204 *Dolan was enthusiastic*: Author interview with Anthony Dolan, October 23, 2017; also Anthony R. Dolan, "Four Little Words," *Wall Street Journal*, November 8, 2009.

204 *"Those were Reagan's words"*: Howard Baker, oral history with Stephen Knott, August 24, 2004, Ronald Reagan Oral History Project, UVA Miller Center/Ronald Reagan Presidential Library.

205 *"You know, Dick"*: Richard Allen, oral history with Stephen Knott, May 28, 2002, Ronald Reagan Oral History Project, UVA Miller Center/Ronald Reagan Presidential Library.

205 *"It's funny"*: Frederick J. Ryan, Jr., oral history with Stephen Knott, May 25, 2004, Ronald Reagan Oral History Project, UVA Miller Center/Ronald Reagan Presidential Library.

205 *"When the President"*: Malcolm Moos, oral history with T. H. Baker, November 2, 1972, Columbia University Oral History Project/ Dwight D. Eisenhower Library.

205 *"One day this ugly wall will disappear"*: Robinson, *How Ronald Reagan Changed My Life*.

206 *The NSC's Peter Rodman*: Peter Rodman, correspondence, Ronald Reagan Presidential Library.

206 *"The Brandenburg gate speech"*: Peter Rodman, letter to Colin Powell, June 2, 1987, Ronald Reagan Presidential Library.

206 *"The boys at State"*: Author interview with Kenneth Duberstein, October 26, 2017.

206 *"Behind me stands"*: Ronald Reagan, "Remarks on East-West Relations at the Brandenburg Gate in West Berlin," June 12, 1987, Ronald Reagan Presidential Library and Museum.

208 *Reagan was nervous*: Marlin Fitzwater, *Call the Briefing* (New York: Crown, 1995).

209 *She was nervous, too*: Ibid.

209 *Reagan scrawled an annoyed note*: Ronald Reagan, *The Reagan Diaries*, ed. Douglas Brinkley (New York: HarperCollins, 2007).

209 *"She's already bought the groceries"*: Shultz, *Turmoil and Triumph.*

210 *"We were gradually freeing ourselves"*: Mikhail Gorbachev, *Memoirs.*

210 *In a devastating attack*: Ibid.

210 *"He would suddenly appear"*: Ibid.

211 *On November 9*: Ibid.

211 *"President Reagan is little more"*: James Gerstenzang and Robert Shogan, "Conservatives Hit Reagan on Treaty: One Calls President 'A Useful Idiot of Soviets'; Criticism of Accord Mounts," *Los Angeles Times*, December 5, 1987.

211 *"a useful idiot"*: Ibid.

212 *Imagining the embarrassing specter*: Fitzwater, *Call the Briefing.*

212 *"I knew Gennadi Gerasimov"*: Author interview with Marlin Fitzwater, July 19, 2017.

212 *"I have often felt"*: David K. Shipler, "The Summit; Reagan and Gorbachev Sign Missile Treaty and Vow to Work for Greater Reductions," *New York Times*, December 8, 1987.

213 *Reagan began by*: Memorandum of Conversation, President's Meeting with Gorbachev, December 8, 1987, National Security Agency Archives, Washington, DC.

213 *He gave Gorbachev a card*: Ibid.

214 *Gorbachev finally said*: Memorandum of Conversation, President's Meeting with Gorbachev, December 8, 1987, National Security Agency Archives, Washington, DC.

214 *"We can only hope"*: David K. Shipler, "The Summit; Reagan and Gorbachev Sign Missile Treaty and Vow to Work for Greater Reductions," *New York Times*, December 8, 1987.

215 *"May Dec. 8, 1987"*: Reagan, *An American Life.*

215 *"We have listened"*: Memorandum of Conversation, President's Meeting with Gorbachev, December 8, 1987, National Security Agency Archives, Washington, DC.

215 *"An American scholar"*: Ibid.

216 *"Probably, they put more"*: Kathleen Osborne, oral history with Jim Young and Stephen Knott, April 26, 2003, Ronald Reagan Oral History Project, UVA Miller Center/Ronald Reagan Presidential Library.

216–217 *"A boundless world stretches far"*: Shultz, *Turmoil and Triumph.*

217 *Nancy had secured*: Ibid.; see also Nancy Reagan, *My Turn.*

217 *asking Raisa if she knew*: Barbara Bush, *A Memoir* (New York: Simon & Schuster, 1994).

217 *Raisa had a habit*: Nancy Reagan, *My Turn*.

218 *He was bouncing*: Author interview with Kenneth Duberstein, October 26, 2017; also Memorandum of Conversation, President's Meeting with Gorbachev, December 9, 1987, National Security Agency Archives, Washington, DC.

218 *He finally said*: Memorandum of Conversation, President's Meeting with Gorbachev, December 9, 1987, National Security Agency Archives, Washington DC.

218 *But Gorbachev had*: Ibid.

219 *In Russian, Gorbachev recounted*: Ibid.

219 *With vodka and champagne flowing*: Shultz, *Turmoil and Triumph*.

219 *The next morning*: Fitzwater, *Call the Briefing*.

220 *"I thought you'd gone home"*: Author interview with Marlin Fitzwater, July 19, 2017.

221 *Reagan recounted an incident*: Memorandum of Conversation, President's Meeting with Gorbachev, December 10, 1987, National Security Agency Archives, Washington, DC.

221 *That reminded Gorbachev*: Ibid.

221 *Baker whispered*: Shultz, *Turmoil and Triumph*.

222 *"We have not agreed"*: Ibid.; Memorandum of Conversation, President's Meeting with Gorbachev, December 10, 1987, National Security Agency Archives, Washington, DC.

222 *"Well, we're going"*: Ibid.

222 *"Oh, all right"*: Ibid.

222 *"During World War II"*: "Remarks on the Departure of General Secretary Mikhail Gorbachev of the Soviet Union," December 10, 1987, The American Presidency Project; http://www.presidency.ucsb.edu/ws/?pid=33804.

223 *"In bidding farewell"*: Ibid.

223 *"Before," he said*: Gorbachev, *Memoirs*.

CHAPTER 9: THE TRUE MISSION

227 *Kenneth Adelman saw it*: Kenneth Adelman, oral history with Stephen Knott, September 30, 2003, Ronald Reagan Oral History Project, UVA Miller Center/Ronald Reagan Presidential Library.

229 *"As you know"*: "New Year's Messages of President Reagan and Soviet General Secretary Gorbachev," January 1, 1988, The American Presidency Project; http://www.presidency.ucsb.edu/ws/?pid=34831.

229 *"a complete turnabout"*: Ronald Reagan, State of the Union Address, January 25, 1988, Ronald Reagan Presidential Library and Museum.

229 *"Talk about reform"*: Jack F. Matlock, Jr., *Reagan and Gorbachev: How the Cold War Ended* (New York: Random House, 2004).

230 *"What he didn't understand"*: Caspar Weinberger, oral history with Stephen Knott, November 19, 2002, Ronald Reagan Oral History Project, UVA Miller Center/Ronald Reagan Presidential Library.

230 *"Could it be"*: Shultz, *Turmoil and Triumph*.

231 *"My visit to the Soviet Union"*: "President Reagan's Goals for the Summit," in *The Moscow Summit 20 Years Later: From the Secret U.S. and Soviet Files*, National Security Archive, Washington, DC.

231 *"This is an expansionist empire"*: Author interview with Charles Krauthammer, May 2, 2017.

232 *Krauthammer could see*: Ibid.

233 *chose that point*: Larry Speakes, *Speaking Out: The Reagan Presidency from Inside the White House* (New York: Scribner, 1988).

233 *Don Regan exacted his revenge*: Donald T. Regan, *For the Record: From Wall Street to Washington* (New York: Harcourt Brace Jovanovich, 1988).

233 *"an act of spite"*: George F. Will, "Regan's Book Important, If True," *Washington Post*, May 11, 1988.

233 *"I had become"*: Nancy Reagan, *My Turn*.

234 *"I feel terrible about this"*: Ibid.

234 *In a meeting*: Meeting with Non-government Soviet Experts, Ronald Reagan Presidential Library.

235 Land of the Firebird: Suzanne Massie, *Land of the Firebird: The Beauty of Old Russia* (New York: Simon and Schuster, 1981).

236 *Improved bilateral relations*: Meeting with Non-government Soviet Experts, Ronald Reagan Presidential Library.

236 *"As you know"*: "President Reagan's Goals for the Summit," in *The Moscow Summit 20 Years Later: From the Secret U.S. and Soviet Files*, National Security Archive, Washington, DC.

237 *"In the past"*: Ronald Reagan Remarks to the World Affairs Council of Western Massachusetts in Springfield, April 21, 1988, Ronald Reagan Presidential Library.

237 *"We applaud the changes"*: Ronald Reagan, "Remarks and a Question-and-Answer Session with Members of the National Strategy Forum in Chicago, Illinois," May 4, 1988, The American Presidency Project; http://www.presidency.ucsb.edu/ws/?pid=35783.

237 *"I'm going to tackle him"*: Ronald Reagan, *The Reagan Diaries*, ed. Douglas Brinkley (New York: HarperCollins, 2007).

237 *"What Reagan was doing"*: Author interview with Marlin Fitzwater, July 19, 2017.

238 *"There is no true"*: Shultz, *Turmoil and Triumph*.

CHAPTER 10: CRY FREEDOM

239 *"The streets had been cleaned"*: Don Oberdorfer, *From the Cold War to a New Era: The United States and the Soviet Union 1983–1991* (Baltimore: Johns Hopkins University Press, 1998). (Updated from Oberdorfer's 1991 book, *The Turn.*)

239 *Still, the human rights*: Ibid.

240 *"If, as you say"*: Ibid.

241 *"The two were like actors"*: Matlock, *Reagan and Gorbachev: How the Cold War Ended*.

242 *"It's like a gas mask"*: Memorandum of Conversation, First Plenary Meeting between President Reagan and General Secretary Gorbachev, May 30, 1988, in *The Moscow Summit 20 Years Later: From*

the Secret U.S. and Soviet Files, National Security Archive, Washington, DC.

243 *"It's been said"*: Memorandum of Conversation, The President's Meeting with Monks in Danilov Monastery, May 30, 1988, Ronald Reagan Presidential Library, in *The Moscow Summit 20 Years Later: From the Secret U.S. and Soviet Files*, National Security Archive, Washington, DC.

244 *The plight of the Ziemans*: Nancy Reagan, *My Turn*.

244 *Soon Jack Matlock was summoned*: Matlock, *Reagan and Gorbachev*.

245 *"I came here"*: Ronald Reagan, "Remarks to Soviet Dissidents at Spaso House in Moscow," May 30, 1988, The American Presidency Project; http://www.presidency.ucsb.edu/ws/?pid=35894.

245 *"I don't know"*: From the US. standpoint, the gathering was a success; a Department of State cable was entitled "The President's Human Rights Reception a Success," May 31, 1988; see also "Full List of Attendees at President's Reception for Refuseniks/Dissidents," in *The Moscow Summit 20 Years Later: From the Secret U.S. and Soviet Files*, National Security Archive, Washington, DC.

246 *"As wartime allies"*: Ronald Reagan, "Reagan's Remarks at Dinner," March 31, 1988, Ronald Reagan Presidential Library.

246 *"As I watched"*: Igor Korchilov, *Translating History: 30 Years on the Front Lines of Diplomacy with a Top Russian Interpreter* (New York: Scribner, 1997).

246 *At one point, he turned*: Nancy Reagan, *My Turn*.

247 *Before they started their discussion*: Memorandum of Conversation, The President's Second One-on-One Meeting with General Secretary Gorbachev, May 31, 1988, in *The Moscow Summit 20 Years Later: From the Secret U.S. and Soviet Files*, National Security Archive, Washington, DC.

249 *Gorbachev then launched*: Ibid.

249 *"better dead than beautiful"*: Korchilov, *Translating History*.

250 *Shultz suggested that Reagan say*: Shultz, *Turmoil and Triumph*.

250 *"There were all these collections"*: Author interview with Marlin Fitzwater, July 19, 2017.

251 *There was a side story*: Al Kamen, "When Reagan Met Putin in Red Square?," *Washington Post*, March 6, 2014; see also author interview with Marlin Fitzwater, November 14, 2017.

252 *"Do you still think"*: Multiple sources, including James Mann, *The Rebellion of Ronald Reagan: A History of the End of the Cold War* (New York: Penguin, 2009); Stanley Meisler, "Reagan Recants 'Evil Empire' Description," *Los Angeles Times*, June 1, 1988; also Shultz, *Turmoil and Triumph*.

252 *"It made them pay attention"*: Matlock, *Reagan and Gorbachev*.

CHAPTER 11: THE SPEECH

253 *Josh Gilder*: Author interview with Josh Gilder, February 23, 2018.

254 *"Marlin, when you get here"*: Author interview with Marlin Fitzwater, July 19, 2017.

255 *Anthony Dolan viewed*: Author interview with Anthony Dolan, October 23, 2017.

256 *"Josh had a great understanding"*: Ibid.

256 *"Most of us"*: Author interview with Josh Gilder, February 23, 2018.

256 *"I know you must be"*: Ronald Reagan, "Remarks and a Question-and-Answer Session with the Students and Faculty at Moscow State University," May 31, 1988, Ronald Reagan Presidential Library; https://www.reaganlibrary.gov/sites/default/files/archives/speeches/1988/053188b.htm.

256 *the speechwriters had lobbied*: Igor Korchilov, *Translating History: 30 Years on the Front Lines of Diplomacy with a Top Russian Interpreter* (New York: Scribner, 1997).

257 *"Standing here before a mural"*: Ronald Reagan, "Remarks and a Question-and-Answer Session with the Students and Faculty at Moscow State University," May 31, 1988, Ronald Reagan Presidential Library.

261 *"You could see at first"*: Author interview with Kenneth Duberstein, October 26, 2017.

262 *"Here's a guy"*: Ibid.

262 *"It may have been"*: "With Lenin Watching," *New York Times*, June 1, 1988.

262 *The "odd couple"*: "Press conference Fitzwater-Gerasimov," May 31, 1988, Ronald Reagan Presidential Library.

264 *The summit could feel surreal*: Author interview with Anthony Dolan, October 23, 2017.

264 *"You could have stored meat"*: Helen Thomas, *Front Row at the White House: My Life and Times* (New York: Scribner, 1999).

265 *"Mrs. Gorbachev was"*: Edward Rowny, oral history with Stephen Knott, May 17, 2006, Ronald Reagan Oral History Project, UVA Miller Center/Ronald Reagan Presidential Library.

265 *She was overwhelmed*: Nancy Reagan, *My Turn*.

CHAPTER 12: MORNING IN MOSCOW

266 *When the meeting began*: Memorandum of Conversation, Second Plenary Meeting Between President Reagan and General Secretary Gorbachev, June 1, 1988, in *The Moscow Summit 20 Years Later: From the Secret U.S. and Soviet Files*, National Security Archive, Washington, DC.

266 *"Proceeding from their"*: Marlin Fitzwater, *Call the Briefing* (New York: Crown, 1995).

267 *Reagan had glanced at it*: Multiple sources for the signing statement conflict. Primary sources: author interviews with George Shultz, December 2, 2017, and Marlin Fitzwater, November 14, 2017, who were in the room.

268 *"I thought Reagan"*: Fitzwater, *Call the Briefing*.

269 *"This enabled Gorbachev and Reagan"*: Igor Korchilov, *Translating History: 30 Years on the Front Lines of Diplomacy with a Top Russian Interpreter* (New York: Scribner, 1997).

270 *"maybe one rung or two"*: Ibid.

270 *"probably did more"*: Jack Matlock, *Reagan and Gorbachev.*

270 *"To hear that song"*: Ronald Reagan, *An American Life.*

271 *But as they passed*: Nancy Reagan, *My Turn.*

271 *At a friendly departure ceremony*: Korchilov, *Translating History*; see also Gary Lee, "Reagan Lauds Gorbachev in Farewell," *Washington Post*, June 3, 1988.

272 *Riding to the airport*: Author interview with Ken Duberstein, October 26, 2017.

272 *"We arrived in Moscow"*: Ibid.

272 *"Reagan felt he had"*: Ibid.

274 *"In my view"*: Mikhail Gorbachev, *Memoirs.*

274 *"As some of you"*: "Reagan Return Moscow Summit, June 3, 1988," video; c-span.org.

276 *"He [Bush] had pledged"*: Jon Meacham, *Destiny and Power: The American Odyssey of George Herbert Walker Bush* (New York: Random House, 2015).

276 *According to Colin Powell*: Colin Powell, oral history with Russell Riley et al., December 16, 2011, George H. W. Bush Oral History Project, UVA Miller Center.

277 *"Everybody walks into"*: Author interview with Kenneth Duberstein, October 26, 2017.

277 *Secret documents made public*: Reagan, Gorbachev, and Bush at Governors Island: Previously Secret Documents from Soviet and U.S. Files on the 1988 Summit in New York, National Security Archive Electronic Briefing Book, ed. Dr. Svetlana Savranskaya and Thomas Blanton.

278 *Gorbachev might have been feeling*: Ibid., including record of Gorbachev's conference with advisors to write the speech and media response; also Anatoly C. Chernyaev, *My Six Years with Gorbachev* (University Park: Pennsylvania State University Press, 2000).

278 *"The Russian steamroller"*: "Gorbachev Eases Europe's Fears," *The Guardian*, December 8, 1988.

278 *"Perhaps not since"*: "Gambler, Showman, Statesman," *New York Times*, December 8, 1988.

279 *"Gorbachev's UN speech had established"*: Brent Scowcroft, oral history with Philip Zelikow et al., December 31, 2009, George H. W. Bush Oral History Project, UVA Miller Center.

279 *Lunch at the Coast Guard*: "Reagan, Gorbachev and Bush at Governors Island: Previously Secret Documents from Soviet and U.S. Files on the 1988 Summit in New York, 20 Years Later," National Security Archive Electronic Briefing Book No. 261, December 8, 2008.

279 *"He turned to Reagan"*: Author interview with Kenneth Duberstein, October 26, 2017.

280 *"In 1985, when I first"*: "Reagan, Gorbachev and Bush at Governors Island: Previously Secret Documents from Soviet and U.S. Files on the 1988 Summit in New York, 20 Years Later," National Security Archive Electronic Briefing Book No. 261, December 8, 2008.

280 *"I will miss you"*: Nancy Reagan, *My Turn.*

281 *"I think the meeting"*: Ronald Reagan, *The Reagan Diaries*, ed. Douglas Brinkley (New York: HarperCollins, 2007).

CHAPTER 13: THE FALL

285 *"Tomorrow I stop being President"*: Ronald Reagan, *The Reagan Diaries*, ed. Douglas Brinkley (New York: HarperCollins, 2007).

285 *Earlier that evening*: Jim Kuhn, *Ronald Reagan in Private: A Memoir of My Years in the White House* (New York: Sentinel, 2004).

285 *"Of all the things"*: Michael Giorgione, *Inside Camp David: The Private World of the Presidential Retreat* (Boston: Little, Brown, 2017).

286 *"Coming into"*: Remarks at a Question-and-Answer Session with Members of the Center for the Study of the Presidency, March 25, 1988. Ronald Reagan Presidential Library and Museum.

286 *"Nothing can prepare you"*: Nancy Reagan, *My Turn*.

286 *"He was the same man"*: James Kuhn, oral history with Stephen Knott, March 7, 2003, Ronald Reagan Oral History Project, UVA Miller Center/Ronald Reagan Presidential Library.

287 *"What a wave of affection"*: Ronald Reagan, *An American Life*.

287 *"My view is that"*: Ronald Reagan, "Farewell Address to the Nation," January 11, 1989, Ronald Reagan Presidential Library and Museum.

289 *"Mr. President, you fundamentally ended"*: Author interview with Kenneth Duberstein, October 26, 2017.

290 *"For a moment alone"*: Kuhn, *Ronald Reagan in Private*.

290 *"The world is quiet today"*: Ibid.

290 *"a friendly takeover"*: Barbara Bush, *A Memoir* (New York: Simon & Schuster, 1994).

290 *"Nancy does not like Barbara"*: George H. W. Bush Daily Diary, 1989–90, UVA Miller Center for Public Affairs.

291 *"When I became Governor"*: Ibid.

291 *"I thought this must be"*: Maureen Dowd, "The 41st President: Speech Writer; A Stirring Breeze Sparks Feelings, Then Words for a Presidential Vision," *New York Times*, January 21, 1989.

292 *Bush's director of communications*: David F. Demarest, Jr., oral history with Russell Riley, January 28, 2010, George H. W. Bush Oral History Project, UVA Miller Center.

292 *"I don't like"*: Ibid.

292 *"It was sad"*: Barbara Bush, *A Memoir*.

292 *Fitzwater recalled that*: Marlin Fitzwater, *Call the Briefing* (New York: Crown, 1995).

293 *"Look, dear"*: Author interview with Ken Duberstein, October 26, 2017.

293 *When Bush entered the Oval Office*: Author interview with Marlin Fitzwater, November 14, 2017.

294 *"Brent was so tired"*: Robert M. Gates, oral history with Tim Naftali, December 31, 2009, George H. W. Bush Oral History Project, UVA Miller Center.

295 *"He won't let you be"*: Colin Powell, oral history with Russell Riley et al., December 16, 2011, George H. W. Bush Oral History Project, UVA Miller Center.

295 *Some advisors were*: Campbell Craig and Fredrik Logevall, *America's Cold War* (Cambridge, MA: Harvard University Press, 2012).

295 *"I'll be darned"*: George Bush, *All the Best, George Bush: My Life in Letters and Other Writings* (New York: Simon and Schuster, 2014).

296 *"the worst mistake"*: Fitzwater, *Call the Briefing.*

296 *"Imagine that an alien spaceship"*: "Take Me to Your Leader," *New York Times*, May 21, 1989.

296 *Scowcroft would later admit*: Brent Scowcroft, oral history with Philip Zelikow et al., December 31, 2009, George H. W. Bush Oral History Project, UVA Miller Center.

297 *"Life punishes harshly"*: Mikhail Gorbachev, *Memoirs.*

298 *"Do you want to make"*: Fitzwater, *Call the Briefing.*

299 *"Well, I didn't know"*: "Ronald Reagan Celebrates Fall of the Berlin Wall, November 9, 1989," video, ABC News, YouTube.

299–300 *"He got a lot of grief"*: James A. Baker III, oral history with Jim Young, March 17, 2011, George H. W. Bush Oral History Project, UVA Miller Center.

300 *"The Berlin Wall has collapsed"*: Anatoly C. Chernyaev, *My Six Years with Gorbachev* (University Park: Pennsylvania State University Press, 2000).

301 *"Twice in the twentieth century"*: Michael Beschloss and Strobe Talbot, *At the Highest Levels: The Inside Story of the End of the Cold War* (Boston: Little, Brown, 1993).

301 *"Decades have passed"*: Mikhail Gorbachev, *Memoirs.*

301 *"I think both Brent and I"*: Robert M. Gates, oral history with Tim Naftali, December 31, 2009, George H. W. Bush Oral History Project, UVA Miller Center.

302 *"The Gorky was"*: Fitzwater, *Call the Briefing.*

303 *When they met*: Carl Bernstein, "The Holy Alliance," *Time*, June 24, 2001.

303 *"He's my best friend"*: Paul Kengor, *A Pope and a President: John Paul II, Ronald Reagan, and the Extraordinary Untold Story of the 20th Century* (Wilmington, DE: Intercollegiate Studies Institute, 2017).

304 *There were small signs*: James A. Baker III, *Work Hard, Study . . . and Keep Out of Politics!* (Evanston, IL: Northwestern University Press, 2008).

304 *He spoke to Gorbachev*: Transcript of Gorbachev–John Paul II Meeting, Vatican City, December 1, 1989, National Security Archive Electronic Briefing Book, "Bush and Gorbachev at Malta," ed. Dr. Svetlana Savranskaya and Thomas Blanton.

305 *"We are not here"*: Author interview with Marlin Fitzwater, July 19, 2017.

305 *"There are people"*: Transcript of the Malta Meeting, December 2–3, 1989, National Security Archive Electronic Briefing Book No. 298, ed. Svetlana Savranskaya and Thomas Blanton.

306 *"The president walked out"*: Fitzwater, *Call the Briefing.*

307 *"an embattled leader"*: Jack Matlock cable, "Preparing for Malta: Trade Policy Toward the USSR," November 14, 1989, National Security Archive Electronic Briefing Book.

307 *The most difficult conversation*: Transcript of the Malta Meeting, December 2–3, 1989, National Security Archive Electronic Briefing Book No. 298, ed. Svetlana Savranskaya and Thomas Blanton.

309 *"the USSR and the United States"*: Chernyaev, *My Six Years with Gorbachev.*

309 *"The discussion that took place"*: "Reagan," *The American Experi-ence*, February 23, 1998.

310 *Riding the president's golf cart*: Giorgione, *Inside Camp David*.

310 *Reagan and Gorbachev beamed*: John-Thor Dahlburg, "Reagan Greeted with Hearty Bearhug by Gorbachev: Reunion: President Feels like Rip Van Winkle. He Tells Leaders Not to Lose Heart, Lectures on Capitalism," *Los Angeles Times*, September 18, 1990.

311 *"Yeltsin created parallel structures"*: Condoleezza Rice, *No Higher Honor: A Memoir of My Years in Washington* (New York: Crown, 2011); see also Leon Aaron, *Yeltsin: A Revolutionary Life* (New York: St. Martin's Press, 2000).

311 *Gorbachev was exhausted*: Gorbachev, *Memoirs*.

313 *Chernyaev, who was staying*: Chernyaev, *My Six Years with Gorbachev*.

313 *"Soldiers, officers, generals"*: Aaron, *Yeltsin*.

314 *"My God, I'm glad"*: Meacham, *Destiny and Power*.

315 *"This was one"*: Robert M. Gates, oral history with Tim Naftali, December 31, 2009, George H. W. Bush Oral History Project, UVA Miller Center.

315 *"I'm feeling absolutely calm"*: Conor O'Clery, *Moscow, December 25, 1991: The Last Day of the Soviet Union* (New York: Public Affairs, 2011).

316 *"We're now living"*: "President Reagan's 83rd Birthday," video, C-Span Historical Archives.

316 *"Eighty years is a long time"*: Robert Reinhold, "4 Presidents Join Reagan in Dedicating His Library," *New York Times*, November 5, 1991.

CHAPTER 14: WITHOUT FIRING A SHOT

318 *Dick Cheney received a visitor*: Richard B. Cheney, oral history with Philip Zelikow, March 16 and 17, 2000, George H. W. Bush Oral History Project, UVA Miller Center.

319 *In late 1993*: Peggy Grande, *The President Will See You Now: My Stories and Lessons from Ronald Reagan's Final Years* (New York: Hachette, 2017).

319 *When they walked*: Ray Moseley, "Reagan Gets His Shot at the Berlin Wall," *Chicago Tribune*, September 13, 1990.

319 *"May you live 100 years"*: Frederick J. Ryan, Jr., Reagan's postpres-idency chief of staff, recounted this story in *Reagan Remembered*, a compilation of memories of Reagan created by Gilbert A. Robinson (New York: International Publishers, 2015).

319 *"Ronald Reagan won"*: Margaret Thatcher first made this statement in 1991; she repeated it at her eulogy for Ronald Reagan in 2004; https://www.margaretthatcher.org/document/110360.

320 *"Pragmatism without principles is cynicism"*: James A. Baker, III, *Work Hard, Study . . . and Keep Out of Politics!*

321 *"Generally speaking"*: Brent Scowcroft, oral history with Philip Zelikow et al., December 31, 2009, George H. W. Bush Oral History Project, UVA Miller Center.

321 *"He learned that"*: Peter Hannaford, oral history with Stephen Knott et al., January 10, 2003, Ronald Reagan Oral History Project, UVA Miller Center/Ronald Reagan Presidential Library.

322 *"He painted in primary colors"*: Author interview with Kenneth Du-
    berstein, October 26, 2017.
322 *"I never thought"*: Ronald Reagan, "Farewell Address to the Nation,"
    January 11, 1989, Ronald Reagan Presidential Library and Museum.
323 *"the forty-fourth anniversary"*: Ronald Reagan, "Text of Letter Written
    by President Ronald Reagan Announcing He Has Alzheimer's Disease,"
    November 5, 1994, Ronald Reagan Presidential Library and Museum.
323 *"As most of you know"*: "President Reagan's 83rd Birthday," video,
    C-Span Historical Archives.
323 *"I now begin the journey"*: Ronald Reagan, "Text of Letter Written by
    President Ronald Reagan Announcing He Has Alzheimer's Disease,"
    November 5, 1994, Ronald Reagan Presidential Library and Museum.
324 *Margaret Thatcher revealed*: Alex Russell and Andrew Sparrow,
    "Thatcher's taped eulogy at Reagan's funeral," *The Telegraph*, June 7,
    2004.
324 *Mourning his friend*: Even *Pravda* published an article, "This Week
    America Mourns the Death of Ronald Reagan," June 7, 2004, liber-
    ally quoting Gorbachev's words of praise for the president.
324 *In a* New York Times: Mikhail Gorbachev, "A President Who Lis-
    tened," *New York Times*, June 7, 2004.

THE LAST WORD

327 *"Does the president"*: White House Press Briefing, February 20, 2018.
330 *"I looked the man"*: Press Conference by President Bush and Russian
    Federation President Putin, June 16, 2001, the White House.
330 *Asked by the BBC*: Steve Rosenberg, "Mikhail Gorbachev: The Man
    Who Lost an Empire," BBC, December 13, 2006.
331 *"I want to tell"*: Travis Fedschun and Lucas Tomlinson, "Russia Un-
    veils Nuclear Weapons Putin Claims Are Immune to Interception,"
    Fox News, March 1, 2018.
332 *"Americans, Poles and the nations"*: "Remarks by President Trump to
    the People of Poland," July 6, 2017, whitehouse.gov.
334 *"Reagan took all that"*: Author interview with Marlin Fitzwater, No-
    vember 14, 2017.
334 *"When you can't make them"*: Kenneth W. Thompson, *Leadership in
    the Reagan Presidency Part II: Eleven Intimate Perspectives* (Madi-
    son Books, 1993).
335 *"I am convinced"*: Mikhail Gorbachev, *The New Russia* (UK: Polity
    Books, 2016).
336 *"When the Lord calls me"*: Ronald Reagan, "Text of Letter Written by
    President Ronald Reagan Announcing He Has Alzheimer's Disease,"
    November 5, 1994, Ronald Reagan Presidential Library and Museum.

APPENDIX

341 *"Thank you, Rector Logunov"*: Ronald Reagan, "Remarks and a Ques-
    tion-and-Answer Session with the Students and Faculty at Moscow
    State University," May 31, 1988, Ronald Reagan Presidential Library;
    https://www.reaganlibrary.gov/sites/default/files/archives/speeches
    /1988/053188b.htm.

INDEX

ALSO BY **BRET BAIER**

THREE DAYS IN JANUARY
Dwight Eisenhower's Final Mission

"Bret Baier has given history a great gift: a riveting account of Dwight Eisenhower's determination to call on his vast experience to prepare America for the perils of the new war--the cold war."
—Tom Brokaw, author of *The Greatest Generation*

The blockbuster #1 national bestseller, now updated with a new preface and postcript: Bret Baier, the Chief Political Anchor for Fox News Channel and the Anchor and Executive Editor of *Special Report with Bret Baier*, illuminates the extraordinary yet underappreciated presidency of Dwight Eisenhower by taking readers into Ike's last days in power.

THREE DAYS IN MOSCOW
Ronald Reagan and the Fall of the Soviet Empire

"Forceful. ... It is curious how many Reaganesque themes find a contemporary echo... [and] it is worth recalling both Reagan's celebration of freedom and his understanding of democracy."
—*Wall Street Journal*

In his acclaimed bestseller *Three Days in Moscow*, Bret Baier takes readers behind the scenes of President Ronald Reagan's extraordinary three day visit to the Soviet Union in 1988. Baier explores the dramatic endgame of the Cold War and Reagan's central role in shaping the world we live in today.

COMING FALL 2019
Three Days at the Brink
FDR's Daring Gamble to Win World War II